The
ABCs of
How We Learn

The
ABCs of
How We Learn

26 Scientifically Proven Approaches,
How They Work, and When to Use Them

Daniel L. Schwartz,
Jessica M. Tsang,
and Kristen P. Blair

W.W. Norton & Company
Independent Publishers Since 1923
New York | London

Note to Readers: Models and/or techniques described in this volume are illustrative or are included for general informational purposes only; neither the publisher nor the author(s) can guarantee the efficacy or appropriateness of any particular recommendation in every circumstance.

For information about permission to reproduce selections from this book, write to Permissions, W. W. Norton & Company, Inc., 500 Fifth Avenue, New York, NY 10110

For information about special discounts for bulk purchases, please contact W. W. Norton Special Sales at specialsales@wwnorton.com or 800-233-4830

Manufacturing by Edwards Brothers Malloy
Book design by Anika Steppe
Production manager: Christine Critelli

Library of Congress Cataloging-in-Publication Data

Names: Schwartz,
Daniel L., author. | Tsang, Jessica M., author. | Blair, Kristen P. author.
Title: The ABCs of how we learn : 26 scientifically proven approaches, how they work, and when to use them / Daniel L. Schwartz, Jessica M. Tsang, and Kristen P. Blair.
Description: First edition. | New York, NY : W.W. Norton & Company, Inc., 2016. |
Series: Norton books in education | Includes bibliographical references and index.
Identifiers: LCCN 2015047247 | ISBN 9780393709261 (pbk.)
Subjects: LCSH: Learning. Classification: LCC LB1060 .S375 2016 | DDC 370.15/23—dc23
LC record available at http://lccn.loc.gov/2015047247

W. W. Norton & Company, Inc.
500 Fifth Avenue, New York, N.Y. 10110
www.wwnorton.com

W. W. Norton & Company Ltd.
15 Carlisle Street, London W1D 3BS

4 5 6 7 8 9 0

DEDICATION

I am deeply grateful to the three Johns who served as my mentors: John Bransford, John Rieser, and John Black. Nobody makes it on their own. I am also indebted to the enthusiasm and encouragement of the Core Mechanics classes of 2012, 2014, 2015, and even the over-the-top class of 2013. —*DLS*

To my professional mentors (a certain co-author included), and to my family—my mom and dad for supporting me, my husband, Scott, for sharing the adventure, and my daughters, Alissa and Madeline, for upping the ante on the chaos and the fun. —*KPB*

This work is dedicated to the Oakland public schools, for giving me education, inspiration, and perspective. And to my littles, Oliver and Julius, who are also my biggest bigs. —*JMT*

Contents

Acknowledgments

This work depended on the support of the AAALab@Stanford and the generous patience and contributions of Dr. Doris Chin. We would also like to thank Kate Joy for managing the production of the figures. Finally, we thank Neil Levine for his creative genius. He produced the letter art work and supplied us with gorgeous socks (http://www.xoab.us).

The
ABCs of
How We Learn

Introduction

HAVE YOU TAUGHT?

That is a rhetorical question. Of course you have.

Humans have a basic need to teach one another. Teachers do it; so do parents, friends, siblings, gossips, and employers. People even teach themselves. Today alone, among our many teaching experiences, we showed a toddler how to peel a banana, familiarized an out-of-town visitor with the commuter train, returned written feedback on a statistics assignment, and coaxed a puppy to sit, yet again.

Given that you have taught, you might also recall a time when it did not work very well. So, you tried another approach and it worked better. Here is a common example: Someone asks you for directions to a building or store, and you reply, "Sure!" because you certainly know where it is. But soon enough, you find yourself gesturing ineffectually as confusion crosses the listener's face. Finally, you just draw a map.

What is the moral of this story? It is not that perseverance pays off, though that is often true. The moral is that there are many different ways we teach one another. Moreover, different ways of teaching are suited to different types of learning. For instance, the visual system is very good at learning spatial material, and that is why a map usually works better than words when it comes to spatial directions.

Learning is not a single thing—there is no central processing unit responsible for all learning, and the brain is not a homogenous lump of neurons. The brain has many learning systems each of which has a different neural structure and a unique appetite. Effective instruction depends on choosing pedagogical moves that nourish the right learning system for the desired outcomes. If you want people to learn to respond appropriately to frustration, give them a chance to observe a role model, don't just tell them to buck up. If you want people to change their bad habits, use reinforcement, not willpower.

The purpose of this book is to help people understand learning and to creatively develop methods of instruction suited to their learning goals, whether for .themselves or another.

At Stanford University, we teach an applied course that emphasizes learning theories that can be put into practice. The course draws beginning and advanced teachers, undergraduates, master students, doctoral students, lawyers, physicians, engineers, business men and women, and people who want to design learning technologies. The variety of students is evidence that people want to know about learning.

About five years ago, we abandoned the available textbooks. They never quite united theory, research, and practice in a way that was spot-on actionable for the variety of goals that teachers—all of us—bring to education. Instead, we organized the course by describing a number of important learning mechanisms, why they work, what they are good for, and how to use them.

The course is called the Core Mechanics of Learning. The expression—core mechanic—comes from games, where there are specific interactions that drive a game forward. In golf, strike a ball into a hole. In Tetris, rotate falling pieces to land in place. Similarly, there are specific interactions that drive different types of learning forward. Good teaching is to arrange for those interactions.

A single course has limited time. We selected mechanisms that exemplify the most well developed learning theories, such as behaviorism (R is for Reward), social psychology (O is for Observation), perceptual psychology (C is for Contrasting Cases), cultural psychology (P is for Participation), and cognitive psychology (S is for Self-Explanation). (As cognitive psychologists, we think about thinking, and we learn about learning.) Once we switched to this format, students regularly requested a second course, so they could learn additional core mechanics. Human learning is fascinating!

Building on the demand, we decided to write the ABC book. We wrote it to be accessible and enjoyable for any person interested in learning and how to improve it. We also wanted it to be suitable as a textbook when elaborated with additional readings and appropriate tasks. For instance, a good task after reading a few chapters is to analyze a piece of instruction, such as an online math game, with the eye of a learning scientist. Students can analyze which learning mechanisms the experience enlists or misses, and how effectively they are brought to bear.

We chose 26 core mechanics that have strong evidence, comprehensible theories, and clear implications. We made some hard decisions about what to include. For example, we chose A is for Analogy, but we could have written A is for Attention. The book is not exhaustive. How could it be? The science of learning has exploded in the past 15 years, in part because of a $500 million investment by the National Science Foundation into centers dedicated to the science of learning. (We were members of the center, *Learning in Informal and Formal Environments*—LIFE.) We chose the 26 chapters based on our own experiences as educators and researchers of learning, and our sense of what people want to know about. Someday, we might write a book called, *The Other ABCs*.

Each chapter is organized the same way. Our basic assumption is that knowing how something works, seeing the evidence for why it works, and providing multiple examples will help people generate their own insights and effective applications. The structure is as follows:

- **What it is.** A basic statement of the learning mechanism and why it is important.
- **How it works.** The science and theory, including accessible descriptions of seminal research.
- **How to use it.** Examples of activities that recruit the learning mechanisms.
- **What it is good for.** The outcomes that the learning mechanism is especially good for.
- **Its risks.** Common mistakes that lead to undesirable consequences.
- **Examples of Good and Bad Use.** Quick examples to help solidify the ideas.
- **References.** A mix of classic and contemporary papers on the topic.
- **A Cheat Sheet.** An elaborated outline that summarizes the main ideas of the chapter with brief examples—useful as a reminder months or years after reading.

Educators often want people to achieve multiple learning outcomes for a single topic. For instance, one might want students to memorize scientific formulas, understand why they work, and develop an interest in becoming a scientist. Our hope is that the book gives a more differentiated picture of the many kinds of learning outcomes and the many strategies and techniques that can be combined to help learners achieve these multi-faceted outcomes. Good instruction can combine techniques from several chapters. For instance, for science, one might develop a lesson that enlists GAP—Generation, Analogy, and Participation, or maybe MET—Making, Elaboration, and Teaching. The possible combinations are limitless.

Even for a single outcome, several complementary mechanisms can be enlisted. For instance, if the desired learning outcome is memorization, the chapters E, G, X, and Z may be especially useful. Here is a starter list of how the chapters align with some familiar outcomes. Many other chapters address each outcome as well, but the list is a good place to get started given a specific interest.

Conceptual Understanding	A is for Analogy J is for Just-in-Time Telling U is for Undoing
Memory	E is for Elaboration G is for Generation X is for eXcitement
Motivation	Y is for Yes I Can R is for Reward I is for Imaginative Play
Expertise	D is for Deliberate Practice K is for Knowledge M is for Making
Study Skills	S is for Self-Explanation Z is for ZZZs E is for Elaboration
Sense of Inclusion	B is for Belonging N is for Norms P is for Participation
Problem Solving	W is for Worked Examples Q is for Question Driven F is for Feedback
Collaboration	L is for Listening and Sharing O is for Observation T is for Teaching
Discovery	H is for Hands On C is for Contrasting Cases V is for Visualization

Producing the conditions of learning can be a wonderfully creative act. This book will equip readers with the tools to design effective learning experiences. You may also find great satisfaction in discovering how learning works and how teaching leads to learning. After all, learning and teaching are what make us human.

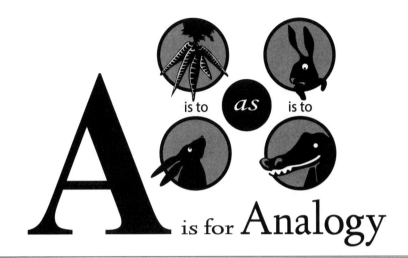

A is for Analogy

is to *as* is to

Finding the general principle

DRAWING AN ANALOGY involves finding the underlying similarity between diverse instances. Analogies help people learn principles and apply those principles in new situations.

If you have taken a standardized test, and in America the odds are about 100 percent, then you are probably familiar with analogical reasoning questions. Just in case, here is an example:

Deluge is to Droplet as:

(a) Beach is to Wave
(b) Desert is to Oasis
(c) Blizzard is to Icicle
(d) Landslide is to Pebble
(e) Cloudburst is to Puddle

Analogical reasoning tests are variously used to evaluate people's vocabulary, intelligence, and creativity. Don't worry—we explain the answer below. No single question can ever assess a person's abilities or knowledge.

Setting tests aside, analogies can be a powerful way to learn new concepts and principles. Providing tasks where students find the analogy between two examples improves understanding of the underlying principle. It also increases the chances that students will spontaneously use that principle in a novel situation. Moreover, people can even learn to use analogical reasoning to learn.

I. How Analogies Work

Many people choose the answers (a) or (e) to the analogy above. These options share *surface features* with the prompt, because they all involve water. Surface features refer to readily perceived properties. Answer (d) is correct: it shares the same *deep structure* as the prompt. The common deep structure might be summarized as "a disaster can result from an accumulation of many harmless events." Deep structure refers to the relations among elements. So, even though one involves water and the other involves rocks, the two examples have an analogous structure. This is the key to using analogies to learn: find the common principle despite differences at the surface. The Venn diagram in Figure A.1 summarizes the idea. It reflects a basic truth about human learning: *two examples are better than one.*

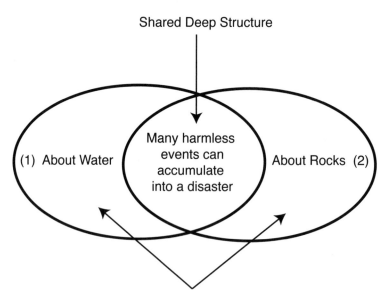

Figure A.1. Drawing an analogy depends on finding the deep structure between two instances despite differences in surface features.

II. How to Use Analogies to Enhance Learning

There are two main ways to use analogies for instruction. The first is to explain a novel idea by making an analogy to a more familiar one. Some common examples are teaching the idea of blood vessels by making reference to highways, and explaining that the layers of the earth are like layers of a peach. Science has many examples of discoveries that were based on an analogy from something familiar to something new. One of the most impressive comes from Johannes Kepler, who developed the concept of gravity to explain planetary orbits (Gentner et al., 1997). He worked out his theory of gravity by drawing an analogy to the rays of the sun. The rays of the sun become weaker at a distance, so by analogy, gravity does too. Of course, he did not do this in a single flash of insight. It took many years for him to fully map the analogy between light and gravity to explain elliptical orbits. Discovering a good analogy for something that one does not yet understand can be quite difficult. However, teachers can provide good analogies so students can build on what they already know.

The second way to use analogies is to provide students with two (or more) examples and ask them to induce the underlying structure. This turns out to be extremely powerful for learning. In fact, having students find the analogous structure is much better than giving them one example and explaining the structure! Pay attention to this point, because giving a single example with an explanation is the standard approach in most U.S. classrooms, and we can do better (Richland, Zur, & Holyoak, 2007). In a classic study, researchers tried to determine what would help people solve Duncker's radiation problem, short of telling them the answer (Gick & Holyoak, 1983). Here is Duncker's radiation problem:

> A patient has a tumor that needs to be irradiated. If the doctor uses a beam that is powerful enough to kill the tumor, it will kill healthy cells as it passes on the way to the tumor. If the doctor uses a radiation beam that is weak enough that it will not hurt healthy cells, then it will not kill the tumor. What can the doctor do?

> The answer: The doctor can use multiple weak beams from different angles that simultaneously converge on the tumor.

To see what would help people solve this problem, the researchers constructed several analogies to the radiation problem. For example, in one analog, a general wanted to attack a fortress and had to split up his troops to converge from different angles so they would not be too heavy for any one bridge. In another, firefighters needed to use multiple hoses to put out a fire. The researchers also wrote out the general principle: split up forces to converge on a central target. Given these materials, the researchers tried different combinations to see which one would lead students to later solve the radiation problem on their own. The college students in the study received packets. On the last page of all the packets was the radiation problem, and there were no cues that this problem was relevant to what came before in the packet. The experimental manipulation involved the earlier pages. The pages in the packet could include zero, one, or two of the analogies (fortress and fire problems). Half of the packets also included a statement of the principle, while the other half did not. The table below shows the percentages of students who solved the radiation problem.

Packet contents	Percent who solved the radiation problem	
	Read principle	Did not read principle
Received No analogy	28%	18%
One analogy	32%	29%
Two analogies	62%	52%

Reasoning through two analogous problems more than doubled performance on the radiation problem compared with no analogy, and solving two analogies without an explanation of the principle led to better performance than receiving one analogy plus the principle. This latter result can seem counterintuitive. Explaining a principle with the aid of a single example can be a fine way to help people grasp a concept. The problem is that grasping a concept does not mean people know when to use it. The reason that the single analogy and the principle did not work very well is that students did not learn the range of variation that might appear for this particular principle. For example, those students who learned only about the story of attacking the fortress from multiple bridges, even with the statement of the principle, had no way of knowing that it can apply to lots of situations. Seeing two examples helps people appreciate that the idea can apply to lots of situations. The variability of the surface features is important.

III. The Outcomes of Analogical Learning

Analogies help students sort out the wheat of deep structure from the chaff of surface features (if we may make an overused analogy). Often, people rely on surface features too much, and they can miss the deep structure.

In a telling study (Ross, 1984), college students learned probability formulas, such as for computing combinations and permutations. (Imagine a bag of red and blue chips, and you pull out two chips. There are three possible combinations: two reds, two blues, or one red and one blue. Permutations further consider the possible order they are pulled out of the bag, so there are four possible permutations: red → red, blue → blue, red → blue, blue → red.) As part of the study, students were taught how to compute the number of combinations using an example that involved one kind of object, such as cars. They were taught how to compute the number of permutations with a different object type, such as dice. On a posttest with several problems, students performed very well when the object of the problem was the same as the object used in the original instruction. For example, they did well when they received a combination problem involving cars if they had learned the combination formula with a cars example. So far so good.

The issue showed up when students received a problem that crossed the objects. For instance, they did terribly when they received a posttest combination problem involving dice instead of cars. In fact, they did much worse when the objects were crossed than when the test problems used objects that had never appeared during instruction. One explanation is that the students did not learn the deep structure of combinations and permutations. When they had to figure out what formula to use for a problem, they relied on the object in the problem (dice) as their cue. They mistakenly thought, "Dice means permutation. This is a permutation problem." This type of error is called *negative transfer*. People use something they have memorized but in the wrong situation. This often happens because people do not learn to recognize the deep structure of a problem but instead use the obvious surface features as the cue for which solution to apply.

Analogies can help students make a *positive transfer*. For Duncker's radiation problem, the students who received two analogies made a positive transfer. They appropriately applied what they had learned in a new situation. If we wanted to help the poor statistics students in Ross's study, we would have given them examples of permutations using both dice and cars, and we would ask them what the examples have in common. Ditto for combinations. Afterward, we would tell students the principles and formulas.

One of the best ways to measure the benefits of teaching with analogies is to provide students a transfer task that has the same deep structure as the analogies but differs on the surface. Give them a novel problem, and do not tell them that it is relevant to what they had learned before. If they spontaneously use what was covered in the analogies, then you know they have learned the deep structure. For example, researchers had eighth-grade students find the analogy between density and speed (Schwartz, Chase, Oppezzo, & Chin, 2011). You may be asking yourself right now, what is the analogy between density and speed?! They both involve the use of ratio: d = mass/volume and s = distance/time. Later they had students work on a problem involving the spring constant (another ratio, k = mass/distance). The students spontaneously transferred the idea of using ratio to solve the spring constant problem.

The key outcome of learning through analogy is the ability to transfer the key concept to a new situation. This is a critical outcome because we want students to problem solve on their own, even when there is no teacher around to tell them which concept they should be using.

IV. Can People Learn to Teach Themselves with Analogies?

It is possible to teach people to think analogically so they can help themselves learn. A wonderful example comes from studies of three- and four-year-old children (Brown & Kane, 1988). These experiments used play sets for the instruction. In one play set, the farmer had a problem. He needed to reach something on the top shelf. The children were asked how the farmer could solve the problem. After they tried, they were shown that the answer is that he could stack hay bales on top of one another so he could climb up. The second play set in the pair involved a garage with a mechanic who needed to reach something on a high shelf. Children would try to solve this problem, and if they could not, the experimenter would show the answer (the mechanic could stack tires to climb up). The children completed two more problem pairs like this. For example, in another pair, the solutions involved using something long to reach beyond arm's length.

For the first pair they encountered, children did not use the solution from the first problem of the pair (stack hay bales) to help them solve the second problem (stack tires). However, by the third pair, the preschool-age children had learned to look for the analogy between the first problem and the second. They learned to look for analogies between problems, rather than treating them as two completely separate situations. Ideally, helping children learn to look for analogies can improve their future learning from examples.

V. Risks of Analogies

There are two risks of analogies. The first is that students may not be able to draw the analogy to find the deep structure, or they may find a deep structure that was unintended by the original selection of the examples. For example, given the atom and the solar system, students might conclude that the deep structure is that everything involves round balls, and they might miss the orbits or the relatively large amount of space compared with mass. This is not a terrible problem, because even if students do not find the analogy, the search for the deep structure can prepare them to understand the principle more deeply when explained afterward (see Chapter J).

A more serious problem is that one may have a bad analogy. The modern conception of the atom is no longer analogous in the least to planetary orbits. This leads to the second risk: the analogies may not be precisely aligned. For instance, people often use the analogy of water filling a pipe when explaining electrical current. This helps students understand the idea of current, but it also introduces misconceptions. For instance, students may use the analogy to conclude that the last bulb on a string of Christmas lights will come on last, because the electricity (water) gets there last. The problem here is not poor analogical reasoning. Rather, the problem is a poor analogy. A better analogy is that the pipe is already filled with water and turning on the power moves all the water simultaneously. It is important for instructors who use analogies to pick the right ones. Sometimes it makes sense to begin with a simple starter analogy that can be replaced with a better analogy as student understanding becomes more sophisticated. But be careful about introducing misconceptions, because they can be hard to undo (see Chapter U).

Asking students to come up with their own analogies may seem like a good idea on the face of it. The problem is that students will tend to make analogies to what they already know instead of learning new aspects of the deep structure. For example, if we were to ask you for analogies of DNA, you might say a blueprint or a set of computer instructions or a braided rope. But you already knew those, so the analogy activity did not help a whole lot. If you want to use analogy generation tasks, a better approach is to ask a class to generate several analogies and then help them work through which analogies fit the target structure the best. This will help them learn the criteria for a precise analogy while also helping them find the deep structure of the target concept.

VI. Examples of Good and Bad Use

Imagine that you are teaching about brain pathways and you use the following analogy:

Highway Systems	:	**Cars**
	as	
White Matter Tracts	:	**Neural Signals**

GOOD FEATURES
- The base pair describes a well-known relationship.
- The target pair parallels the base in multiple ways:
  - Both relationships can be summarized as ". . . are long pathways traveled by . . ."
  - For both, the traveling entities join and exit the pathways via smaller paths.
  - For both, the pathways have set entrance and exit locations.

BAD FEATURES

Sometimes people know *so* much about a base pair that they accidentally transfer mistaken nuances to the target pair's relationship. For instance, in this example, a highway is *one* road that cars enter and exit via *other* roads. But white matter tracts are bundles of many pathways called axons that run parallel to each other. Neural signals travel within only one axon from their origin to their destination. People learning about brains from this example may accidentally think that neural signals can jump from one axon to another (like highway lanes) to travel to wherever they want to go.

If imprecision in the mapping of the analogs is not pointed out, people can develop misunderstandings. Generally, exact analogies are better. However, there is no need to avoid imprecise analogies as long as misleading aspects are pointed out.

VII. References

Brown, A. L., & Kane, M. J. (1988). Preschool children can learn to transfer: Learning to learn and learning from example. *Cognitive Psychology, 20*(4), 493–523.

Gentner, D., Brem, S., Ferguson, R. W., Markman, A. B., Levidow, B. B., Wolff, P., & Forbus, K. D. (1997). Analogical reasoning and conceptual change: A case study of Johannes Kepler. *Journal of the Learning Sciences, 6*(1), 3–40.

Gick, M. L., & Holyoak, K. J. (1983). Schema induction and analogical transfer. *Cognitive Psychology, 15*(1), 1–38.

Richland, L. E., Zur, O., & Holyoak, K. (2007). Cognitive supports for analogies in the mathematics classroom. *Science, 316* (5828), 1128–1129.

Ross, B. H. (1984). Remindings and their effects in learning a cognitive skill. *Cognitive Psychology, 16*(3), 371-416.

Schwartz, D. L., Chase, C. C., Oppezzo, M. A., & Chin, D. B. (2011). Practicing versus inventing with contrasting cases: The effects of telling first on learning and transfer. *Journal of Educational Psychology, 103*(4), 759–775.

A IS FOR ANALOGY

What is the core learning mechanic?
Finding the similarity between two or more examples despite differences on the surface.

What is an example, and what is it good for?
What is the same about an insect that looks like a stick and a golden lion that crouches in tall dry grass? Asking students to find the analogy helps them learn the key idea (e.g., camouflage), rather than focusing on irrelevant features like how majestic a lion looks. Analogies improve understanding of the underlying principle and increase the chances that students will spontaneously transfer that principle to a new situation. This is a top goal of education: enabling students to take what they learn in school and use it outside of school.

Why does it work?
Drawing analogies allows students to make sense of a new concept by relying on a familiar one, taking advantage of their prior knowledge. Analogies are also powerful because they help students to find the common principle despite surface differences of examples.

What problems does the core mechanic solve?
- Students having a difficult time understanding a new concept.
  - A student cannot grasp the size of the sun compared to the earth.
- Students seem to focus on details but miss the big idea or principle.
  - In a lesson about animal protective color, a child focusses on the specific color of an animal, instead of the way that coloring lets it blend in with its environment.
- Students fail to use what they learned for a new problem.
  - Students do well on quizzes but poorly on the final exam.

- A student learns to find a linear slope for problems involving speed (d/t) but cannot find the slope for a new problem involving density (m/v).

Examples of how to use it
- Use a familiar example to explain a novel concept that is intangible.
  - Electricity is like water in a filled pipe.
- Ask students to explain the similarity across several diverse instances of a big idea.

- What is the same about how butterflies, jellyfish, and pollen travel great distances?
- How is drawing marbles from a jar like rolling dice?

Risks

- Analogies may introduce misconceptions—infinity is not really just something very big.
- Students may fail to grasp the deep structure of the analogy, especially if the relation is not transparent or the original domain is poorly understood.

B is for Belonging

Silencing anxiety and buying in

BELONGING IS THE perception of being accepted, valued, and included. Belonging can help learning by increasing effort and decreasing negative distracting thoughts.

A student has recently begun to opt out of class, sinking down in his chair at the back of the room. One explanation is that he finds the class boring, or perhaps he is feigning disinterest to mask a lack of effort. While these certainly could be true, a very common problem is that the student feels like he does not belong. He may believe that he cannot participate or that "his kind" does not belong there. Amy Cuddy, a prominent professor of social psychology at Harvard, recounts the story of a student who never participated in her class and was in danger of failing (Cuddy, 2012). From the outside, it could appear that this student did not prepare for class or was simply unmotivated. Calling the student to her office to discuss the situation, the student said, "I'm not supposed to be here." Cuddy, who herself almost quit graduate school because she felt like an imposter, recognized that the student lacked a feeling of belonging, and this was why she did not participate. This insight led to a productive way forward for the student. In this case, the challenge for the teacher was recognizing that belonging was the issue.

Belonging is one of our most fundamental needs. Everyone has experienced the joy of planning a group party and the sting of being left out of a conversation. Young or old, a person's sense of belonging has powerful effects on learning. On the positive side, engendering a sense of belonging in a learning group (e.g., a math class) can bolster motivation and engagement, as well as persistence in the face of difficulties. On the negative side, highlighting that a person does not belong by pointing out stereotypes about gender or race can increase anxiety and depress learning and test performance. Fortunately, there are simple ways to increase people's feelings that they belong and to mitigate destructive beliefs that they do not.

I. How Belonging Works

Learning is social. It takes place in social contexts, such as classrooms and workplaces. Even quietly reading a textbook is social. The text was written by someone and may present a society's adopted view of the world, including subtle information about who are valued producers of knowledge in society. Additionally, the purpose for reading often includes social goals, such as doing well in school.

A characteristic of human affairs is the existence of social groups. These can range from families to nations to people who drive fast. Humans can construct social groups based on just about any attribute one might care to think of. Kraft Foods ran a successful ad campaign, 'Are You Miracle Whip?' which created social groups of people who love versus hate the condiment.

Membership in some social groups, like Miracle Whip lovers, is unlikely to shape one's life outcomes. Membership in other groups, however, can confer broad material advantages, or disadvantages, to learning. Eliminating inequities between groups will require dramatic societal changes. In the meantime, it is also possible to work at the psychological level to ameliorate the negative and enhance the positive effects of group membership. This involves increasing people's sense of belonging in a learning setting.

With social groups comes the question of whether one belongs to a group or not. Group membership is socially constructed, so it often depends on people's attributions or beliefs. People attribute group memberships to themselves and to others. Attributing group membership is a form of identification. One way this occurs is through an individual's self-identification—I am a basketball player. A second way this occurs is through other people's attributions about one's identity—you are a basketball player.

Sometimes people may not identify with a learning group. For instance, a person may believe he does not belong in college, despite attending. One can imagine a scenario in which this belief is reinforced by others, such as an unsupportive teacher. More subtly, one can also imagine a scenario in which the student is surrounded by supportive teachers who simply do not recognize that belonging could be an issue for this student. They never encountered the problem themselves and cannot recognize the student's anxiety. What you don't know can hurt others, too. Without support for a sense of belonging, there can be loss of engagement, anxiety, and avoidance.

A second major concern is more insidious and involves stereotypes. Sometimes there is a belief that being a member of one group excludes people from belonging to another group. For instance, let us imagine there is a group called "women," and there is a group called, "good at math." A woman wants to identify with and belong to both groups. Other people, however, may believe a person cannot belong to both the "women" group and the "good at math" group. (Perhaps the reader recalls a talking Barbie Doll that stated, "Math is hard.") The attribution that women cannot do well in math causes *stereotype threat*. Even though the stereotype has no basis in fact, it can still cause the woman to dwell on whether she belongs to the group that does well in math. The anxiety can be conscious, or it may be diffuse and not explicitly recognized. In either case, it can be distracting and siphon cognitive resources, leading to poorer math performance and learning. Without the anxiety, the woman would do just fine. The negative social attribution causes the poor performance, not anything about the woman's math abilities.

The triggers of stereotype threat can be subtle and hard to anticipate. In a classic study, Steele and Aronson (1995) found that simply asking African-American college students to indicate their race at the front of a test booklet caused their performance to drop. Because stereotype threats are ubiquitous and often hard to identify, it can be difficult to remove all the triggers that can cause stereotype threat. In this situation, it may help to work at the level of people's beliefs rather than exhaustively changing the environment (although that, too, is a good thing to do). One useful solution is to help people simply appreciate that they do belong.

II. How to Influence Belonging to Enhance Learning

Two major types of belonging interventions improve learning. One type focuses on changing students' attributions about whether they belong. These kinds of interventions are generally short but powerful, and they focus on shifting individuals' perceptions of their own belonging. The second type of intervention involves changing the environment and social structure to engender social connectedness and belonging. In both types of interventions, the benefits are most pronounced when people face challenging conditions, such as solving difficult problems, taking high-stakes tests, or overcoming setbacks.

Importantly, belonging interventions assume one can belong to multiple groups. No interventions ask people to forgo membership in one group to belong to another (e.g., you do not have to sacrifice your identity as an athlete to be high achieving in school).

CHANGING ATTRIBUTIONS

One way to increase a sense of belonging is to help students reframe beliefs about their place in a community, particularly when it comes to setbacks. People can misinterpret short-term failure as reflecting that they do not belong, when in fact it may be very common to the group. Helping students reframe setbacks so they are not viewed as a reason for exclusion can be very powerful. Walton and Cohen (2011) conducted a study with college freshmen. In one of two conditions, the freshmen did an activity to boost their sense of belonging, by reading ostensible survey results from more senior college students. The survey indicated that most senior students had worried about whether they belonged their first year of college but that they became more confident in their belonging as time went on. The students read quotes from individual students and wrote a short essay about how their own experiences echoed the survey, which they read in front of a video camera to help future students. Freshmen in the second condition served as a control and did a neutral version of the activity where the survey and essay topics were unrelated to social belonging. The belonging booster was expected to especially help African American students, who more often express higher levels of uncertainty about belonging in college and are at risk for the negative consequences of feeling that they do not belong.

Figure B.1 shows the effect of the study as measured by the students' grade point averages. GPAs generally went up from the start of college to the end, even for the neutral group. However, focusing on the African American students reveals a telling story. At the start of college, the African Americans in both conditions had lower GPAs than their European American counterparts. Three years later, the GPAs of African American students who did the neutral activity still exhibited a large achievement gap. In contrast, the students who completed the belonging booster made significant gains, cutting the achievement gap by 79 percent. Followup surveys indicated that the one-hour intervention particularly helped the African American students to reframe their interpretation of the daily adversities of being in college—rather than seeing adversity as symbolizing that they do not belong, they reframed the setbacks as simply setbacks. "The intervention robbed adversity of its symbolic meaning for African Americans, untethering their sense of belonging from daily hardship" (Walton & Cohen, 2011, p.1449). It is of note that the intervention did not influence the European American students. Presumably, this is

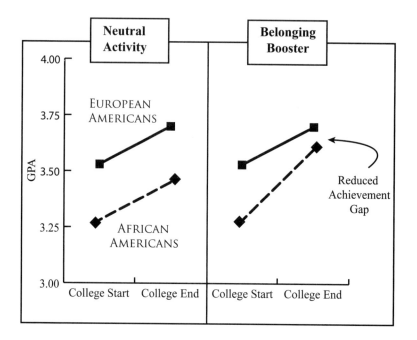

Figure B.1. Grade point averages during the first and last semesters of college. African Americans who participated in a brief exercise to help them appreciate that they do belong in college realized more of their academic potential over the four years than did African Americans who did not receive the exercise. The European Americans did not exhibit any effects of the belonging treatment, because they already felt they belonged in college. Based on data from Walton and Cohen (2011).

because they already felt they belonged at college, so they did not take early difficulties as evidence that they did not belong.

In addition to setbacks, there are ambiguous situations, which students will interpret based on their prior experiences. Figure B.2 shows how past experiences may lead students to different interpretations of an ambiguous classroom experience, such as a constructive criticism from the teacher (Aguilar, Walton, & Wieman, 2014). The students may see the critique as reflecting an area in which they have the capacity to improve (positive) or as an indication that they are not good at the subject (negative). These in turn can feed a cycle of increased effort, comfort, and success or of increased stress and anxiety, and poor performance, which will likely influence how the student interprets future interactions. The role that psychological belonging interventions can play is to help students reinterpret these ambiguous situations to avoid the negative cycle.

There are several ways to help people reframe or change their beliefs to

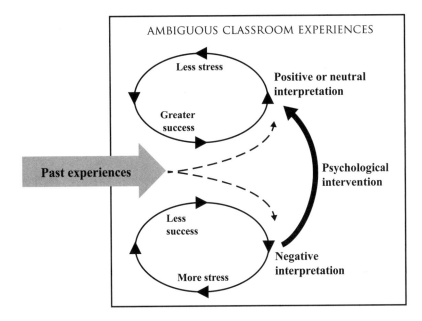

Figure B.2. Belonging cycle. (Reproduced from Aguilar, Walton, and Wieman, 2014)

reduce concerns about not belonging. In one set of studies, one group of women performed worse than men on a challenging math test. A second group of women were told beforehand that the test was gender-fair and would not produce gender differences. This group of women performed as well as the men (Spencer, Steele, & Quinn, 1999). Other studies have found that helping people to think about themselves as having multiple identities, in particular, focusing on those facets of their identity that are in-group (e.g., college student) rather than out-group (e.g., female), improves performance for those at risk of stereotype threat (Rydell, McConnell, & Beilock, 2009; for more examples, see http://www.reducingstereotypethreat.org).

CHANGING THE ENVIRONMENT

The second approach works on improving the environment. This can occur at the level of the whole classroom, the relationship between student and teacher, and the relationships among students. At the classroom level, it is valuable to establish shared classroom goals, norms, and values (see Chapter N). Remember, students need to adopt the goals and norms to feel a sense of belonging, so simply imposing them may not be sufficient. It can be more beneficial if students work together to negotiate a set of classroom goals and rules for the year.

The development of shared norms may be facilitated when students

Which are more important for being a good student? Rank them, putting the most important at the top, the least important on the bottom.

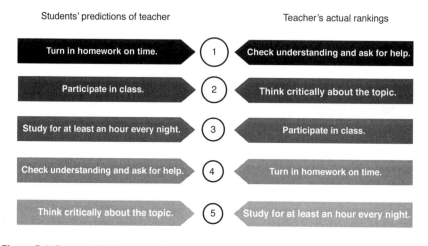

Figure B.3. Rate and Relate, an online environment in which students and teachers rank the importance of various activities and beliefs and also predict one another's rankings.

understand one another's perspectives. In particular, students and teachers may have different values or assumptions of which they are unaware. To help facilitate discussions about classroom norms and values, we developed an online environment called R2, for Rate and Relate, as shown in Figure B.3. The teacher produces a question and five possible relevant answers. Students anonymously rank the answers, and so does the teacher. The students also predict the teacher's ranking, and the teacher predicts the students' rankings. Afterward, the system reveals how well each party predicted the other's rankings. This creates an environment of perspective taking, facilitating an open discussion of why people thought what they did.

Research shows that, within the environment of the classroom, the relationships among people are very important (Goodenow, 1993; Osterman, 2000). A caring relationship between the teacher and students improves a sense of belonging. In particular, teachers who support students while allowing them to develop a sense of autonomy have shown the greatest benefits in motivation. Among students, a sense of belonging can be fostered through cooperative learning activities, discussion, and acting toward shared goals (see Chapter L).

In some instances, such as online courses, close physical proximity is limited, and self-motivated persistence is required. It is important to engineer the environment to support a sense of belonging. In online courses, one way to build community is to emphasize dialog and discussion in class forums, for example, making it a central part of student grades. Additionally, the instructor should appear active and visible, for example, through detailed feedback where possible, or facilitation of the discussion forums. Building trust among students by promoting honest peer feedback and discussion is another valuable addition.

III. The Outcomes of Belonging Interventions

The feeling that one belongs is wonderful. The feeling that one does not is awful. The key outcomes of belonging interventions are increased effort, greater persistence in the face of challenges, and decreased dwelling on whether one fits in or not. In turn, these proximal effects can further yield important distal outcomes such as better learning and performance.

Early studies of belonging showed that students with a greater sense of school belonging also had higher motivation, grades, and effort (Goodenow, 1993). The outcome of persistence is especially important, because it is precisely when tasks become difficult that people begin to question themselves. The importance of belonging for persistence shows up at early ages. For example, in one study (Master & Walton, 2013), preschoolers alone in a room received a very challenging puzzle to complete. In one condition, preschoolers simply received the puzzle. In another, they wore a shirt with the number 3 on it. They were told, "You're child number 3. You are the puzzle child." In a third condition, they wore a blue T-shirt and were told, "You're part of the blue group. The blue group is the puzzles group." Although all children did the puzzle alone, those who heard they were in the puzzles group persisted about 40 percent longer than the other two conditions. Identifying with the "puzzle group" increased persistence, even though the children never saw any other members of the group. In a related study (Butler & Walton, 2013), preschoolers (again, alone in a room) received a puzzle with one piece already completed and learned that another child in a different room had been working on it. One group of preschoolers were told they were taking turns with that child to complete the puzzle. The other preschoolers were told that they were working together with the child to complete the puzzle. Those who thought they were working together persisted longer and said they liked the puzzle better than those who thought they were taking turns. Similar research in adults shows the same patterns. For example, adults received a challenging math puzzle. They also wore an identification sticker. For one condition, the sticker indicated they were part of a "puzzles group." For the second condition, the sticker indicated they were a "puzzles person." The adults who thought they were part of the puzzles group persisted longer (Walton, Cohen, Cwir, & Spencer, 2012). Feeling social connection or part of a group increases persistence on challenging tasks, even when working alone.

IV. Can People Learn to Modify their Sense of Belonging?

Most belonging studies have asked people to engage in specific thought exercises or changed the environment for the people. Thus, it is unknown whether people can successfully modify their own sense of belonging or reduce their feelings of stereotype threat. However, it seems possible that people could learn to engage in some of the relevant exercises on their own. For instance, people can create study areas that have posters showing positive role models that mitigate stereotype threat (e.g., include posters of successful female scientists rather than only posters of male scientists). There may also be forms of value affirmations that can be learned. A study with middle school students found that having students do self-affirmation at the beginning of the semester, where they wrote about their most cherished values, reduced the effects of stereotype threat for African Americans. This led to improved performance in the class where they did the self-affirmation and in their other classes as well (Cohen, Garcia, Apfel, & Master, 2006). (See Chapter Y for additional techniques.) The belonging cycle (Figure B.2) indicates that belonging has a bootstrapping effect that can lead to a greater sense of belonging. In some situations, however, it may be too difficult for people to reimagine themselves as belonging, which leads them to withdraw further. In this case, outside social and environmental changes may be necessary.

V. Risks of Belonging Interventions

Belonging interventions, if done poorly, can backfire. One risk involves identification with poor role models. For instance, female role models can help women identify with otherwise male-dominated communities (e.g., computer science). However, if the female role models display low competence, it can hinder women's performance (Marx & Roman, 2002). Moreover, role models can inadvertently communicate stereotypes. Researchers discovered that having a female math teacher with math anxiety increased kindergarten girls' belief that boys are better than girls in math, and the girls' performance declined; the boys were unaffected (Beilock, Gunderson, Ramirez, & Levine, 2010).

A second risk is that belonging interventions may not feel authentic, which can lead to further alienation. People can put up their defenses when they feel they are being manipulated. It is also important to consider collateral effects. The Harvard Business School employed a program aimed at promoting gender equality. It resulted in improvements in women's grades and participation in top programs, a very positive outcome. However, it also raised new challenges, and there was a backlash against the intervention by some male students, who found it forced and intrusive (Kantor, 2013).

A third risk is that belonging interventions targeted to particular cultural groups may call attention to negative stereotypes or reinforce feelings of being different, inadvertently making students feel less like they belong or feel like they need special help because of their cultural backgrounds.

Lastly, students may not want to belong to a particular group. For example, it may be undesirable to belong to the "smart kids" group at school, and students may resist imposed identities or may suffer conflicts with other groups to which they wish to belong. In some cases, this may be a complex social issue not easily solved. In others cases, it may be possible to help students expand their view of the group, such that they could envision themselves belonging. For example, Boaler and Greeno (2010) found that even among students who have been successful in math, their vision of mathematics was at odds with their visions of themselves as a creative thinker. Being creative and being a math person are not at odds in reality, only in the views students constructed based on their experiences.

VI. Examples of Good and Bad Use

Many of the research studies on belonging use brief interventions intended to inoculate students against feeling excluded. An invigorated sense of belonging is going to fade if learners find themselves in an environment that is hostile. The teacher has responsibilities too. Here are some examples of classroom structures that do and do not support belonging.

BAD

Imagine a classroom in a school that tracks students by ability. Already there is an implicit in-group (the high track) and out-group (the low track). The teacher wants to help students aspire to the higher track by making it more attractive. To do this, the teacher spends more time with the high-track children. The teacher further implements a competition in the low track, whereby the winners can make it into the high track. Rather than inspiring children to try for the high track, these moves are more likely to make the low track a group to which no student wants to belong. Students will begin to opt out of the activities of the low track.

BAD

Imagine a diverse classroom where the teacher wants to foster belonging and knows that feeling belonging, in some sense, means feeling the same as others in the group. To establish this feeling among his students, on the first day of school he tells them, "I am color-blind, gender-blind, and religion-blind, and I don't care if you're poor or rich, foreign or native, fat or skinny. You are all students learning in this class." Unfortunately, his plan ignores the reality that his students do feel they belong to their respective groups. The point is not to get rid of students' differences but, rather, to help students understand that their differences do not present a barrier for belonging or succeeding in class. Honoring differences is particularly important in schools where succeeding has come to be associated with "acting white."

GOOD

Imagine a classroom where the teacher has explicitly created an atmosphere of respect and community. The teacher listens to students and acknowledges what they have to say. Students have agreed-upon norms and work cooperatively together to solve problems. Creating a space that fosters belonging is not easy. It takes time to build trust, and students may enter the classroom with a host of problems that make belonging difficult for them. However, it can be a powerful learning tool that is worth the effort.

VII. References

Aguilar, L., Walton, G., & Wieman, C. (2014). Psychological insights for improved physics teaching. *Physics Today, 67*(5), 43–49.

Beilock, S. L., Gunderson, E. A., Ramirez, G., & Levine, S. C. (2010). Female teachers' math anxiety affects girls' math achievement. *Proceedings of the National Academy of Sciences of the USA, 107*(5), 1860–1863.

Boaler, J., & Greeno, J. G. (2000). Identity, agency, and knowing in mathematics worlds. In J. Boaler (Ed.), *Multiple perspectives on mathematics teaching and learning* (pp. 171–200). Westport, CT: Ablex.

Butler, L. P., & Walton, G. M. (2013). The opportunity to collaborate increases preschoolers' motivation for challenging tasks. *Journal of Experimental Child Psychology, 116*(4), 953–961.

Cohen, G. L., Garcia, J., Apfel, N., & Master, A. (2006). Reducing the racial achievement gap: A social-psychological intervention. *Science, 313*(5791), 1307–1310.

Cuddy, A. (2012, June). Your body language shapes who you are. Retrieved October 1, 2015 from http://www.ted.com/talks/amy_cuddy_your_body_language_shapes_who_you_are

Goodenow, C. (1993). Classroom belonging among early adolescent students: Relationships to motivation and achievement. *Journal of Early Adolescence, 13*(1), 21–43.

Kantor, J. (2013, September 7). Harvard Business School case study: Gender equity. *New York Times.* Retrieved October 1, 2015 from http://www.nytimes.com/2013/09/08/education/harvard-case-study-gender-equity.html?pagewanted=all

Marx, D. M., & Roman, J. S. (2002). Female role models: Protecting women's math test performance. *Personality and Social Psychology Bulletin, 28*(9), 1183–1193.

Master, A., & Walton, G. M. (2013). Minimal groups increase young children's motivation and learning on group⊠relevant tasks. *Child Development, 84*(2), 737–751.

Osterman, K. F. (2000). Students' need for belonging in the school community. *Review of Educational Research, 70*(3), 323–367.

Rydell, R. J., McConnell, A. R., & Beilock, S. L. (2009). Multiple social identities and stereotype threat: Imbalance, accessibility, and working memory. *Journal of Personality and Social Psychology, 96*(5), 949–966.

Spencer, S. J., Steele, C. M., & Quinn, D. M. (1999). Stereotype threat and women's math performance. *Journal of Experimental Social Psychology, 35*(1), 4–28.

Steele, C. M., & Aronson, J. (1995). Stereotype threat and the intellectual test performance of African Americans. *Journal of Personality and Social Psychology, 69*(5), 797–811.

Walton, G. M., & Cohen, G. L. (2011). A brief social-belonging intervention improves academic and health outcomes of minority students. *Science, 331*(6023), 1447–1451.

Walton, G. M., Cohen, G. L., Cwir, D., & Spencer, S. J. (2012). Mere belonging: The power of social connections. *Journal of Personality and Social Psychology, 102*(3), 513–532.

B IS FOR BELONGING

What is the core learning mechanic?

Feeling that one belongs will increase effort and decrease distracting thoughts of inadequacy or alienation.

What is an example, and what is it good for?

Imagine you have just moved to a new state, and you are arriving at a new school for the first time. What is going through your head? "Will I fit in? Will I make friends? Will I be embarrassed in class?" When people make special efforts to make sure you feel like you belong, you will try harder to participate and learn. For example, a teacher might help you understand that everyone who is new, not just you, finds the schoolwork difficult at first. This way, you can realize that the difficulties you experience do not make you different from the group and that others in your situation have overcome the difficulties in the past.

Why does it work?

People try harder when they belong, and they are not distracted by a sense of alienation. Sometimes people feel they do not belong because they already belong to a group that is negatively stereotyped, such as "girls are bad at math." Increasing a student's sense of belonging to the learning community can soften the negative effects of stereotype threat.

What problems does the core mechanic solve?
- A student opts out of participation in class.
  - The student may feel like she does not belong and cannot participate fully.
  - The student may not want to identify with a particular group or topic.
- A student underperforms on tests compared to how he does in class.
  - An African American student may feel anxiety stemming from negative stereotypes about his race's academic abilities, which interferes with concentration on the test.
- A student feels out of place.
  - A successful female electrical engineering student is considering changing her major.

Examples of how to use it
- Change the environment to make it easier to belong.

- In a classroom, establish shared norms and encourage collaborative problem solving.
- In an online environment, encourage students getting to know one another in the forums.
- Help students reframe their sense of belonging.
  - Give students opportunities to see diverse role models who prove they too can belong.
  - Have students gain perspective on the many groups to which they successfully belong.

Risks

- Students may feel that belonging to a certain group (e.g., computer scientists, college-bound students) is in conflict with their current identity.
- Belonging interventions may inadvertently increase feelings of not belonging, or may call attention to it as a problem for students who did not initially think it was.
- Belonging interventions may wrongly place the burden of belonging on the student (e.g., "just change your attitude," or "just try harder to feel like you belong here").

C is for Contrasting Cases

Discerning critical information

CONTRASTING CASES ARE close examples that help people notice features they might otherwise overlook. They increase the precision and usability of knowledge.

Consider an example provided by Bransford and McCarrel (1974). Figure C.1 shows a solitary pair of scissors. You probably notice basic-level properties—it has two blades, two handles, and a center point that allows the scissors to close. You can imagine it opening and closing. This is what a novice sees, which you probably are (at least when it comes to scissors).

Next, consider the same scissors when contrasted with other examples (Figure C.2). Spend a minute looking at the examples, and keep this question in mind: why is pair D especially good for cutting toenails?

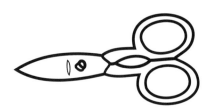

Figure C.1. A pair of scissors. (From Bransford and McCarrel, 1974.)

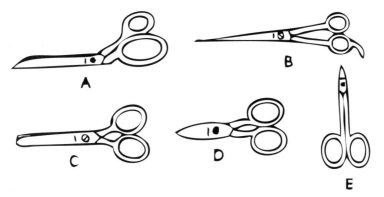

Figure C.2. Contrasting cases of pairs of scissors. (From Bransford and McCarrel, 1974.)

The contrasts may have helped you notice that pair D has a number of features for applying a large force—the blades are thick to cut tough toenails, the handles are large for multiple fingers, and the screw is close to the blades to maximize the leverage of the handles. Looking at some of the other scissors, one can begin to notice what makes them special, too. Pair A is for cutting cloth where the bottom blade slides along the table. Pair C is for children, so it has rounded tips to protect against unwanted pokes. Pair B is for cutting fine hair and the little hook on the handle is for extra control with the pinky. Pair E is for cutting cuticles. You can probably notice the features that make pair E perfect for cuticles.

Contrasting cases are close examples that help people discern what makes each instance distinctive. Tasting wines side by side is the classic example. Contrasting cases help people learn to perceive what they previously could not. Increasing the features that learners notice has a host of benefits that include better abilities to recognize what is important, a better understanding of abstract ideas, and increased recognition of when to use a piece of knowledge.

I. How Contrasting Cases Work

People often think of experts as having a great deal of abstract knowledge. Experts can also perceive more detail in their domain of expertise. Novices see their world in terms of *basic-level categories*—cat, dog. Experts see important subtleties that go beyond the basic categories of novices—Norwegian forest cat, Belgian shepherd. This is true of all types of expertise. Sommeliers can differentiate a Zinfandel from a Syrah, whereas most of us would just notice "red wine" (Solomon, 1990). Archeologists can differentiate types of dirt that novices completely overlook (Goodwin, 1994). For adult readers, the letters

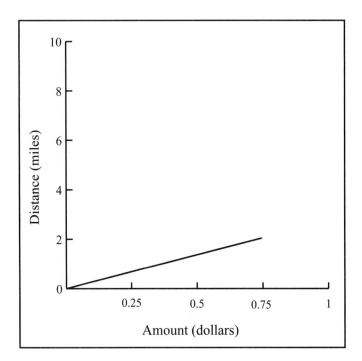

$$y = \frac{-0.75}{2} x + 10 \qquad y = \frac{2}{0.75} x \qquad y = \frac{0.75}{2} x$$

Figure C.3. Contrasting cases to help students discern the structure of equations. (Adapted from Kellman, Massey, and Son, 2010.)

'b' and 'd' and clearly quite distinct, whereas for young children these are not well differentiated and easily confused. Expertise depends on the ability to perceive features that beginners do not normally notice or recognize as important.

Experts develop their precision by comparing many examples over the years. Contrasting cases shorten the time to learn by using carefully juxta-posed examples. For instance, Kellman, Massey, and Son (2010) developed brief online modules to support perceptual learning in mathematics. Students make quick decisions for 120 problems, like the one shown in Figure C.3. Notice how each of the equations include similar numbers, forcing students to discern which structural relation best reflects the graph, not which numbers. After choosing an answer, students simply see the correct answer

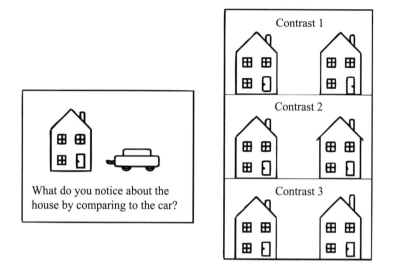

Figure C.4. Different contrasts highlight different features. Look at the house compared to the car in the left of the figure. Next, compare the house to each of the other houses to the right. Notice how contrasts 1–3 each help lift out a different feature of the original house.

without explanation. The goal is to have the students see the structure, not explain it. (Students also judge the other direction: they receive a single equation and pick which of three graphs characterize it.) Twelfth-grade students who completed the module nearly tripled their abilities to translate between graphs and equations, despite the fact that they had all previously completed algebra courses. The contrasting cases put them on a better trajectory to expertise.

Contrasts help people notice what is important. Each contrast lifts out a different feature. The left drawing of Figure C.4 shows a typical drawing of a house. It yields the basic-level interpretation of a house—a house compared to a car. Now notice how each of the close contrasts on the right, between two drawings of houses, pull out a different feature of the original house: contrast 1, the doorknob is on the left, and the door is off the ground; contrast 2, the roof has no eaves; contrast 3, the chimney is below the crown of the roof—a bad design for ensuring the smoke pulls through the chimney. Look back to the house by the car to see how much you originally missed.

The learner's goal for contrasting cases is to discern key features by differentiating one example from another. The Venn diagram on the bottom

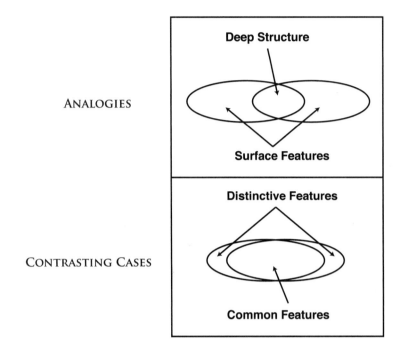

Figure C.5. Two ways to use multiple examples.

of Figure C.5 summarizes the idea. Again, we see a basic truth of learning: two examples are better than one. With the diagram of analogies, shown on top, the goal is to make examples as far apart as possible, so learners find the abstract commonality (see Chapter A). With contrasting cases, the goal is to make the cases as similar as possible, so learners find what makes each one distinct.

II. How to Design Contrasting Cases to Enhance Learning

Contrasting cases arose from research on perceptual learning (Gibson & Gibson, 1955). Perception differs from sensation. *Sensation* occurs when sensory receptors pick up energy from the environment. The eyes pick up light energy; the skin picks up heat energy. Lobsters have iron in sensory receptors that detect the earth's magnetic field—they are great navigators. Sensory signals travel from receptors to the brain. *Perception* is the meaningful interpretation of those signals. If one cannot perceive the patterns in sensation, they will be unavailable to conscious thought. While people may not learn to sense, they do learn to perceive. To help, one can provide carefully chosen contrasts that help learners pick out the relevant signals amid their many sensations.

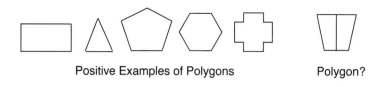

Positive Examples of Polygons   Polygon?

Figure C.6. Polygons

The use of contrasting cases is intuitive: pick examples that differ on select dimensions, and ask students to identify those differences. Surprisingly, its use is rare during instruction. The typical instructional thought process seems to be, "I need people to get good at recognizing this, so I will show examples of this over and over." The flaw in this reasoning is simple: *learning what a thing is also depends on learning what it is not.* Imagine, for example, that a teacher wants students to learn to recognize polygons. A typical approach would be to show several different polygons like those on the left of Figure C.6. Are these examples sufficient to help learners to answer the question to the right of Figure C.6?

Perhaps the reader already knows that polygons cannot have a line through the middle; students who are just learning do not. When students see the example on the right, they might just think that the other examples omitted an instance with a line down the middle. Figure C.7 has a better set of contrasting cases. With these examples, students have a better chance of noticing that polygons are two-dimensional shapes that do not have curves or crossing lines. The sample of non-polygons would be even better if they showed a figure that was open, such that all the line segments did not connect at their endpoints.

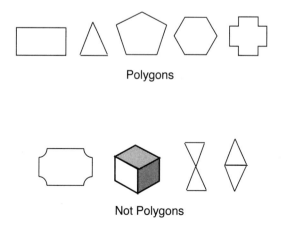

Polygons

Not Polygons

Figure C.7. Polygons and non-polygons.

A common alternative to the use of contrasting cases is to provide only positive instances plus a definition. In the case of the polygons, the assumption seems to be that students can use the positive instance to recognize new instances, and they can use the definition to exclude non-polygons. But if simply stating a definition were sufficient, then why bother with any examples at all? People learn from positive and negative examples.

A simple way to generate contrasting cases is to decide the features that learners need to notice and to pick contrasts on that feature. For instance, maybe you have experienced looking at flower books that have many easily confused daisy-like flowers. To help people discern the features that make each flower unique, it would be useful to see specific contrasts on the identifying features; for example, one contrasting example might have differently shaped leaves, another might have different numbers of petals, and so forth.

III. The Outcomes of Contrasting Cases

The most obvious outcome of contrasting cases is increased precision in noticing. People often hire experts because they observe meaningful detail, for example, when picking mushrooms in the forest or diagnosing a sore knee. An easy way to assess students' precision of noticing is to show a picture or figure of interest. Wait a few minutes, and then ask them to redraw the image. It will be easy to determine what they have learned to perceive by what features they include in their recreations. For instance, if asked to recreate Figure C.1 (without the benefit of studying Figure C.2), many people fail to draw thick blades that are shorter than the handles.

Contrasting cases activities help students learn the applicability conditions for their abstract knowledge (also see Chapter J). Students learn the situational cues that indicate which piece of their abstract knowledge they should apply. A common experience of college students is that they can bring a sheet of formulas to a final exam but cannot figure out which formula applies to which problem. This is not a memory problem—they have the sheet of formulas. The problem is that they never learned to discern the cues for when to use one formula instead of another. The result is inert knowledge: the students know the formulas but cannot use them. Contrasting cases can help students learn to "see" where they should and should not use their knowledge. As a simple example, coming up with a way to characterize home prices for the following two locations could help students later recognize when the median might be more appropriate than the mean as a measure of central tendency.

Pleasantville Homes For Sale	Sunnyside Homes For Sale
$150,000	$200,000
$225,000	$2,600,000
$300,000	$210,000
$275, 000	$170,000
$170,000	$115,000

IV. Can People Learn to Teach Themselves with Contrasting Cases?

Howard Gardner (1982) describes an art museum where the exhibit placed forgeries next to originals. Visitors would notice what made the originals paintings so special. In this case, an expert set up the contrasting cases for the visitors. There is not always a handy expert around to create the contrasting cases. Can people learn to pick their own cases? As a starting point, it can be useful to help students understand that making close comparisons is a valuable learning technique. For instance, when learning to recognize a Chinese written character, rather than just copying it over and over it works better to compare it side by side with similar-looking characters—this helps one notice what makes the character distinctive and helps avoid confusion with other characters.

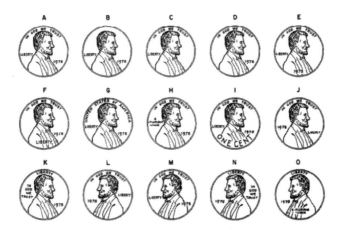

Figure C.8. Can you tell which of the images is correct? People can differentiate a penny from other coins, so they may never notice how little they have really "seen" in a penny. (Reprinted from Nickerson and Adams, 1979.)

A deeper challenge is whether people can learn to produce their own contrasting cases. There are two challenges. The first is that people naturally believe they perceive all that is before them; it never occurs to them that more information may be perceived. For instance, people can see enough about a penny to know it is different from a nickel. Because they can see "enough," they may not realize just how much they are missing, as is made evident by Figure C.8 (Nickerson & Adams, 1979).

The second challenge is that even if people believe there is more to perceive, how could they possibly pick the right contrasting cases to highlight something they do not yet know? It is a version of Meno's paradox: where would you begin to look for something, if you did not already know what you are looking for. There is no ready solution to these challenges, and it will be up to a knowledgeable instructor to construct the cases.

However, people can learn to pick contrasting cases when they know what question to ask. A relatively typical situation involves trying to determine if the presence or amount of a feature makes a difference. For instance, one might wonder if increasing the diameter of a spring affects the springiness. In this case, one would chose to contrast narrow and wide springs. Ideally, one would hold all other variables constant, such as the thickness of the wire and the amount of force applied to each spring. Learning to design effective contrasting cases is at the heart of conducting scientific experiments.

V. Risks of Contrasting Cases

There are two primary risks of contrasting cases: bad cases and bad tasks. Bad cases make it difficult for students to discern the intended features. A familiar version of this problem is comparing apples and oranges. There are so many differences that it is hard to know which comparisons are important. The tighter the contrast, the more likely the learner will notice the desired dimension of variation.

Bad tasks do not point students toward the significance of the contrasts. Asking students to "compare and contrast" does not provide sufficient direction. Students will find too many incidental differences and not consider the implications of what they find. They need a frame that guides their search for differences. For instance, for Figure C.2, asking people to notice the differences among the scissors does not work very well, because they will notice all sorts of unintended differences, such as the position on the page. For this example, it works better to ask learners to contrast the scissors with an eye toward their function. In general, there is a reason that some features are important to notice, and the task orientation should prepare students to appreciate the significance of the features. (For several fleshed out examples in statistics, see the appendix in Schwartz & Martin, 2004.)

VI. Examples of Good and Bad Use

Contrasting cases can also work for situations that do not depend on subtle visual discriminations. Imagine a lesson that involves comparing cell phone rate plans, with the goal to introduce students to the idea of slope and intercept. For instance, one phone might have a plan that charges only for usage (y-intercept: 0, slope: $.25/min), another plan might have a flat fee for unlimited usage (y-intercept: $50, slope: 0), and other plans have some combination of the two (e.g., y-intercept: $40, slope: 0 for the first 500 minutes, then 10 cents/minute). You decide to make four contrasting cases, laying out the costs in the form of cell phone brochure pages.

Bad: You lay out the four plans front to back on two sheets of paper. This is a bad idea, because it means people need to remember what they saw in one plan when they go to the next—if they never noticed the key feature, how will they remember it?

Better: Contrasting cases work better when they are easy to compare at a glance.

Bad: You indicate the cost breakdown for five separate features: data download, number of lines, number of texts, number of minutes, voice mail. This is too many contrasts for four phones. People will have trouble finding the key contrasts you care about, namely, allowance cost (intercept) plus additional usage cost (slope).

Better: Limit the number of variables, so that students can notice the key contrast on allowance plus additional charges. Show only one or two features for the first activity. Then replace those cases with other cases that highlight other features for the next activity. And so on. It often works better to use several small sets of contrasting cases that in turn each isolate a different feature than using one giant set of cases.

Bad: You tell students to compare and contrast the cell phone planes. Students will tend to list discrete pairwise similarities and differences, when you really want them to notice is that there is a trade-off in the intercept and slope.

Better: You give students some typical users, and you ask them which plan would be the best for each. This will lead them to notice the separate roles played by the intercept and slope.

Best: Ask students to make some sort of visualization that helps any user compare which phone is best depending on their typical monthly call usage. This will create a 'time for telling' so that students are prepared to hear the conventional solution (see Chapter J). So, after they have tried, you can show students how well a Cartesian plot solves this very problem.

VII. References

Bransford, J. D., & McCarrel, N. S. (1974). A sketch of a cognitive approach to comprehension. In W. Weimer and D. S. Palermo (Eds.), *Cognition and the Symbolic Processes* (pp. 189-229). Hillsdale, NJ: Erlbaum.

Gardner, H. (1982). *Art, mind, and brain: A cognitive approach to creativity.* New York: Basic Books.

Gibson, J. J., & Gibson, E. J. (1955). Perceptual learning: Differentiation or enrichment? *Psychological Review, 62*(1), 32–51.

Goodwin, C. (1994). Professional vision. *American Anthropologist, 96*(3), 606–633.

Kellman, P. J., Massey, C. M., & Son, J. Y. (2010). Perceptual learning modules in mathematics: Enhancing students' pattern recognition, structure extraction, and fluency. *Topics in Cognitive Science, 2*(2), 285–305.

Nickerson, R. S., & Adams, J. J. (1979). Long-term memory for a common object. *Cognitive Psychology, 11*(3), 287–307.

Schwartz, D. L., & Martin, T. (2004). Inventing to prepare for future learning: The hidden efficiency of original student production in statistics instruction. *Cognition and Instruction, 22*(2) 129–184.

Solomon, G. E. A. (1990). Psychology of novice and expert wine talk. *American Journal of Psychology, 103*(4), 495–517.

C IS FOR CONTRASTING CASES

What is the core learning mechanic?
Noticing the difference between two or more examples that seem the same at a glance.

What is an example, and what is it good for?
Comparing a square knot to a granny knot. The close comparison can help people see the differences, which in turn can prepare them understand an explanation of why the square knot is preferable to the granny knot. Contrasting cases help people notice subtle but important details that they might otherwise overlook. These details help people recognize one thing from another, and they prepare people to understand why the difference is important. Contrasting cases increase the chances that people will use the right knowledge at the right time, because people learn to recognize cues in the environment.

Why does it work?
People learn to perceive patterns in sensation. This occurs by discerning what makes one thing different from another. Contrasting cases juxtapose "near misses" to help students pick out distinctive features.

What problems does the core mechanic solve?
- Students misidentify examples or confuse one thing for another.
  - A student thinks a spider is an insect.
  - Someone believes that all country music sounds the same.
- Students do not understand an explanation precisely.
  - A student does not recognize the difference between force and work.
- Students fail to recognize where to use what they know.
  - A student brings a sheet of formulas to a test but cannot figure out which ones to use.

Examples of how to use it
- Provide "near miss" examples that highlight what a thing is and is not.
  - For an English language learner, contrast the sounds "pa" and "ba."
- Provide collections of examples that highlight critical dimensions of variation.

° Show paintings of the same scene from four different centuries.
° Give four examples of projectile motion that switch between two starting heights and two initial velocities.

Risks

- Contrasting cases may be too complex for students to notice key features.
- Students may not try to make sense of the differences they notice.

D is for Deliberate Practice

Becoming an expert

DELIBERATE PRACTICE IS characterized by a high degree of focused effort to develop specific skills and concepts beyond one's current abilities.

Deliberate practice contrasts with the more common practice of simply participating in an activity or profession to get better. For instance, playing basketball games is one way to get better at basketball. However, as weekend warriors know, just playing games leads to a performance plateau. To escape the plateau, players need to step away from the games that are the very reason for playing basketball and dedicate effort to improve specific shots, moves, and alas, conditioning.

The idea that pushing past performance plateaus takes effortful practice, and not simply repeated performance, comes from the study of experts. Researchers have studied many types of experts—doctors, physicists, artists, chess grand masters, cigar rollers, and even the experts who determine the gender of chick hatchlings (who knew?). While different types of expertise require different constellations of skills and concepts, there have been two common findings across all types of expertise. The first is that it takes about 10,000 hours of engagement to develop exceptional expertise. Famous scientists and artists did not produce their important works until they had been at it for a long time. Expertise, fittingly enough, depends on a lot of experience.

A commercial photographer is currently putting this claim to test: with little golf experience, he quit his job to devote 10,000 hours to practice in hopes of qualifying for the PGA tournament (see http://thedanplan.com). We hope he succeeds both for the science and for his faith in the science.

The second finding is that it is not just the quantity of practice but also the quality. Chess duffers get good by playing. Grand masters get great by further studying famous games. Deliberate practice involves focusing on what is beyond one's current skill set rather than just executing what one is already able to do.

Deliberate practice is effortful. Ericsson, Krampe, and Tesch-Römer(1993) compared violin students at a prestigious Berlin school of music. Some of the students were preparing to become music teachers, and others were preparing for careers as concert violinists. Those with the concert goal practiced alone (and not for fun) about twenty-four hours a week, compared with nine hours for the music teachers. Over many years, these differences accumulate into thousands of hours of practice. This indicates the importance of quantity. Indicating the importance of quality, students from both groups practiced about eighty minutes per session, but tellingly, the concert students had to nap after their practice sessions. This highlights how much concentration and energy they put into their practice. Deliberate practice, if done well, requires a degree of concentration that people cannot sustain. If students are practicing for more than two hours at a stretch, then it is a good bet they are not engaging in deliberate practice.

People often believe that experts rely on innate talent to achieve their status. In reality, what separates the truly great from the rest of us is many (many) more hours spent engaging in deliberate practice. Please pay attention here, because this one of those big points that contradicts popular belief: *whatever the contribution of innate abilities to performance may be, it appears to be small compared with the effects of practice* (Ericsson et al., 1993). The next time someone says, "I do not have the ability to become . . . ," you might consider reinterpreting the statement as, "I do not have the will (or opportunity) to practice enough to become. . . ."

One source of evidence that expertise depends on practice and not innate ability comes from the fact that experts rarely show outsized performance on tasks unrelated to their expertise. For instance, chess grand masters can remember the placement of pieces on a game board extremely well, unless those pieces have been placed at random (Chase & Simon, 1973). They have outsized memories only for game boards that are likely to occur in a chess game, not a generally superior spatial memory. Abacus masters—people who win abacus competitions—have prodigious memories for numbers (Hatano & Osawa, 1983). Hearing a new number every 2.5 seconds, they can compute the following in their heads and in real time without an actual abacus:

$$28,596 + 847,351,654 - 166,291 - 324,008,909 + 74,886,215$$
$$- 8,672,214 + 54,221 - 91,834 - 103,682,588 + 17,274 -$$
$$212,974,008 + 4,081,123 - 56,315,444 + 897,294 - 380,941,248$$

Notably, the abacus masters are no better than the rest of us at memorizing lists of words or fruits. This implies that they do not have a superior general memory capacity that enables their stunning performance. Rather, they practiced and refined specific skills needed for their expertise. They learned to simulate an abacus in their imagination, which helps them keep track of the numbers (by moving around the beads in their imagination). It takes about one year of deliberate practice to add each new column to a mental abacus.

I. How Deliberate Practice Works

Deliberate practice improves learning and performance through two cognitive mechanisms: chunking and knowledge reorganization.

CHUNKING

Chunking involves grouping smaller units of information into larger ones (also see Chapter E). Imagine trying to remember a phone number for the few seconds needed to type it into your phone. If it has a novel area code (so you need to remember ten digits) chances are it will be fairly difficult. This is because working memory (the memory system responsible for short term storage and manipulation of information) has limited capacity. People can consciously hold and manipulate approximately seven pieces of information at any given time. By chunking, the pieces of information can gradually become larger so that people can engage more information simultaneously. It typically proceeds through two phases: proceduralization and automatization. In the first phase, people use verbal control and explicit memory retrieval to guide the steps needed to execute a task. When learning to drive a stick shift, one might state the steps aloud or in one's head to guide action: "Push in the clutch with the left foot, take right foot off of the gas pedal quickly, use the right hand to move the gear shift into neutral, put the gear shift into first, release the clutch slowly with the left foot while increasing the gas slowly with the right foot." Eventually, the steps become procedures that do not need conscious, verbal guidance to execute. The micro steps involved in balancing the clutch release with the increase in gas have become a chunk. During automatization, the chunks link into sequences that fire off automatically. A practiced driver needs only to think one piece of information, "shift gears," and the whole sequence happens without further thought.

Interestingly, once procedures have been automatized, it is difficult for people to recover the original substeps. You probably do not know what your fingers are doing when you type, although once upon a time you thought very hard about each finger. This is what causes the common refrain, "I don't know how I do it—I just do it." While experts exhibit superior performance by definition, they may not be very good at decomposing and explaining their expertise. Being an expert does not entail that one can teach, which helps to explain some of the more awful college classes you took.

The same mechanisms of chunking also apply to conceptual domains. For a research scientist in psychology, the expression "within-subjects crossover design" neatly encapsulates many details about the experimental conditions and empirical hypotheses. A novice requires a laborious delineation of the logic of the research design; the expert understands in a single chunk.

Problem 1.

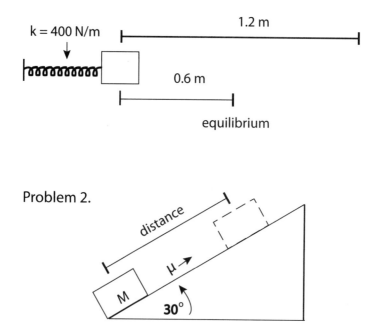

Problem 2.

Figure D.1. Two physics problems. Novices categorize these two situations as different, whereas experts treat them as the same, because they both involve conservation of energy. (Based on work by Chi, Feltovich, & Glaser, 1981

KNOWLEDGE REORGANIZATION

As people advance in a field they confront new problems, and the demands of those problems cause knowledge reorganization. For example, when you look at the two diagrams in Figure D.1 (don't worry, you don't need to solve them), a relative novice might see these as a spring problem and an inclined plane problem. Expert physicists see them differently: they consider these two situations highly similar, because they both involve conservation of energy (Chi, Feltovich, & Glaser, 1981). Conservation of energy is a major principle in physics, so experts reorganize their categorization of the world according to this principle.

Over time, engaging in deliberate practice changes people's knowledge organization, making it more specialized for the tasks they regularly face. For instance, in one study (Loftus & Loftus, 1974), people heard a subdiscipline of psychology (psychoanalysis) and the letter of a psychologist's last name (F). Their task was to generate the name of a psychologist who fit both constraints (Freud). For beginning psychology students, hearing the letter first, before hearing the subdiscipline, led to faster answers. For professors, hearing the subdiscipline first and then the letter led to faster answers. The novices had their memory organized by the generic alphabet structure, so the letter cue helped them execute their memory search faster. The professors had reorganized their knowledge of people according to their subdisciplines, so hearing the subdiscipline first helped them search memory more efficiently.

Deliberate practice isolates specific and often difficult tasks from the flow of the overall activity. This allows for the time and mental effort necessary to support chunking and knowledge reorganization.

II. How to Design Learning Opportunities for Deliberate Practice

Deliberate practice is ideal for people already engaged in authentic activities as a professional or hobbyist. (To get people started in an authentic activity, see Chapter P.) However, deliberate practice should occur outside the demands of the authentic activity. The basketball player who only works on her shots during games is not going to reach peak performance. Deliberate practice requires a narrow focus on difficult skills and concepts without risking the professional consequences of failure. For our driver who has been learning to use clutch, it is a good idea to practice on a steep hill when there are no cars behind. The opportunity to engage in deliberate practice depends on having the resources that permit carving out time for study and not just performance, which is a useful fact for companies that want their employees to continue growing their skills.

Deliberate practice can employ the techniques from nearly all the chapters in this book. It is a high-level theory about the conditions of effective practice rather than the specific techniques one should use to practice. The conditions that support deliberate practice are well-chosen goals and tasks, rich feedback, effort and rest, and copious amounts of motivation.

SETTING GOALS AND CHOOSING TASKS

It takes expertise to make expertise (Bransford & Schwartz, 2009). Expert teachers and coaches are important in helping people chose the right tasks to work on. If a task is too easy or too hard, it will not be effective. Instructors can also play an important role in targeting weak points. Even experts may miss areas that could use some work when practicing. For example, a running coach can point out a stride issue to an elite runner. In well-defined domains such as programming and mathematics, computerized cognitive tutors (Anderson, Corbett, Koedinger, & Pelletier, 1995) can track student performance, identify those skills that have yet to be chunked, and deliver practice for just those skills.

RICH FEEDBACK LOOPS

People must evaluate and improve their practice by seeing the effects of their efforts in the world (a quarterback seeing the spin of a football, a teacher seeing how well her students learned from her lesson). This feedback allows learners to refine and adjust their performance. Feedback from a knowledgeable coach or teacher, who can see what the person cannot, is also invaluable. (See Chapter F for more on how to use feedback to improve performance.)

EFFORT AND REST

Most readers have had the experience of working exceptionally hard to make sense of a difficult text or formula. This experience is quite different from doing just enough to get by. It is not possible to sustain deliberate practice for long stretches of time. (Recall the concert violinists needing to nap after an 80-minute practice.) Often, shorter sessions of intense concentration are better. If a school is giving three to five hours of homework a night, chances are that the students are not engaging in deliberate practice for all that time. Less and more focused practice may be better.

MOTIVATION

Deliberate practice is not always fun. For people advanced in a field, recognizing improvement is its own reward, and it may be all the motivation they need. For others, motivation may be more of a struggle. One way to address this is to incentivize deliberate practice and not just correct answers. In a math class, rewarding accurate 'plug and chug' can lead to mindless symbol pushing, rather than the difficult work of figuring out why the symbols work the way they do. Find ways to incentivize deliberate practice specifically, for example, by rewarding the effort (not success) at trying difficult, bonus problems. A more psychological approach to increase motivation is to encourage a growth mind-set that helps students appreciate that they can grow through practice (Blackwell, Trzesniewski, & Dweck, 2007). When people believe that talent is innately fixed, rather than something that grows, they may conclude that they are not smart enough to improve, or on the flipside, they may think practicing means they are not smart (see Chapter Y for tips on improving self-attributions about learning).

III. The Outcomes of Deliberate Practice

With practice, complex tasks execute seamlessly, so they are more efficient and less prone to forgetting and disruption by other tasks. A chef can chat while chopping an onion, but we would not suggest it for a novice. People can begin to work at the level of the chunk, which frees up working memory for considering other relations and alternatives. The chef can think of different ways to use a roux, whereas the novice is heads down following each step of the roux recipe. Deliberate practice helps people optimize their knowledge organization to fit the most important structures of an activity. The chef knows where to pay the

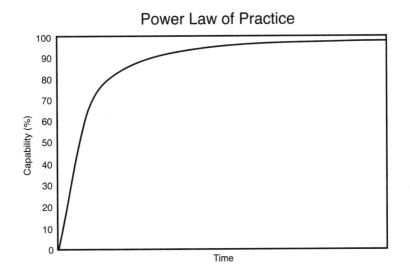

Figure D.2. The power law of practice. People show rapid improvement early, but then the gains attenuate.

most attention when planning a harmonious dinner, whereas a novice may just choose his favorite foods (pizza, peanut butter, and cold cereal).

Deliberate practice helps people elevate above plateaus in performance. Figure D.2 shows the ubiquitous power law of practice that applies to nearly all learning activities. (The term "power law" refers to the shape of the curve.) When just starting, there is tremendous room for improvement. People quickly become faster and more accurate. However, the gains begin to taper because there are fewer and fewer inefficiencies to squeeze out of performance. The power law leads to the famous 80/20 rule: one can learn 80 percent of the content in 20 percent of the time. The 80/20 rule is a great way to become a dilettante.

Figure D.3 shows the effects of deliberate practice over a lifetime of expertise development. Phase I involves general-interest development. Phase II shows the power curve as people begin to practice. Phase III is when people begin to engage in deliberate practice full time. One can see that it elevates people from the power curve of phase II.

It may be easiest to grasp the value of deliberate practice for physical skills, such as playing basketball or the violin. But it applies to all domains of endeavor. Famously, Benjamin Franklin's autobiography describes deliberate practice (Franklin, Woolman, & Penn, 1909). Franklin did not simply write, he engaged in effortful practice to improve his writing spacing. For example, he would take brief notes about the content of an article he admired, and later write his own version of the article based on his notes, attempting to emulate the style of the original author as he did so. When finished, he would compare his version to the original article, identifying and correcting his faults.

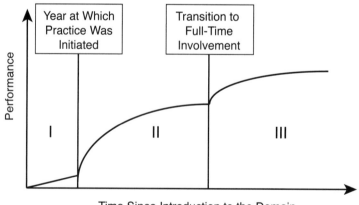

Figure D.3. Development of expertise over a lifetime. (Fom Ericsson, Krampe, and Tesch-Römer, 1993.)

Through deliberate practice, Franklin became one of the most influential writers of his time.

IV. Can People Learn to Teach Themselves with Deliberate Practice?

With enough domain knowledge people can (and do) teach themselves to engage in deliberate practice. For example, expert musicians practice alone every day. They know which skills they need to work on, what goals are appropriate, and how to structure their practice to work on those skills.

Novices find it harder to engage in deliberate practice on their own, because novices often do not have the experience to know what skills they should be working on or how to go about it. If people practice the wrong way, it can become a bad habit that is hard to break. One solution is to get instruction from a teacher or coach and then leave with some drills or tasks to work on at home. College classes often provide homework assignments that are intended to serve as guides for deliberate practice, and it is up to the students to focus and push themselves, rather than doing just enough to get by.

V. Risks of Deliberate Practice

One risk of deliberate practice is that it requires stepping away from the activities that make an endeavor enjoyable. For example, a guitar student might just want to play through all the songs she knows and may not want to work on finger drills during a lesson. There are the dual dangers that students will find a way to sneak around the needed practice or that they will burn out from the practice and stop wanting to engage in the activity altogether.

A second risk involves flexibility. People may become comfortable in their expertise and stop growing. An example might be an engineer who is very good at designing a particular kind of bridge that fits a common set of criteria. If a bridge request falls outside those criteria, the engineer will not take the job. The abacus masters discussed above developed a highly specialized routine, but they did not seek opportunities outside of this routine to expand their expertise. There is a natural gravity to rest on one's successes, because taking on unfamiliar challenges moves one out of a comfort zone and can lead to suboptimal performance, at least in the short run. One solution is to help people develop adaptive expertise (see Chapter K).

VI. Examples of Good and Bad Use

Good: A basketball player starts practice by shooting one hundred free throws. On each shot she focuses on her balance and knee bend, striving for perfect form.

Bad: A basketball player starts practice by shooting two hundred free throws while chatting with a friend and without focus on form. While this player put up more shots, the quality of the practice was neither effortful nor focused.

Good: A teacher focuses on mastering how he presents fractions to his students. He works on his fraction lesson, trying to anticipate how his students will respond to his tasks and what will be the challenging concepts for them. After seeing how the students responded, and informally assessing how well they learned from his lesson, he revises his lesson plan and makes notes for next year.

Bad: A teacher uses the same fractions lesson he used last year, not making changes despite some sticking points causing student confusion.

Good: A student in a physics course mixes up problems from different chapters of the textbook, solving each problem by first trying to determine which concept it embodies and which formula to use.

Bad: A student solves lots of problems simply by plugging in numbers to the given formula. While this student solved more problems, the quality of the first student's practice will make it more valuable.

Good: A guitarist focuses on the specific scores of a song she struggles with, practicing them over and over.

Bad: A guitarist plays through the songs she knows best and finds easiest. While this may be fun, it is not a good example of engaging in deliberate practice.

VII. References

Anderson, J. R., Corbett, A. T., Koedinger, K., & Pelletier, R. (1995). Cognitive tutors: Lessons learned. *Journal of Learning Sciences, 4*(2), 167–207.

Blackwell, L. S., Trzesniewski, K. H., & Dweck, C. S. (2007). Implicit theories of intelligence predict achievement across an adolescent transition: A longitudinal study and an intervention. *Child Development, 78*(1), 246–263.

Bransford, J. D., & Schwartz, D. L. (2009). It takes expertise to make expertise: Some thoughts about why and how and reflections on the themes in chapters 15–18. In K. A. Ericsson (Ed.), *Development of professional expertise: Toward measurement of expert performance and design of optimal learning environments* (pp. 432–448). Cambridge, UK: Cambridge University Press.

Chase, W. G., & Simon, H. A. (1973). Perception in chess. *Cognitive Psychology, 4*(1), 55–81.

Chi, M. T. H., Feltovich, P. J., & Glaser, R. (1981). Categorization and representation of physics problems by experts and novices. *Cognitive Science, 5*(2), 121–152.

Ericsson, K. A., Krampe, R. T., & Tesch-Römer, C. (1993). The role of deliberate practice in the acquisition of expert performance. *Psychological Review, 100*(3), 363–406.

Franklin, B., Woolman, J., & Penn, W. (1909). *The Autobiography of Benjamin Franklin* (Vol. 1). New York, NY: P.F. Collier.

Hatano, G., & Osawa, K. (1983). Digit memory of grand experts in abacus-derived mental calculation. *Cognition, 15*(1), 95–110.

Loftus, E. F., &, Loftus, G. R. (1974). Changes in memory structure and retention over the course of instruction. *Journal of Educational Psychology, 66*(3), 315–318.

D IS FOR DELIBERATE PRACTICE

What is the core learning mechanic?
Applying focused and effortful practice to develop specific skills and concepts beyond one's current abilities.

What is an example, and what is it good for?
A basketball player starts practice by shooting one hundred free throws. On each shot she focuses on her balance and knee bend, striving for perfect form. Engaging in deliberate practice is necessary to develop exceptional expertise. Yet, even for those who do not seek to be world experts, it can increase improvement. For example, a student in a physics course might engage in deliberate practice by mixing up problems from different chapters of the textbook, solving each problem by first trying to determine which concept it embodies and which formula to use. Contrast this with another student who solves lots of problems simply by plugging in numbers to the given formula. While the second student may solve more problems, the quality of the first student's practice will make it more valuable.

Why does it work?
Deliberate practice automatizes skills and concepts so they become faster, more accurate, less variable, and less effortful to execute. This allows people to see new patterns and frees cognitive resources so people can attempt more complex tasks. Additionally, deliberate practice leads to a reorganization of knowledge about a domain, such as a reorganization of physics formulas based on conceptual similarities rather than perceptual similarities.

What problems does the core mechanic solve?
- Students hit a plateau and are no longer improving.
  - A student is not getting faster or more accurate at a skill despite repeating it over and over.
- Even after many hours of homework, a student does not have a strong understanding of a topic.
  - A student is completing many problems, but is just going through the motions rather than engaging in focused effort.

Examples of how to use it
- Focus on specific skills and be goal directed.
  - For writers who want to improve their prose, try to convert every

instance of passive voice into active voice across several of your earlier writings.

- Go beyond current skills.
  - For a guitarist, practice the scores of a song you struggle with most, not those parts you can play with ease.

Risks

- Deliberate practice is difficult and effortful. Beginners may not engage or may burn out.
- People may develop rigid routines that prevent them from adapting to new situations.

E is for Elaboration

Making memories meaningful

ELABORATION IMPROVES MEMORY by making connections between new information and prior knowledge.

The outcome of the following scenario should be familiar. Sandra discovered a potential client while shopping at the mall. As they parted, the client said, "Call me at 422-8888." Sandra eagerly repeated the phone number while walking back to her car. On the way, a passerby asked for the location of a restroom. After answering the passerby, Sandra realized she had utterly forgotten the phone number she had just been repeating so successfully.

Poor Sandra—she should have tried to make meaningful patterns of the numbers. For example, "This would be my fourth client; 4 divided by 2 makes 2 (422), and adding them up makes 8, of which there are 4 again (8888)." By only repeating the phone number, Sandra did nothing to commit the number to long-term memory. Elaboration helps by actively connecting new ideas to ideas that are already in long-term memory, for example, by associating the phone number with the knowledge that this would have been her fourth client, and that $4 \div 2 = 2$. It is a basic truth worth memorizing: *repeating something over and over keeps it in your mind fleetingly, whereas connecting new information to what you already know creates a memory.* So, how will you remember this truth?

I. How Elaboration Works

The human body has many different memory systems, each specializing in a different type of information. The immune system, for example, has a memory. When people receive bone marrow transplants, doctors destroy the existing marrow. The immune system "forgets" all the diseases it has encountered, and it needs to relearn from (painful) experience. The immune system is the poster child for the wisdom that it is much more efficient to remember a solution than figure it out afresh. At the same time, the immune system also cautions us that memory is insufficient for adaptive behavior, because we still need to handle novel problems (new germs) for which we have no exact memories.

Elaboration is a strategy specialized for memorizing declarative information—things about which one can talk. The amount of declarative information that people know is astonishing. Newspaper articles, movies, a bully from second grade, sundry math facts, your friend's preferences, alphabetical order, favorite dinners—it's all in there. It is a good thing people do not remember everything at once! The great trick of memory is to remember the right thing at the right time. Elaboration helps.

To understand how elaboration works, we need to consider two of our many memory systems. One is called working memory. It enables the conscious manipulation of information, for example, when thinking through a problem. Working memory has only temporary storage. Information moves

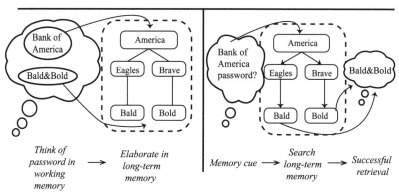

Figure E.1. The benefits of elaborative encoding for retrieval. Elaboration makes connections between an idea in working memory and long-term memory. During retrieval, the increased pathways among ideas improve the chances that the memory will be found.

in and out of working memory depending on the problem at hand. Working memory cannot hold information very long, so people need to keep refreshing the information, for example, by repeating the name of a person they just met. Refreshing the information keeps it available for immediate processing in working memory, but it is a poor technique for storing the information for later use. To file the information away for later use, people need to encode it in long-term memory. Long-term memory holds information indefinitely. Encoding is only half the story, however. To use the stored information, people need to be able to retrieve it from long-term memory to help solve problems and answer questions using their working memory.

Figure E.1 shows the distinction between encoding and retrieval. The left side, which is a massive simplification of what goes on in the brain, shows how someone might use elaboration to remember the password to a Bank of America online account. The elaboration connects both the bank's name and the password (Bald&Bold) to the idea of America, using the associated ideas of brave and eagles.

The right side of Figure E.1 shows the payoff of elaboration. Retrieval is a process of spreading activation. Working memory makes a request of long-term memory, such as "What is my Bank of America password?" This activates a long-term memory, such as *America*. The activation in *America* cascades across associated ideas. The activation spreads through several connections that lead to the desired memories, which become sufficiently active that they become available to working memory.

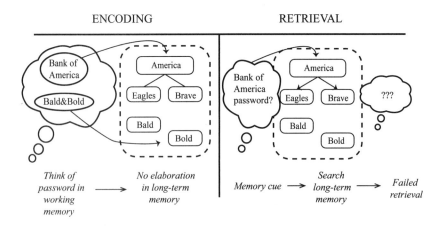

Figure E.2. What happens when people do not use elaboration. During encoding, the new ideas (Bald and Bold) do not connect with other ideas in long-term memory. During retrieval, there is no path back to the original ideas, so they cannot be found in memory.

Figure E.2 shows what happens when people do not elaborate new information. Even though the information may make its way to long-term memory, it remains unconnected to any other ideas. It is hard to search for the memories, because there are no connections to them. As an analogy, it is much easier to find documents in a well-organized filing system than a box filled with mounds of paper.

The formal representation of memory networks can become very complicated. The basic mechanism is simple—ideas that fire together wire together, and ideas that wire together fire together. Elaboration increases the chances that one idea will fire another idea you want to remember.

II. How to Use Elaboration to Enhance Learning

Elaboration is useful for memorizing meaningful material, including new vocabulary words, sentences, people's names, directions, or even phone numbers. Ironically, elaboration does not need to be very elaborate to make a difference. In one study, participants had to memorize one hundred words (Tresselt & Mayzner, 1960). There were three conditions: cross out the vowels, copy the words, and judge the degree to which each word was an instance of the concept "economic" (e.g., *poem* would be low, and *credit* would be high). When asked to remember the words, participants in the judge condition did twice as well as the copy condition and four times as well as the cross-out-vowels condition.

If the goal is to memorize, elaborations do not need to be correct. For instance, given the sentence "A group of woodpeckers is called a descent," people can elaborate the sentence by manufacturing a "because" to finish it out. A group of woodpeckers is called a descent because . . . together they could fell a tree. Of course, it is probably best to elaborate with a true reason so that one does not build up misconceptions (e.g., a group of woodpeckers may actually be called a descent because woodpeckers like to peck trees from the top to the bottom). Nevertheless, to simply remember the woodpecker-descent connection, the accuracy of the "because" does not matter.

The basic strategy for improving memory is to make up relevant connections to what one already knows. There are three complementary approaches: precise and relevant elaborations, chunking, and connecting to well-structured knowledge.

PRECISE AND RELEVANT

Relevant and precise elaborations create better retrieval paths. For instance, in one study people read sentences in one four conditions (Stein & Bransford, 1979):

(a) The tall man purchased the crackers. (no elaboration)
(b) The tall man purchased the crackers. (come up with own elaboration)
(c) The tall man purchased the crackers that were on sale. (irrelevant elaboration)
(d) The tall man purchased the crackers that were on the top shelf. (relevant elaboration)

People read 10 sentences like these. Afterward, they took a memory test in which they had to provide the missing adjective for each sentence: The _____ man purchased the crackers.

The percentages of correctly remembered words were as follows:
(a) 42 percent (No Elaboration condition)
(b) 58 percent (Self-Elaboration condition)
(c) 22 percent (Irrelevant Elaboration condition)
(d) 74 percent (Relevant Elaboration condition)

The relevant elaboration provided a precise connection that marked the relevance of the man's height for reaching the crackers. On average, receiving a relevant elaboration was even more effective than generating a

Figure E.3. Meaningful elaborations can help us remember images. How would you elaborate these images to improve your chances of remembering them later? (Reprinted from Schwartz, 1999.)

self-elaboration. This is likely a result of some people making ineffective elaborations: when people in the self-elaboration condition did generate their own precise and relevant elaborations, their probability of recall was 91 percent (Stein & Bransford, 1979).

Relevant elaboration can also improve memory for pictures. Pretend you need to remember the images in Figure E.3. They may appear as a bunch of very hard to remember squiggles. It would help if you could elaborate by connecting the squiggles to something you already know. Here is a clue: the image in the upper left corner is the head of a baseball player. For fun, we will let you figure out the other three (we provide them below). One handy use of elaborating visual information is to remember people's names. Find a way to connect a name to its owner's facial features. To make up an example, the two Bs in "Burt Bennett" stand for his black beard.

CHUNKING

Chunking depends on uniting discrete ideas (see also Chapter D). For instance, to remember the digits 2 6 2 4 2 2 2 0, one can chunk them as 26, 24, 22, and 20. Although there are still eight digits, it is easier to remember four numbers than eight. (One can go further to elaborate that each chunk is two less than the preceding one.) Chunking depends on elaboration, because it is prior knowledge that enables people to convert two digits into a single number (and to notice the pattern of subtracting by 2). A second example is to chunk words into a sentence: house, dog, car, sprint, spring → Last *spring*, my *dog sprint*ed from the *house* to chase a *car*. Here, the list is elaborated by chunking the words into a single sentence and by connecting the sentence to prior experience.

CONNECTING TO WELL-STRUCTURED KNOWLEDGE

A third elaborative technique associates the new material to well-structured knowledge. The *method of loci* is an example. If people need to remember a series of steps, parts of speech, or other sequential information, they can associate each step to a different room of their house or office. Once they have mentally "placed" the memories in their locations, they can later retrieve the memories by taking an imagined walk through the house. The spatial memory for the house provides a well-known search path for finding the memories. When you try to remember a person's name by working through the alphabet, you are relying on a well-known sequence to help search memory. Did it start with an A, B, C . . .?

A hierarchy is also an example of a well-organized structure. In a famous study (Ericsson, Chase, & Faloon, 1980), a person had to remember long lists of numbers. The person happened to be an active marathon runner. He took sequences of numbers and associated them with known race times. For instance, 3 5 9 1 2 becomes 3 hours 59 minutes and 12 seconds. He then further organized the elaborated chunks into a hierarchy such as race times early and late in his career. This way, he only needed to remember "my early career race times," and it would connect to the chunked times and the digits within each chunk.

The three remaining elaborations for Figure E.3 are James Dean (lower left), a baby (upper right), and Santa Claus (lower right) (Schwartz, 1999).

III. The Outcomes of Elaboration

Elaboration improves memory for declarative information, especially under conditions of *cued recall*. There are different conditions under which one might need to remember something. For instance, one condition merely involves *recognition memory*: "I've seen that painting before." Under conditions of cued recall, a thought or stimulus cues memory for an associated idea. Most school-based memory tests rely on cued recall: Given the name of a vocabulary word, remember the definition. Remember the prime factors of 12. What is an example of an apex consumer? In each case, having more connections between the possible cues and the memory will improve the chances of retrieving the answer.

IV. Can People Learn to Teach Themselves with Elaboration?

As presented here, elaboration is primarily an aid for memory. (To improve understanding, it requires more constrained forms of elaboration, such as self-explanation; see Chapter S.) Elaboration strategies are relatively straightforward to teach and learn. In one study (Weinstein, 1982), researchers told adolescents several elaboration strategies, including create a mental picture, invent a story or sentence, and draw similarities and differences to what they already know. The students practiced with further coaching once a week for five weeks. On the sixth week, they read a passage without coaching. One month later, the students showed better memory for the passage than students who had not received elaboration training.

Even five-year-olds can learn simple elaboration strategies (Yuille & Catchpole, 1973). Children played a game in which they had to remember which objects went together. Researchers trained one group of children to imagine object pairs interacting, such that children learned to generate their own elaborations. The experimenters showed children ten pairs of objects side by side and then showed how the objects in each pair could interact, such as putting a hat on a duck, or a rock on a spoon. After the ten training pairs, the experimenters told the children they would get new pairs of objects to study.

They encouraged the children to think about how the objects in the new pairs might interact, similar to what they had seen in the training pairs. The children then saw a sequence of twenty pairs of objects set side by side.

This group of children was compared with two groups who were not trained to imagine objects interacting. In the Side-by-Side condition, children simply saw the twenty pairs of objects and heard that they "go together." In the Interacting condition, the experimenters demonstrated the twenty pairs of objects interacting together, so that the children saw experimenter-generated elaborations. All the children then completed a cued-recall test. They saw one of the objects (e.g., a rock) and had to pick out the paired object (e.g., a spoon).

Object presentation	Elaboration Training	No Training	
	Side-by-side	Side-by-side	Demonstrated Interacting
Average cued recall	11.6	6.1	12.2

Table E.1. Memory performance of five-year-olds taught and not taught to elaborate twenty pairs of objects (Data from Yuille & Catchpole, 1973)

Table E.1 shows the results of the cued recall test for the twenty study pairs. There are two relevant comparisons. The first is that the children who received the elaboration training nearly doubled the performance of otherwise equivalent children who did not receive training and also saw each pair just side-by-side. The second is that children who learned to elaborate a connection between two objects did nearly as well as the children who saw the experimenter explicitly show the objects interacting. This indicates that the trained children had learned to elaborate quite well, even when not receiving the support of the experimenter to do so. Whether these children continued to elaborate for the rest of their lives when nobody was telling them to imagine is unknown (and unlikely). Nevertheless, the study provides a concrete model for how to help children understand how they can use an elaborative strategy.

V. Risks of Elaboration

Cognitive overload can block opportunities for elaboration. Perhaps you have had the experience of being introduced to someone and forgetting her name within a minute. You were probably putting most of your cognitive resources into the social aspects of the introduction (e.g., saying something intelligent and observing the reaction). You did not have the cognitive resources to spare for elaborating the name and committing it to long-term memory.

Working memory can work with only a few ideas at once. When there is too much information simultaneously, people experience high *cognitive load* and it is difficult to elaborate, because just keeping all the information in working memory is so much work. High cognitive load is a problem during many college lectures. Chemistry and mathematics lecturers are notoriously inconsiderate, because they present many new equations and ideas one after another. The sheer number of new ideas introduced per minute makes it difficult to pay attention to all the new information and elaborate it simultaneously. Professors often forget how hard they worked to make sense of all that they know—after all, it seems so obvious to them now. Consequently, they offer lectures that are suitable for their peers, not for students. Compared with students, their faculty peers can readily follow the lectures, because they already know much of the information being presented and they have well-organized knowledge structures for quickly connecting a new equation or idea to what they know.

A second elaboration risk is that people can misidentify what they need to remember. Imagine that you need to remember the following words: bun, stew, bee, boar, chive, ticks. A reasonable strategy is to elaborate the words into food and creature categories. But what if the recall task demanded remembering the order of the words? Then it would be better to use the peg-word method: one-bun, two-stew, three-bee, four-boar, five-chive, six-ticks. It is important to define one's memory goals before elaborating.

VI. Examples of Good and Bad Use

A common practice asks students to construct sentences using new vocabulary words. When done well, it entails elaboration and improves memory for the vocabulary words and their meaning. When done poorly, it is useless. Here is a series of possible sentences for the word *gloaming* (twilight) ranked from worst to best with respect to elaboration:
- *Gloaming is spelled g-l-o-a-m-i-n-g.*
  - Not meaning focused
- *Gloaming means twilight.*
  - Rehearsal, not elaboration
- *Gloaming could be a name for my dog. Sit, Gloaming, sit.*
  - Irrelevant elaboration to prior knowledge

- *Gloaming is when the horrible mosquitoes finally went to bed during my recent hike.*
  - Relevant elaboration to prior knowledge
- *The lovers glowed as they stole a kiss under the gloaming fringe of the night's cloak.*
  - Precise, double elaboration comprising the sound of the word and its meaning

VII. References

Ericsson, K. A., Chase, W. G., & Faloon, S. (1980). Acquisition of a memory skill. *Science, 208*(4448), 1181–1182.

Schwartz, D. L. (1999). The productive agency that drives collaborative learning. In P. Dillenbourg (Ed.), *Collaborative learning: Cognitive and computational approaches* (pp. 197–218). New York: Pergamon.

Stein, B. S., & Bransford, J. D. (1979). Constraints on effective elaboration: Effects of precision and subject generation. *Journal of Verbal Learning and Verbal Behavior, 18*(6), 769–777.

Tresselt, M. E., & Mayzner, M. S. (1960). A study of incidental learning. *Journal of Psychology, 50*(2), 339–347.

Weinstein, C. E. (1982). Training students to use elaboration learning strategies. *Contemporary Educational Psychology, 7*(4), 301–311.

Yuille, J. C., & Catchpole, M. J. (1973). Associative learning and imagery training in children. *Journal of Experimental Child Psychology, 16*, 403–412.

E is for Elaboration

What is the core learning mechanic?
The process of elaboration involves explicitly connecting new information to what one already knows. Elaboration increases the chances of remembering the material later.

What is an example, and what is it good for?
A student needs to memorize a problem-solving cycle that has the following elements: identify problems, define goals, explore strategies, anticipate outcomes, look back to learn. An elaboration strategy is to find a way to connect each of these steps and relate them to one's prior knowledge. One solution is to generate the acronym *IDEAL* and connect it to the idea of an ideal problem solver.

Why does it work?
Human memory is vast. Remembering depends on finding the right memory at the right time. Elaboration makes connections among memories when learning, so it is easier to find a path to the stored information later. For instance, when asked how a "good" problem solver operates, one might think good → ideal → IDEAL → identify problems, define goals. . . .

What problems does the core mechanic solve?
- Students forget too much.
  - They have trouble remembering vocabulary words and their definitions.
  - They cannot remember the steps in a procedure.
- Teachers cannot remember student names.
  - A teacher rereads the student roll sheet but cannot remember who is who.

Examples of how to use it
- To learn vocabulary words.
  - Create a sentence that reflects the meaning of the word *precisely.*
- To remember a long speech or a long sequence of actions.
  - Associate each section/step with way stations on a route that one travels frequently.
- To memorize a set of rules.
  - Make up an acronym that summarizes the rules. The acronym *FOIL* (first, outer, inner, last) helps people remember the rules for multiplying binomials.

Risks

- Teachers (and videos) may move so quickly that students do not have time to elaborate.
- People may fail to identify what they are supposed to remember and elaborate.

F is for Feedback

Supporting self-improvement

FEEDBACK IS INFORMATION that flows back to learners about the quality of their ideas and behaviors. Learners can then use the feedback to make adjustments.

A kindergarten teacher of our acquaintance asked us to finish the following sentence:

Practice makes _____.

We took the bait and said, "Perfect." He said, "No! Practice makes permanent. Practice with feedback makes perfect!"

It is a poor idea to try improving at archery without ever seeing where your arrows land. Nevertheless, many learning systems may not build in feedback. For instance, more experienced clinical psychologists do not produce better client outcomes than less experienced clinicians. This is because the structure of the professional system does not deliver reliable, objective feedback about patient outcomes. It is hard for the clinicians to learn what works. They are left to make their own judgments, which may be biased toward seeing success rather than places to improve (Saptya, Riemer, & Bickman, 2005).

Feedback improves learning at the individual, group, and institutional level. This chapter discusses informative feedback. *Informative feedback* indicates a discrepancy between the current outcome and the desired goal, so learners can take steps to improve. This differs from reinforcement feedback, which employs rewards and punishments to change the likelihood that learners will repeat a behavior in the future (see Chapter R).

I. How Feedback Works

Feedback appears in very many forms, for example, verbal corrections from others, noticing that your behaviors are not working, or a little voice in your head telling you that you just said the wrong thing. Control theory (Powers, 1973) provides a theory of feedback that can be exemplified by a softball fielder catching a fly ball. The fielder uses her eyes to collect feedback about whether the ball is on track toward the glove. When the feedback indicates that the ball's trajectory and the glove are mismatched, the fielder moves her glove accordingly. According to control theory, the only informative feedback is *negative feedback*, which indicates a discrepancy from a goal state (negative does not mean punishing). *Positive feedback* indicates there is no need to change, so there is no need for new learning or behavior—the ball is on track to hit her glove. Most human behavior is more complex, and both positive and negative feedback can be informative for learning. For instance, when preparing a speech it can be helpful to know which sections people appreciate so you can revise around those strengths. The key point is that to be effective, informative feedback needs to be . . . well, informative.

Figure F.1 shows a continuum of the information value of feedback. "No feedback" is at the far left, as it offers no information to the learner. Feedback that indicates a "right" behavior is a little more informative, because it signals that people can continue whatever behavior they have been doing. Next is feedback that indicates "wrong" behavior, signaling a need for new learning. Farther to the right is feedback that indicates a specific discrepancy: knowing that your essay had too few supporting statements is more useful than knowing that your essay was wrong. Next is elaborative feedback, which further includes a verbal explanation of where the error resides and, ideally, why.

Figure F.1. A continuum of the information content in feedback. As is often the case in learning, there is a sweet spot that resides somewhere between too little and too much.

When correcting an essay's prose, a teacher might elaborate by explaining that the phrase "in order" adds wordiness without substance—so, ~~in order~~ to reduce wordiness, don't use it. Finally, there is feedback that provides so much information that learners cannot make sense of it: "Purpose can be expressed with the prepositional phrase in order followed by an infinitive clause or a that-clause (almost always with a modal may or might). The prepositional phrase in order is often omitted in informal speech."

The sweet spot for feedback depends on the learner's knowledge. Very knowledgeable learners completing a familiar task may need only right/wrong feedback. They can fill in the mental blanks about what went wrong and how to correct. For novices, the sweet spot resides between discrepancy and elaborative feedback. We provide multiple examples below. The choice of whether to add an explanation to discrepancy feedback depends on how disruptive the explanation will be. For example, receiving an explanation about a mistake in a video game can ruin the flow the video game is trying to produce. Most video games are designed so that people can eventually figure things out just using discrepancy feedback.

II. How to Use Feedback to Enhance Learning

Anytime instructors teach anything, no matter how good their curriculum or teaching skill, students will sometimes learn imperfectly and will make mistakes. How should the instructor handle this? One common solution is to repeat the instruction—slower and louder—hoping that it will work the second time. Another possibility is to include a second, back-up method of instruction; when students do not learn from initial instruction, maybe a second method will work better. This is an expensive solution, because one has to develop the same lesson in two different ways. The feedback solution is to focus on the information you provide to students, so they can self-correct. *It is striking how many educational programs have well-conceptualized instruction yet fail to include provisions for effective feedback.*

The key task for the design of effective feedback is to enable learners to solve the assignment-of-credit problem. Imagine a computer that plays chess and tries to learn from its mistakes. The computer loses a game. It needs to trace backward through all its earlier moves to figure out which move was the big mistake. The assignment-of-credit problem involves identifying the specific condition, behavior, or idea that eventually led to the undesirable outcome. Feedback that is specific, timely, understandable, and nonthreatening can help students solve the assignment-of-credit problem. To this list, we add one more proviso: people need an opportunity and reason to revise. Together, these features form the lovely acronym STUN-R.

Figure F.2. *Critter Corral* (a free iPad math app) provides discrepancy feedback and opportunities for informed revision. A child choses five fish to deliver to seven patrons. The display allows the child to see how far off he is. The child then receives a chance to revise his answer by increasing or decreasing the number of fish.

SPECIFIC

Good feedback helps learners locate the discrepancy between the desired goal and the actual outcome. Feedback delivery systems often fail to do this. In a review of mathematics software for three- to six-year-olds, we found that a large majority of the programs did not provide discrepancy feedback: children learn only that they are right or wrong; they do not receive any information about where the error resides. This is an easy problem to fix. For instance, an iPad game called *Critter Corral* lets students see how far their answer is from correct (Figure F.2). In one of the games, children need to decide how much food to serve to the restaurant patrons, and they can see if they served too much or too little. Ideally, this helps children learn the relative sizes of the numbers while also providing some guidance for how to revise. With only right/wrong feedback, learners can only guess at how to fix a mistake.

Technology is a good vehicle for delivering specific feedback. Mundane technologies, such as paper-and-pencil tests, can help pinpoint areas for additional work. Less mundane technology, such as pedometers, can give feedback by tracking, for example, how many steps people take a day. And least mundane, current investigations into how to use biofeedback may help sufferers of chronic pain: a patient can see a real-time readout of the activation levels in the brain's pain regions by watching a symbolic flame on a screen, which provides a much more sensitive and specific feedback signal than the general feeling of pain. This technology also comes with specific instructions on how to use the feedback to benefit the patient. Their task is to bring the flame down. While patients do not know how they do it, they learn to bring down the flame, which can enable them to bring down their actual pain in the future (for a review, see Chapin, Bagarinao, & Mackey, 2012).

TIMELY

Feedback needs to occur within a time frame that allows learners to figure out which event led to the error. When students take a test, it is useful to deliver feedback while they can still remember how they solved the problems. Otherwise, they will not be able to remember which of their thoughts was responsible for the error. After a delay they might not care, either—you know the case of the student (maybe you) who was dying to know how he or she did on a paper right after it was turned in but may hardly look at the feedback when returned after winter break.

As a thought experiment, imagine a person learning to play chess. You detect the person has made a mistake that will eventually lose the game. Should you provide feedback immediately after the mistake, or wait until the game ends? On the one hand, you want learners to identify the responsible action and correct it, and you do not want them to waste time on a doomed trajectory. Immediate feedback would be ideal for these goals. On the other hand, you may want learners to have an opportunity to see the implications of their mistakes, so they begin to understand how a particular idea or action fits within a larger system. For this goal, a small delay would be better. If you provide feedback at the immediate point of an error, students will avoid that specific move in the future, but they may never know why it was a mistake in the first place. For an algebra problem, sometimes it is worth letting students reach the answer $0 = 0$ before pointing out that they made a mistake in canceling out the variables.

There is no hard-and-fast rule for deciding when to deliver informative feedback, except to make sure it is close enough in time that learners can solve the assignment-of-credit problem yet still forsee the consequences of the error.

UNDERSTANDABLE

With life streaming past us so fast, it can be difficult to detect and interpret feedback signals in the flow. There are two effective ways to make feedback stand out for learners. One is supervised feedback, where another person (or computer) gives feedback to the learner. When teachers score a test, they are providing supervised feedback that tries to make sure the students can notice and interpret their error. In performance domains, recording and discussing a video of a performance is an excellent way to deliver feedback.

A second solution is to help people learn to comprehend feedback without supervision. To do this, learners need a recognizable standard of performance and a way to detect whether they have achieved it. For instance, in a course on psychological research, one objective was to help the students set internal standards for what it means to understand a research article. One possible standard is the ability to recapitulate what it was like to be a participant in the study from start to finish. The accompanying method of self-detection would be, "Can I imagine exactly what it was like to be a participant in the study?" This provides both a standard and an easy way for students to generate their own feedback about what they do not know.

NONTHREATENING

Experienced designers know they will iterate a design many times, and they adopt a "fail early, fail often" mantra. They expect early feedback to be negative, and they seek it to improve their design for the next iteration. For the rest of us, negative feedback stings, and we can have maladaptive responses. We might interpret the feedback as a sign that we are inadequate, or we may blame an unfair environment. We are probably assigning credit to the wrong source of error. A better solution is to assign the "blame" to a component of the specific task performance. For example, the knot was unsecured. Little tricks can go a long way in defusing people's tendency to take negative feedback as a threat to their self-esteem. Have students work in teams to report a group answer; thus, students will not feel personally threatened by negative feedback. It also helps to create a supportive, nonthreatening environment (see Chapters B and Y). We describe several more techniques in Section V in this chapter.

REVISABLE

For feedback to be maximally effective, people need a reason and opportunity to adapt. An interview with an adolescent summarizes the issue. We asked him what he would do if his math test came back with lots of red marks and a bad grade. He explained that he would be disappointed, but in the next week there would be a new topic, and he could try harder then. We then asked what he would do if he missed six free throws in a basketball game. He explained that he would practice each Saturday for twenty minutes. He would try to improve by one free throw every few months. If it went well, he could make the freshman team when he got to high school. Educational systems often fail to foreshadow a trajectory of growth that depends on revision. Simply providing a roadmap that shows student improvement over time can help create a mindset favoring revision and improvement rather than a series of discrete pass-fail scenarios. (Note, however, that making the roadmap public, for example, with a classroom star chart, can invite social comparison and lead to feelings of inadequacy.)

III. The Outcomes of Feedback for Learning

There have been very many studies about feedback, each with a unique characterization of feedback, unique learning goals, and unique ways of delivering the feedback. While all this variability in research can make it difficult to pinpoint any single feedback feature, it can work in our favor to indicate the robustness of the general idea of using feedback across many variations. Researchers can combine all these unique studies into a single analysis, called a *meta-analysis*. A meta-analysis evaluates the average effect across many studies that differ in details but are similar in their broad comparisons. Of special relevance, Kluger and DeNisi (1996) conducted a meta-analysis of 131 studies that compared learning with and without feedback (see their 1998 paper for a more digestible report). The analysis demonstrated that on average, feedback interventions raised student scores compared to interventions that did not include opportunities for feedback. Going even more meta, Hattie and Timperley (2007) reported the results of a meta-anaysis of meta-analyses (get your head around that one), which indicated that including feedback had, on average, a large positive effect on student learning. When done well, adding feedback is a powerful way to help learners improve their performance, regardless of the topic.

Feedback typically assists one of two types of learning. The most common helps people make incremental adjustments. This would be the goal of most homework feedback. The less common type of feedback signals the need for complete overhaul. For this latter kind of reorienting feedback, people are unlikely to figure out the required change based on feedback alone. Receiving feedback that a dolphin is not a fish is insufficient for children to learn that a dolphin is a mammal, especially if children do not understand the biological classification system. In cases of major change, feedback needs to be supplemented (or replaced) with a level of instruction more appropriate for learning novel content (see also Chapter U).

IV. Can People Learn to Teach Themselves with Feedback?

Everyone has pockets of specific expertise—sports, art, work, blogging. In those areas, people typically have a strong repertoire of precise goals that serve as standards for evaluating performance—a chef can tell when a dish is overcooked. In these pockets of expertise, people spontaneously use feedback for quality control and self-improvement.

Novices present a different story. An important component of early learning involves developing standards of performance (goals) and the ability to perceive when performance falls short. Yoga instructors help their clients learn to feel their body posture, so they can detect when they fall short of the goal. Trombone students have a difficult feedback problem: their skulls vibrate with their music, so it is hard for them to discern how a note sounds to the audience. It takes years to learn to interpret the feedback that is relevant to the audience's experience. (The same is true for writing, where authors need to learn what their writing sounds like outside their own heads.)

A major challenge for learners of a foreign language is that they cannot hear their pronunciation mistakes in the new language. Japanese uses a sound that resides between R and L (e.g., somewhere between *lavender* and *ravishing*). When learning English, it is hard for a Japanese speaker to hear the distinction between R and L, so they cannot tell if they have said *lavender* correctly. Contrasting cases provide one technique for helping people learn to notice the relevant information (see Chapter C). For instance, one can provide exaggerated contrasts of the sounds of L and R, so the learner can begin to hear the differences. The contrast can be slowly reduced until the speaker can hear the difference between L and R in typical speech. Once speakers can detect the difference, they can learn from feedback about their own speech, and their pronunciation improves.

Beginners often need to rely on others for feedback. They need feedback that goes beyond what they already know, and to be effective, the feedback should include constructive criticism. Can people learn to seek negative feedback of this sort? Simple tricks, such as a temporary mindset to think more broadly, can lead people to seek information that they might otherwise try to dismiss (Belding, Naufel, & Fujita, 2015). But this is a short-term effect that depends on putting the learner in the "right mood." Can we help people learn to seek constructive criticism more generally?

We addressed this question by making a game-based assessment called *Posterlet*. In the game, players create posters for booths at a funfair. They choose a booth and then design a poster. When done, they select a focus group of animal characters to assess their design. Each member of the focus group shows up with two thought bubbles, as shown in Figure F.3. One says, "I

Figure F.3. In a game-based assessment, players choose whether they want constructive criticism ("I don't like") or praise ("I like"). (Reprinted from Cutumisu, Blair, Chin, and Schwartz, 2015.)

don't like . . . " and one says, "I like . . ." Players can choose either the constructive negative feedback or the positive feedback about their graphic design for each character, but not both. Students then get a chance to revise if they want. Finally, they send their poster to the booth, and they learn how many tickets sold. Students repeat the cycle three times. All told, players have nine chances to choose between constructive criticism and praise (three per poster). The assessment is unique because the goal is not to test students' factual or procedural knowledge but, rather, to assess students' free choices relevant to learning (see Schwartz & Arena, 2013).

Researchers asked hundreds of students at schools in New York City and Chicago to play the game (Cutumisu, Blair, Chin, & Schwartz, 2015). The results were definitive. Students who sought more constructive criticism learned more about graphic design principles (there was a brief posttest to see what they learned from the game). Of special interest, the researchers also had access to the students' academic achievement scores in reading and math. Students who chose more constructive criticism in the game had also done better on their most recent state tests of academic achievement across both mathematics and reading, and the effect was stable across the different standardized tests used in Illinois and New York. Put another way, children who seek positive feedback do worse in school than students who seek negative feedback, whether in New York or Chicago. In a follow-up study, we conducted a teaching experiment. Students received explicit lessons that seeking constructive criticism is worthwhile for learning, even if it stings a little in the short run. Later on, these students chose more constructive criticism than did students who had not received the instruction.

V. Risks of Feedback

Learners often interpret feedback with an ego focus rather than a task focus. With an ego focus, learners will dwell on their self-regard rather than using the feedback to learn. Hattie and Timperley explain that when a student perceives feedback episodes as directed at the self, the episodes "have a negative effect on learning because they include or lead to self-handicapping, learned hopelessness, or social comparison. The related [task] feedback itself is usually discounted or dismissed, and goals of low challenge are adopted" (2007, p. 97). It is important for educators to keep learners' eyes on the task and not on their ego. One way to do this is to ensure the feedback is directed at the task or behavior and not at the people themselves. Don't say, "You are good poem writer, Johnny." Say, "The use of alliteration is very effective in this poem."

Deliver negative feedback in ways that encourage students to take it constructively rather than destructively. In a study with seventh-grade social studies students, teachers wrote constructive critical feedback on student essays (Yeager et al., 2014). Before returning the essays, researchers randomly appended one of two notes to each essay. In the "Wise" Feedback condition, the note stated, "I'm giving you these comments because I have high expectations and I know that you can reach them." In the Placebo condition, the note said, "I'm giving you these comments so that you'll have feedback on your paper." The researchers measured the frequency that students revised their essays. Students at the greatest risk for a misattributing the negative feedback as a self-indicator showed the greatest benefits of the treatment. Among these students, 72 percent revised their essays in the wise feedback condition, compared with 17 percent of the placebo students. Providing a way for students to view negative feedback as an opportunity for growth is key.

A second threat is that learners may not have sufficient knowledge to detect and interpret the feedback. Uninterpretable feedback is a recipe for frustration. Educators need to avoid overestimating what beginners can make of feedback.

VI. Examples of Good and Bad Use

The delivery of effective feedback often depends on a good guess about what students had in mind when they made the error. That way, it is possible to address the source of the problem and not just the outward error. Here are some simple examples of feedback that do and do not help students solve the assignment-of-credit problem in figuring out the source of the error.

BAD

Child answers: 3 x 2 = 5

Feedback: "That's wrong, dummy. The answer is 6." No one would actually do this, except maybe a cruel sibling.

Child answers: 3 x 2 = 6

Feedback: "That's right. You must be very clever." This is more plausible. However, there are a couple of reasons this could have unintended consequences. First, the attention of the feedback is directed at the student rather than the task. In the future, when the student answers incorrectly and gets feedback, he might also see that feedback as reflecting something bad about himself, rather than a correctable error in behavior. Additionally, praising ability ("you're clever") can lead students to believe that learning is based on innate smarts rather than effort, which can decrease motivation and perseverance.

GOOD

Child answers: 3 x 2 = 5

The amount of information you provide will likely depend on the expertise of the student.

Low-information feedback: "That's incorrect." This type of feedback is appropriate for knowledgeable students, who just need a small nudge to self-correct.

Medium-information feedback: "Five is too small. Three groups of two are six." This is better for people who need a little more support.

High-information feedback: "Five is too small. Perhaps you were adding the numbers together. Multiplying 3 x 2 means taking 3 groups of 2 [demonstrating a strategy for solving the problem]." This level of information is great for beginners, where it may be helpful to complement feedback with further instruction.

VII. References

Belding, J. N., Naufel, K. Z., & Fujita, K. (2015). Using high-level construal and perceptions of changeability to promote self-change over self-protection motives in response to negative feedback. *Personality and Social Psychology Bulletin, 41*(6), 822–838.

Chapin, H., Bagarinao, E., & Mackey, S. (2012). Real-time fMRI applied to pain management. *Neuroscience Letters, 520*(2), 174–181.

Cutumisu, M., Blair, K. P., Chin, D. B., & Schwartz, D. L. (2015). Posterlet: A game-based assessment of children's choices to seek feedback and revise. *Journal of Learning Analytics, 2*(1), 49–71.

Hattie, J., & Timperley, H. (2007). The power of feedback. *Review of Educational Research, 77*(1), 81–112.

Kluger, A. N., & DeNisi, A. (1996). The effects of feedback interventions on performance: A historical review, a meta-analysis, and a preliminary feedback intervention theory. *Psychological Bulletin, 119*(2), 254–284.

Kluger, A. N., & DeNisi, A. (1998). Feedback interventions: Toward the understanding of a double-edged sword. *Current Directions in Psychological Science, 7*(3), 67–72.

Powers, W. T. (1973). *Behavior: The control of perception.* New York: Wiley.

Saptya, J., Riemer, M., & Bickman, L. (2005). Feedback to clinicians: Theory, research, and practice. *Journal of Clinical Psychology, 61*(2), 145–153.

Schwartz, D. L., & Arena, D. (2013). *Measuring what matters most: Choice-based assessments for the digital age.* Cambridge, MA: MIT Press.

Yeager, D. S., Purdie-Vaughns, V., Garcia, J., Apfel, N., Brzustoski, P., Master, A., . . . Cohen, G. L. (2014). Breaking the cycle of mistrust: Wise interventions to provide critical feedback across the racial divide. *Journal of Experimental Psychology: General, 143*(2), 804–824.

F IS FOR FEEDBACK

What is the core learning mechanic?
Feedback allows people to sense the discrepancy between what they did and what they should have done, which enables them to adjust future actions.

What is an example, and what is it good for?
When a child incorrectly claims that $9 - 7 = 3$, the teacher uses blocks to lay out the correct answer and the child's answer and then points out the difference between them ("Three is too many!"). Feedback helps people identify a discrepancy and ideally points out what to fix.

Why does it work?
People would have a hard time learning something new if they never knew whether they were on the right track. They could perhaps copy a model, but even so, there would be aspects they would miss. Feedback, particularly constructive negative feedback, guides people toward what they can do to improve and learn.

What problems does the core mechanic solve?
- People are uncertain about what they are doing.
  - In physical therapy, a patient recreates the pose from an exercise diagram but doesn't know if he's positioning his body correctly.
- People receive reinforcement but do not improve.
  - An employee is scolded for poor performance but does not improve.
- People keep making the same mistake.
  - A student repeatedly fails at comparing decimals because he thinks that 0.10 is more than 0.9.
- People are headed down the wrong path, literally or figuratively.
  - In a report on the history of computers, a student spends most of her time reading a biography of Mark Zuckerberg, the founder of Facebook.

Examples of how to use it
- Help a native Japanese speaker hone in on English speech sounds for L and R by asking him to categorize many L-words and R-words by their initial letter sound. Give feedback after each attempt. This helps him learn to distinguish two sounds he previously thought were identical.

- Give students constructively critical feedback on their written essays, prefaced with a note stating that you have high expectations for them and you know they can do their best. The feedback gives the students information by which to improve, and the contextual note guards against the students interpreting the feedback as personal criticism.

Risks

- Negative feedback can be interpreted as personal criticism rather than a constructive tip.
- People are scared of negative feedback.
- The feedback may be too cryptic for a novice to understand.

G is for Generation

Building lasting memories

GENERATION IS A memorization technique that relies on the fact that remembering something makes it easier to remember the next time.

Flash cards are the canonical example. You read a cue on one side, and you try to remember the target on the other side. With practice, you get better each time through the flash cards. The invention of flash cards surely belongs in the pantheon of breakthroughs in learning technologies—simple, effective, and available to all.

Flash cards work because of the generation effect. The expression comes from a famous study in which people learned word pairs (Slamecka & Graf, 1978). You can get a feel for the study by looking at the three columns of word pairs below. For the finished pairs, your task is to read each pair silently. In the cases where there are missing letters, you should generate the word. For instance, if you know that the second word is the opposite of the first, and you receive happy : s _ d, the appropriate generation is sad.

SYNONYMS	ANTONYMS	RHYMES
fast : r _ p _ d	flavorful : bland	rain : g _ _ _
pain : ache	sleep : a _ _ k _	dime : time
witty : c _ _ v _ _	give : t _ _ _	stink : link
jump : leap	leave : come	graph : l _ _ _ _

If you wait a few minutes and then try to write down all the words (without peeking back), you will likely remember about 25 percent more of the words that you had to generate compared with words you directly read. For instance, you should remember *rapid* and *clever* better than *ache* and *leap*. You are also likely to remember the word *rapid* better than the word *fast*, even though they are part of the same pair. This is because you had to generate *rapid*, whereas you only read *fast*.

Generation is very useful for improving recall. It is also very general—it works for memorizing motor movements as well as equations. Knowing some of its subtleties can help avoid common memorization mistakes by enforcing two simple constraints: *make sure that students generate the target memory (not read it), and space the memorization practice over time (don't cram).*

I. How Generation Works

Generation works on the retrieval side of memory. It is not a technique for encoding, or getting information into one's head (see Chapter E). You already knew all the words in the preceding example. Instead, generation is a technique for making it easier to retrieve the memories. The distinction between encoding and retrieval is implicit in much classroom instruction. Teaching promotes the encoding of information; homework promotes its retrieval. Homework typically involves some form of generation whereby people practice remembering the information by accessing it to solve relevant problems or simply through rote practice.

How does generation work? The analogy to strengthening a muscle works well when considering the generation effect. Generation involves practicing exactly what you need to do in the future—exert effort to retrieve a memory from cues. For instance, try to remember a single word that can go with each the following words: *cottage, cake, Swiss*. The words are the cues. The correct memory, which takes some effort to find, is *cheese*. The successful effort to find the word strengthens your memory for *cheese* (lucky you). Now, if we had just told you *cottage cheese, cheesecake*, and *Swiss cheese*, you would not have needed to do any mental heavy lifting, and your memory for *cheese* would not have improved.

Also like muscles, memories weaken over time with disuse, so they become harder to retrieve. A well-defined forgetting function describes how memories decay and become more difficult to retrieve. Memories fade the most in the first few days and weeks after their acquisition but then flatten out to a very slow decay pattern, so they never fully disappear (forgetting follows a power law; see Chapter D).

The time course of memory acquisition influences the forgetting

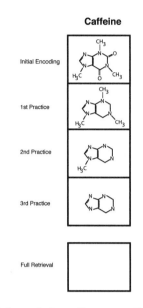

Figure G.1. Expanded practice: generating more and more from memory over time.

function through an important mechanism called the *spacing effect*. Spacing your memory acquisition over time will make the memory last longer in the future. It is better to practice vocabulary words ten minutes a day for two days (spaced practice) than to study the words once for twenty minutes (massed practice). Spacing one's practice over two days buys about a 10 percent improvement in memory a month later (Cepeda, Pashler, Vul, Wixted, & Rohrer, 2006). There are competing explanations for the spacing effect, but a simple one is that it takes more effort to retrieve a memory a day later (spaced practice) than one second later (massed practice). The greater effort creates a stronger memory trace, which in turn takes longer to decay.

The spacing effect helps explain a common experience. Once upon a time, you must have crammed for a midterm test. You did all the studying the night before the test in a big burst of effort. You remembered the material for the test the next day and felt very clever about the whole thing. But now you cannot remember very much, and you may even have forgotten most everything by the time of the final exam. This is because your memory coded the information as something you do not need to retrieve very often, and the memory decayed quickly. Spaced practice solves this problem.

II. How to Use Generation to Enhance Learning

Tasks that require retrieving a memory based on a partial cue improves the strength of the memory. There are ways to optimize the generation effect. The first is to keep the task at a desirable difficulty level (Bjork, 1994). You want people to succeed at remembering, but you do not want it to be so easy that they do not have to work to remember. One nice approach is to use *expanded practice*, where each subsequent round of practice requires remembering all the prior information plus a new piece of information. For example, with a deck of flash cards, it works well to do card 1, then cards 1 and 2, then cards 1 and 2 and 3, and so on. Figure G.1 provides a concrete example. The goal is to remember the molecular composition of caffeine. In the first round, people study the molecule. Ideally, they would use elaboration to help encode the molecule; for instance, H shows up three times with three Hs (see Chapter E). When people move to retrieval practice, they only need to remember and draw a few of the missing atoms and bonds on the first try. In the second round, they need to remember everything from before plus a new set of removed atoms and bonds. The process of expanding the memory task continues until finally, given the cue "caffeine," people can remember the full molecular structure.

A second important consideration is that people increase the strength of the memory trace that they generate but not the cue that triggers the memory. (People remember the target *rapid* better than the cue *fast* in this chapter's initial example.) The implication is that sometimes it is important to swap the cue and the target memory. If you want to remember a definition for a word, you should use the word as the cue and generate the definition from memory. However, if you want to remember the word given a definition, then you should use the definition as the cue and generate the word from memory. People often forget that they need to practice in both directions.

The third important consideration is temporal spacing. As described above, it is better to practice over several sessions than to cram it all into one session. There is also a second temporal issue: sleep. People consolidate their memories during sleep (see Chapter Z). It is a good idea to do memorization practice, get a good sleep, and then practice again to build on top of the consolidation. It is another reason that practicing for two days is better than one.

III. The Outcomes of Generation

Generation works for all types of memories and tasks, but it is especially useful for memory tasks that require free recall. *Free recall* refers to tasks where there is not a strong external stimulus cuing your memory, for instance, if you are trying to remember what somebody told you in a conversation last month, or if you have a final exam where you need to write down all the formulas you can remember from algebra.

One natural implication of the generation effect is that simply taking a test will improve memory (Karpicke & Blunt, 2011). Taking a test requires retrieving memories and therefore improves the accessibility of those memories later, for example, on a future test. Of course, the implication is not that students should only take repeated tests; rather, they should practice remembering what they know. Much school-based instruction focuses on encoding and elaborating information to make it meaningful. This is one important side of the memory equation, but people also need to practice the retrieval side.

IV. Can People Learn to Teach Themselves with Generation?

People learn all sorts of memorization techniques, so it is not difficult to get them to learn generation strategies. People often think that wanting to remember something will help. There is little evidence that the desire to remember, for example, to do well on a test, improves memory (Hyde & Jenkins, 1973). Instead of wishing themselves to a good memory, people must invoke deliberate memorization strategies such as generation and elaboration.

V. Risks of Generation

The primary risk of generation is that people can generate the wrong thing, which will strengthen an "incorrect" memory. A common experience is driving up to an intersection and not remembering whether to turn left or right. After some deliberation, you take a turn only to realize that (a) it is the wrong direction, and (b) it is the direction you turned the last time you were at the same intersection. Blame it on the generation effect! Because you generated the turn last time, you were more likely to remember it again this time. In fact, by taking the wrong turn yet again, you strengthened the incorrect memory trace further!

VI. Examples of Good and Bad Use

Imagine you have used your yellow marker to highlight a sentence in a text. Let us imagine you highlighted *Generation works on the retrieval side of memory.* When you go back to study your text, you make a point of rereading the highlighted sentence. This is a poor, but common, strategy. By rereading the sentence, you are not practicing remembering, because it is right there for you to read. It would be much better if you tested your memory by only reading the first half of the sentence and generating the rest from memory: *Generation works on the . . . .* Perhaps people would remember more if they only highlighted part of the sentence and used that as a cue to remember the rest.

VII. References

Bjork, R. A. (1994). Memory and metamemory considerations in the training of human beings. In J. Metcalfe and A. Shimamura (Eds.), *Metacognition: Knowing about knowing* (pp. 185–205). Cambridge, MA: MIT Press.

Cepeda, N. J., Pashler, H., Vul, E., Wixted, J. T., & Rohrer, D. (2006). Distributed practice in verbal recall tasks: A review and quantitative synthesis. *Psychological Bulletin, 132*(3), 354–380.

Hyde, T. S. & Jenkins, J. J. (1973). Recall for words as a function of semantic, graphic, and syntactic orienting tasks. *Journal of Verbal Learning and Verbal Behavior, 12*(5), 471-480.

Karpicke, J. D., & Blunt, J. R. (2011). Retrieval practice produces more learning than elaborate studying with concept mapping. *Science, 331*, 772–775.

Slamecka, N. J., & Graf, P. (1978). The generation effect: Delineation of a phenomenon. *Journal of Experimental Psychology: Human Learning and Memory, 4*(6), 592–604.

G IS FOR GENERATION

What is the core learning mechanic?
Practicing the retrieval of target memories given partial cues or hints improves future retrieval.

What is an example, and what is it good for?
Flash cards are the original example. On one side a card says *jocund*, and on the other side it says, *cheerful and lighthearted*. To work on memorizing the definition, people read the vocabulary word (the cue) and practice generating the definition (the target) without looking at the other side. This improves memory for the definition. If people simply flip the card over to read the definition, instead of trying to remember the definition first, there will be little improvement in memory.

Why does it work?
Retrieving a memory increases the strength of the memory, so it is easier to retrieve later. Spreading out memorization practice over several days increases memory strength compared with memorizing in only one session.

What problems does the core mechanic solve?
- Students have trouble memorizing arbitrary facts and conventions.
  - They cannot remember correct spelling.
  - They cannot remember the names of the presidents.
- Students have trouble recalling information without strong reminders.
  - They cannot remember the definition of a word without giving them multiple hints.
- Students forget too easily.
  - Students do well on a weekly test but forget the information for the final exam.

Examples of how to use it
- To learn vocabulary words and their definitions.
  - Use flash cards going both directions. Given the word, remember its definition. Given a definition, remember the word.
- To remember an organic molecule.
  - Show all of the molecule except a couple of atoms and bonds, and ask students to remember the missing pieces. Show the molecule again, but remove additional atoms and bonds. Ask students to

remember all the missing pieces. Continue until the students can remember the complete molecule when only hearing its name.

Risks

- People may generate the wrong thing, which will strengthen the "incorrect" memory.
- People tend to read the answer before trying to generate it, which undermines the effect.

H
is for Hands On

Recruiting the body's intelligence

HANDS-ON LEARNING OCCURS when people use their bodies and senses in the learning process. It recruits perceptual-motor intelligence to give meaning to words and symbols.

Language is so important to our thought processes that we often forget the incredible intelligence of our bodies. Need proof? Try to solve the problem in Figure H.1. Does the thin or wide cup pour first, or do they both start to pour at the same angle of tilt? If you are like 80 percent of people, you will give the wrong answer (assuming we had not just told you that your first answer is probably wrong). In contrast, imagine that you hold the thin cup. There is no actual water, just a line indicating the imagined water level. With your eyes closed, you tilt the cup until the imagined water just starts to pour over the lip. You can try this by just holding out your hand and turning it, imagining it is holding a cup of water. You then do the same thing with the wide cup. With your eyes closed and simply imagining the water, not feeling it, the odds are nearly 100 percent that you would produce the right answer (Schwartz, 1999). You would tilt the thin cup farther than the wide cup.

Hands-on learning harnesses the intelligence of the body to help make sense of abstract concepts. Acceleration is just a symbol in the equation $F = ma$. It gains meaning when accelerating in a car and feeling the "push" into the seat.

If you tilt both cups together, which one starts
to pour first, or do they pour at the same time?

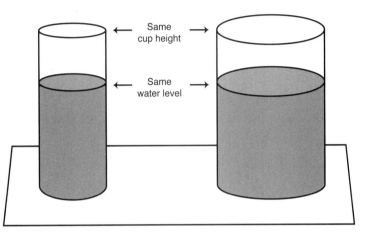

Figure H.1. A problem that is hard for verbal reasoning but easy for the motor system.

Hands-on learning is not a panacea. In the water-pouring example, people physically tilt the cups correctly, but they still do not understand why the wide cup pours first. (Figure H.2 provides an explanation.) The trick to hands-on learning is to help learners recognize the key aspects of their perceptual-motor experiences and hook them up with verbal or mathematical explanations.

I. How Hands-On Learning Works

The theory that our bodies—our perceptual-motor systems—can inform abstract thought is called *embodied cognition*. The theory arose in response to models of cognition that compared human thought with the computer, and instructional approaches that overemphasized pushing symbols. To give a sense of how embodiment can provide meaning, consider the following problem:

> A hollow ball and a solid ball are at the top of a ramp. They are identical weight and size. If you let go of them at the same time, will they reach the bottom of a ramp at the same time?

The hollow ball has greater rotational inertia. Therefore, it will speed up more gradually. The filled ball will reach the bottom of the ramp first.

Did that explanation work for you? No? Maybe drawing on your embodied

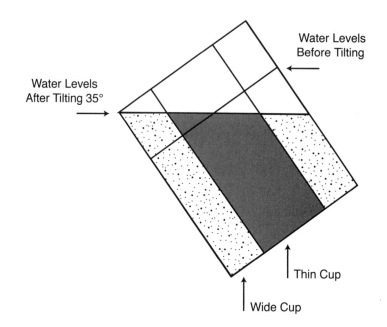

Water Levels
Before Tilting

Water Levels
After Tilting 35°

Thin Cup

Wide Cup

Figure H.2. Why a wide glass pours out water sooner than a thin glass. (Adapted from Schwartz, 1999).

experience helps. If you have a spinning chair, ask someone to give you a spin. Begin with your arms out, and then pull them inward while spinning. Do you notice that you speed up? If you do not have a chair handy, recall what happens to a twirling ice skater when he brings in his arms—he speeds up. Putting the weight closer to the axis of rotation makes an object spin more quickly. Conversely, if more weight is near the outside, the object spins more slowly because it is harder to swing the weight around—it resists changes in rotation more because it has greater rotational inertia. The hollow ball rolls down the ramp more slowly because the weight is farther from the center of ball like the ice skater with his arms out. A hands-on activity, or in this case an embodied memory, can help ground an otherwise abstract concept in a physical experience.

Perceptual-motor intelligence is also at work in mathematics. Here's an easy problem for this demonstration: as fast as you can, decide whether there are fewer dots on the left of each pair:

(a)   •   •••••
(b)   ••••   •••••

People are faster to answer problem (a) because the difference between one and five dots is greater than the difference between four and five dots in (b). It is an easier comparison for your perceptual system. Now, here are some comparisons that use symbolic digits instead:

(c) 1   5
(d) 4   5

People are faster to answer (c) than (d), even though there is nothing about the physical size of the digits to indicate which is more. It is as though people consult their perceptual system just as they do for the dots. In fact, that is what happens. Moyer and Landauer's (1967) pathbreaking research showed that people engage their perceptual sense of magnitude to reason about symbolic magnitudes. Not only does the perceptual system give meaning to the sizes of 1 and 5, but it also provides structure so that 1, 2, 3, and so on make an orderly system of increasing magnitudes.

People do not experience any imagery or other markers of perceptual processing when comparing symbolic digits. People do not translate a "5" into five dots in their imagination. The contribution of perception is more profound—it creates the very sense of magnitude; knowing that 5 is relatively large compared with 1 depends on a perceptual, albeit subconscious, comparison. Current thinking is that mathematics recruits evolutionarily old perceptual systems to give meaning and structure to symbolic number (Dehaene & Cohen, 2007). Who knew that the ability to decide if that animal on the horizon is bigger than you is what gives rise to basic mathematical abilities?

Hands-on learning works by helping people to recruit useful perceptual-motor computations and coordinate them with symbolic and verbal representations. A clear example comes from research on helping fourth-grade children learn about the integers (positive and negative numbers, plus zero). The integers are a good test case, because they are very abstract—people do not bump into negative quantities in the forest. How could perceptual-motor abilities render negative numbers meaningful?

One answer is visual symmetry. People are extremely good at detecting and experiencing symmetry, and the positive and negative numbers are symmetric about zero. By studying people's reaction times as they solve integer problems, as well as looking at their patterns of brain activity, researchers found that adults recruit perceptual symmetry capacities when doing simple integer tasks such as deciding the greater of -2 and 1 or finding the midpoint of -8 and 6 (Tsang & Schwartz, 2009; Tsang, Rosenberg-Lee, Blair, Schwartz, & Menon, 2010; Varma & Schwartz, 2011). A good hands-on

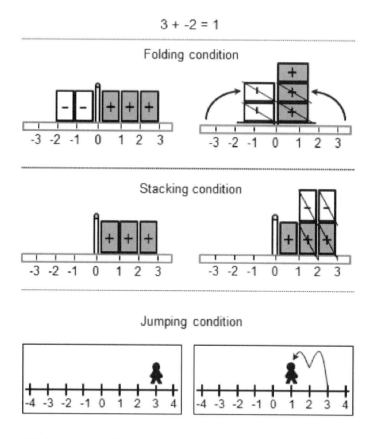

Figure H.3. Hands-on manipulatives for learning to add integers. Top panel: The folding manipulative was developed to help students notice symmetry about zero. To solve the problem 3 + –2, students set out three positive blocks to the right of zero and two negative blocks to the left of zero. The manipulative has a hinge at zero. Students fold the two sides together at the point of integer symmetry (zero) to make them into juxtaposed columns. The number of extra blocks on either side gives the answer, in this case +1. (From Tsang, Blain, Bofferding and Schwartz, 2015.)

activity might help learners recruit symmetry to organize their understanding of the integers. To test this idea, Tsang, Blair, Bofferding, and Schwartz (2015) created a new hands-on manipulative shown in the top panel of Figure H.3. The manipulative incorporates a folding mechanism with a hinge at zero that helps students recruit their native abilities with symmetry, and the numbers on the platform help them coordinate the sense of symmetry with the symbolic digits.

Fourth graders used the folding manipulative for two days and then

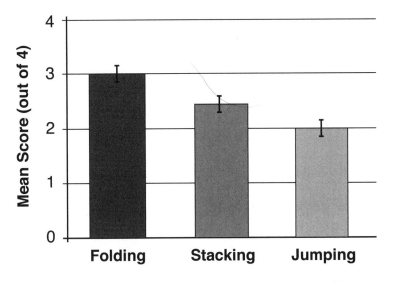

Figure H.4. Performance on a conceptual test of the ability to use integers to solve novel problems. In the Folding condition students received hands-on instruction that emphasized the symmetry of the positive and negative numbers about zero. Errors bars are ± SEM. (From Tsang, Blair, Bofferding, and Schwartz, 2015.)

switched to a computerized version that provided faster practice with addition problems and helped children connect their physical actions to written number sentences. By the end, the children were solving problems without any hands-on or visual support. They were even able to apply their knowledge to make sense of new types of problems they had not yet learned, for example, putting positive and negative fractions on a number line. As Figure H.4 shows, students who used the folding manipulative did substantially better on these novel problems than students who had used stacking or jumping manipulatives, which did not emphasize symmetry. With the folding tool, students learned to use symmetry to coordinate complex thinking about integers.

II. How to Use Hands On to Enhance Learning

Hands-on experiences are fun and mentally nutritious, too (Sowell, 1989; Moyer, 2001). They help prevent symbol pushing without understanding. A bus can carry ten children, and there are twenty-five children; how many drivers are needed? Many people answer 2.5, not realizing that half-drivers are in short supply. Gravemeijer and Doorman (1999) promoted realistic mathematics. Their fundamental insight was that learners need to think about sym-

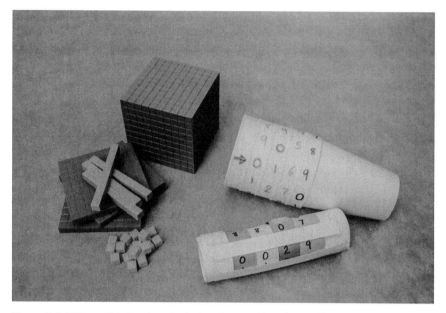

Figure H.5. Different kinds of manipulatives for teaching place value emphasize different conceptual elements.

bolic, mathematical relations in terms of their real world (perceptual-motor) properties and not just their syntactic rules of manipulation.

There is no one-size-fits-all hands-on activity. Unlike flash cards, which work for just about any memorization task, each hands-on learning topic requires its own specially designed experience. The designer of hands-on experiences needs to figure out the specific perceptual-motor experiences that best capture the significant concepts. This is a nontrivial task and often requires deep knowledge of the topic.

Imagine you want to teach the base-10 place value system to students. Figure H.5 shows two kinds of manipulatives that emphasize different properties of place value. The cubes on the left rely on visual dimensionality: 1 is a point (0 dimensions), 10 is a line (1 dimension), 100 is plate (two dimensions), and 1,000 is a cube (three dimensions). The cup and tube manipulatives on the right take a completely different approach. They embody the idea of exhausting a supply of symbols and rolling over like an odometer, emphasizing the symbolic structure of place value and the need for zero.

Hands-on activities can highlight properties that people may otherwise overlook. An excellent example involves the book-on-a-table problem (Clement, 1993). When a book is sitting on a table, the table is exerting a (normal) force against the book that exactly balances out the force of gravity. This is a difficult concept, because the table is inanimate, so how could it exert a force, let alone change the amount of force depending on the weight of the book? People often import their embodied sense of muscular effort when considering physics. A good hands-on activity might help learners switch their conceptual focus. Instead of thinking of the table as an inanimate object, they can think of it as a spring. For instance, students can put a heavy object on a spring and note that it compresses. Then, students can put the same weight on a flexible board, instead of the spring, to help draw the analogy that the board is like the spring. After using boards and springs of varying strength, one would finally use a spring that does not compress and a board that does not bend. DiSessa (1993) argued that the main task of learning physics is to sort out which perceptual-motor experiences (springiness) map to which class of situation (tables). Hands-on activities can be very powerful here.

Does a hands-on activity need to be hands on? There are many computer simulations of hands-on activities that include mathematical and science manipulatives (see, e.g., the National Library of Virtual Manipulatives at http://nlvm.usu.edu/en/nav/vlibrary.html, and PhET Interactive Simulations at http://phet.colorado.edu). The answer to this question depends on whether learners can elicit the right perceptual-motor experiences without physically touching.

In mathematics, where many of the relevant perceptual-motor primitives are visual, physical touch is less important. In the integer example, hands-on materials were primarily used as an engaging way to make sure students pay

Figure H.6. An activity where people need hands-on experience, because they cannot imagine the consequences of angular momentum when trying to tilt a spinning wheel.

attention to symmetry—the eyes often follow the hands. A computer program might have worked as well.

In science, many concepts depend on physical causes, which need to be felt and not just seen. Here the question is whether people can recall a relevant physical experience, or whether they need hands-on experience at the time of instruction. You were probably able to imagine the spinning ice skater in the earlier example of rotational inertia, so spinning in a chair was unnecessary. In contrast, Figure H.6 shows an example of rotational behavior that one needs to experience to believe. (When you hold a spinning wheel and try to tilt it, the wheel feels like it is forcing itself back to the original position.)

When deciding whether to use a hands-on activity, consider whether students need to feel the target concept through their body. Of course, hands-on activities are fun, too, which can be a sufficient reason to use them.

III. The Outcomes of Hands-On Learning

Hands-on learning helps people recruit perceptual intelligence to give meaning to the symbolic world of signs and words. Martin and Schwartz (2005) studied nine- to ten-year-olds learning to solve partitive-whole fraction problems (e.g., one-fourth of 8). The children solved some problems using tiles and other problems with a picture of tiles (Figure H.7). Regardless of order, children were three times more accurate when they worked with the hands-on materials than with the pictures.

What explains these results? In the Picture condition, the children relied on their familiar knowledge of natural numbers. For example, they would circle one chip, four chips, or both one and four chips. They interpreted the "1/4" as referring to the natural numbers 1 and 4. In contrast, when the children had an opportunity to manipulate the pieces, they saw new possibilities emerge. The intelligence of their hands for grouping objects led the way. Children often moved several pieces at the same time, and this may have helped them recognize that several pieces could be counted as one group. Once they started to perceive groups, they were on their way to solving the problem (finding one of four equal groups). Manipulating the environment helped release the children from an overreliance on old interpretations to help them develop new ones (Blair & Schwartz, 2012). There are two bits of information in this finding. The first is that manipulation can help people discover meaningful structure. The second is that one or two hands-on experiences can be insufficient for students to develop a stable meaning for complex symbolic relations. Otherwise, the children would have done better on the picture problems after the hands-on prob-

Show 1/4 of these 8 pieces.

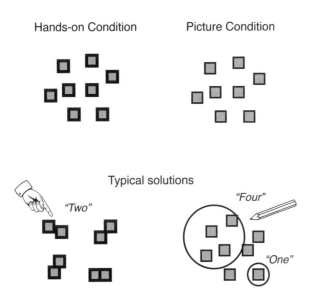

Figure H.7. Children completed fraction problems with pictures of pieces or with hands-on pieces. On average, a child was three times as likely to give the right answer with the hands-on materials. (Based on Martin & Schwartz, 2005.)

lems, which they did not. Binding symbols and perceptual intelligence can often require many experiences.

Once there is a strong connection between perceptual-motor meaning and symbols, the hands-on support can fade. When you first learned the word *doggy*, you needed to see an example of a dog, because it is your perceptual system that gives you the rudimentary meaning of dog. Now, you no longer need to see a dog. Similarly, solving arithmetic problems with one's fingers is a fine idea when first learning; it gives meaning and order to addition and subtraction. Once that meaning is in place, it is useful to transition to more efficient symbolic manipulations and memories. It is easier to solve 33 + 89 symbolically than to figure it out using fingers. The embodied component will not get lost in the move to symbols. The deep meaning is still in there, even if people are no longer using their hands or imagery. People know that 33 is too small to be the sum of 24 + 29, even without exact computation. *The great outcome of hands-on learning is sense-making* (pun intended). Our physical senses help us make conceptual sense of abstract symbols.

IV. Can People Learn to Teach Themselves with Hands-On Learning?

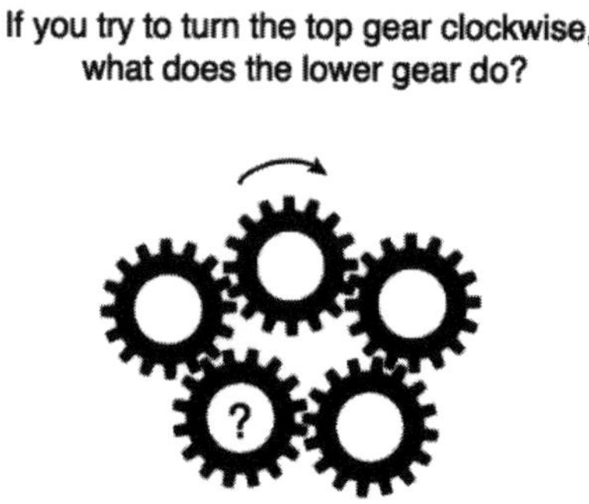

If you try to turn the top gear clockwise,
what does the lower gear do?

Figure H.8. A problem that often leads people to rely on their perceptual-motor intelligence.

People naturally use hands-on learning, when they are not afraid of touching. When there is no way to touch something, people will even use perceptual-motor mental simulations. Try out the problem in Figure H.8.

Counterclockwise is an incorrect answer. Try again. Clockwise is also an incorrect answer. Try again. If you are like most people, you made gestures to work on the problem (Schwartz & Black, 1996). You may have modeled gear movements with your hands, or just used little finger or head movements. The answer is that the gears lock and do not turn at all.

People gesture so naturally that it can reveal their thinking. Gestures can even indicate a conflict between people's embodied knowledge and their verbal knowledge. Documenting a phenomenon known as speech-gesture mismatch, Goldin-Meadow, Alibali, and Church (1993) gave children problems such as 12 + 6 = 10 + __. When first learning, children often think their task is to add up all the numbers instead of making the two sides equal. The interesting case is when children say the add-them-all-up strategy and give the associated answer (28), yet their hands make a balancing gesture. For example, they might put their hands, palms up, on either side of the equal sign. When students make a mismatch between what they say and what they gesture, researchers found that they are in a transitional state and are especially ready to learn the correct balancing strategy, which would give the answer 8. Their perceptual-motor system has gotten into the game, which means the verbal explanation of the balancing strategy will make more sense.

V. Risks of Hands-On Learning

Three risks of hands-on materials help clarify how to use them effectively: missing the key properties, taking the activity as just another procedure to follow, and overscaffolding.

MISSING THE KEY PROPERTIES

Learners may not notice the intended perceptual properties. In a class we taught, students had been using base-10 cubes (Figure H.5). We raised a single small cube, and asked how many. The students said, "One!" We then held up a stick of ten cubes, and they said, "Ten!" For a flat made of ten sticks, they said, "One hundred." Finally, we held up a solid cube comprised of 10 hundred-piece flats. Many said, "six hundred." Despite having handled the heavy cube before, the students perceived it as having six sides of hundred-piece flats, not a cube of stacked flats. The take-home message is to make sure students are experiencing what you intend.

JUST ANOTHER PROCEDURE TO FOLLOW

The point of hands-on material is to find meaning and structure rather than copy a symbolic procedure. Students need an opportunity to explore good questions with hands-on materials. People often use base-10 blocks to mimic the right-to-left symbolic procedure of addition. Start by adding the ones, then the tens, and then hundreds. However, there is no reason students could not start by adding the tens and then add the ones or move back and forth between tens and ones. Giving students a chance to explore the structure of the cubes by solving problems in many ways could be a better starting point than dictating a specific sequence of steps to copy.

OVERSCAFFOLDING

Students may persist with slow hands-on solutions when they should move to the symbolic world of efficiency. Moreover, hands-on materials can inadvertently block students from engaging key issues (Blair & Schwartz, 2012). Plastic pie pieces are commonly used to teach fractions. They can help students understand different-size fractions and combinations. They always provide the whole (one pie equals one whole), which helps students focus on relative wedge size. However, this can be an example of overscaffolding—doing so much work for the learner, they fail to think about the topic themselves. Students who only use pie representations often feel lost in cases in which the whole is not predetermined for them by a circle (such as one-fourth of eight pennies). This is one reason it is often useful to use multiple representations; the strengths of one can compensate for the weaknesses of the other.

VI. Examples of Good and Bad Use

An interesting use of hands-on learning involves games. Imagine a video game with a controller that players can use to jump a character around the screen. How might we turn this into a useful embodied experience for teaching very early math?

Bad: The game presents the digit 4, and children have to jump on the corresponding expression: 2 + 2, 3 + 2, 1 + 5. This could be fun exercise, but there is nothing about jumping on the right answer that relates to the magnitude of 4 or addition.

Good: There is a game board that shows 1, 2, 3, 4, 5. . . . The game presents 2 + 2. The children have to jump two squares plus two more to land on 4. This captures both the magnitude of 2 and the idea of adding to make a bigger number.

Better: The same as before, but eventually the game starts to fade the embodied support. For example, the children have to jump all the way to 4, calculating the result of 2 + 2 in their heads.

VII. References

Blair, K. P., & Schwartz, D. L. (2012). A value of concrete learning materials in adolescence. In V. F. Reyna, S. B. Chapman, M. R. Dougherty, & J. Confrey (Eds.), *The adolescent brain: Learning, reasoning, and decision making* (pp.95-122). Washington, DC: American Psychological Association.

Clement, J. (1993). Using bridging analogies and anchoring intuitions to deal with students' preconceptions in physics. *Journal of Research in Science Teaching, 30*(10), 1241–1257.

Dehaene, S., & Cohen, L. (2007). Cultural recycling of cortical maps. *Neuron, 56*(2), 384–398.

DiSessa, A. A. (1993). Toward an epistemology of physics. *Cognition and Instruction, 10*(2–3), 105–225.

Goldin-Meadow, S., Alibali, M. W., & Church, R. B. (1993). Transitions in concept acquisition: Using the hand to read the mind. *Psychological Review, 100*(2), 279–297.

Gravemeijer, K., & Doorman, M. (1999). Context problems in realistic mathematics education: A calculus course as an example. *Educational Studies in Mathematics, 39*(1–3), 111–129.

Martin, T., & Schwartz, D. L. (2005). Physically distributed learning: Adapting and reinterpreting physical environments in the development of the fraction concept. *Cognitive Science, 29*, 587–625.

Moyer, P. S. (2001). Are we having fun yet? How teachers use manipulatives to teach mathematics. *Educational Studies in Mathematics, 47*, 175–197.

Moyer, R. S., & Landauer, T. K. (1967). The time required for judgments of numerical inequality. *Nature, 215*, 1519–1520.

Schwartz, D. L. (1999). Physical imagery: Kinematic versus dynamic models. *Cognitive Psychology, 38*, 433–464.

Schwartz, D. L., & Black, J. B. (1996). Shuttling between depictive models and abstract rules: Induction and fallback. *Cognitive Science, 20*, 457–497.

Sowell, E. J. (1989). Effects of manipulative materials in mathematics instruction. *Journal for Research in Mathematics Education, 20*, 498–505.

Tsang, J. M., Blair, K. P., Bofferding, L., & Schwartz, D. L. (2015). Learning to "see" less than nothing: Putting perceptual skills to work for learning numerical structure. *Cognition and Instruction, 33*(2), 154–197.

Tsang, J. M., Rosenberg-Lee, M., Blair, K. P., Schwartz, D. L., & Menon, V. (2010, June). Near symmetry in a number bisection task yields faster responses and greater occipital activity. Poster presented at the 16th annual meeting of the organization for human brain mapping, Barcelona, Spain.

Tsang, J. M., & Schwartz, D. L. (2009). Symmetry in the semantic representation of integers. In N. Taatgen & H. van Rijn (Eds.), *Proceedings of the 31st annual conference of the cognitive science society* (pp. 323–328). Austin, TX: Cognitive Science Society.

Varma, S. & Schwartz, D. L. (2011). The Mental Representation of Integers: An Abstract-to-Concrete Shift in the Understanding of Mathematical Concepts. *Cognition, 121, 363-385.*

H IS FOR HANDS ON

What is the core learning mechanic?
Making sense of abstract concepts through perceptual-motor activities.

What is an example, and what is it good for?
Students sit in a spinning chair while stretching their arms in and out. They feel how they speed up and slow down (like a twirling ice skater). This experience can anchor a discussion of angular momentum. Without the perceptual-motor experience, students would learn about angular momentum only through a series of declarative statements and equations.

Why does it work?
The perceptual-motor system contains tremendous intelligence. This intelligence provides meaning for simple symbols and words. For example, without perceptual experience, it would be hard to understand the concepts of large and small. Hands-on learning recruits the perceptual-motor system to coordinate its meaning with symbolic representations.

What problems does the core mechanic solve?
- Students treat mathematics as symbol pushing.
  - For the problem 11 x 19, students do not realize that 50 is a worse answer than 100.
- Students cannot make sense of a science concept.
  - People do not understand how a table can exert a force equal to the weight of a book sitting on it.

Examples of how to use it
- Provide physical manipulatives that highlight key perceptual-motor properties in mathematics.
  - Design integer manipulatives to highlight symmetry around 0.
- Give learners an opportunity to experience physical phenomenon directly.
  - To introduce the concept of torque, have students compare the difficulty of holding a weight with their arms at different angles.

Risks
- A manipulative may fail to help learners notice the most useful perceptual-motor properties.

- The hands-on activity may become a procedure for finding an answer rather than a source of sensemaking.
- Students may become too dependent on the hands-on activity. At some point, we want students to stop using their fingers to do addition.

I is for
Imaginative Play

Developing cognitive control

IMAGINATIVE PLAY INVOLVES creating a story that is different from the world at hand, often letting one thing stand for another (e.g., a stick becomes a swooshing plane). Theoretically, imaginative play should improve a number of developmental outcomes, such as verbal abilities, symbolic creativity, intelligence, cognitive control, and social competence. (Below we explain why we say "theoretically.")

A salivating dog watches a sausage moving back and forth. A puppy gets nipped by another puppy and bites back. A child uses a sausage for an airplane. A child gets punched by his brother and stops to consider whether to cry, punch back, or tattle. In both dog examples, the action is stimulus driven: the environment is pulling the dog's behavior along. In contrast, the child is exerting cognitive control: in the imaginative case, the sausage stands for something other than food; in the aggression case, the child is resisting the immediate response of physical retaliation. Imaginative play exercises children's developing abilities to free themselves from stimulus-driven responses and to construct alternatives in their imagination.

Action figures and dolls are great fuel for imaginative play. A Superman figurine is not really a living Superman, but children know just enough about Superman to build grand stories to save the world (which may actually be an apple).

The great anthropologist Claude Lévi-Strauss argued that statues are usually bigger or smaller than what they portray, because it helps people think about the real thing, yet the odd size releases their imagination (Lévi-Strauss, 1966).

Imagination is just one of many forms of play. Aggressive play is ubiquitous and appears in most mammals. Mammals often emit signals that help their partners differentiate play fighting from true combat. Aggressive play may help animals learn to inhibit species-defeating responses, for example, when competing for a mate. By becoming less stimulus driven in their responses to bumps and bruises, the animals do not strike a killing blow in defense. Other theories exist, too, including the ideas that play fighting improves physical coordination and social competence or creates a dominance hierarchy. There is no clear evidence supporting one evolutionary theory over another for why mammals fight in play.

The same is true for imaginative play in humans. Sigmund Freud claimed that play serves the function of stress reduction. Lev Vygotsky claimed that play drives the development of symbolic abilities. Others believe play is a way to work out real-life challenges in the space of make-believe. The evidence does not adjudicate among these theories (Lillard et al., 2013). There is little consistent evidence that imaginative play improves cognitive control, intelligence, creativity, social competence, or symbolic abilities. It may serve all of them, or none.

Given that imaginative play is ubiquitous, why is it so hard to discover its function? One possible reason is that defining the purpose of play is like defining the purpose of the mouth. The mouth eats, talks, kisses, tastes, breathes, feels, whistles, and emotes. Play, too, does many things at the same time. When children imagine a tea party, they are creating a symbolic world; they are rehearsing social roles and norms; they are imagining both sides of an interaction; they are planning an event; and the list goes on. It is hard to isolate any one aspect of play and connect it to long-term developmental outcomes. For example, Connolly and Doyle (1984) found that children who engaged in more social fantasy play also exhibited superior social skills. Yet, as with all correlational studies, it is impossible to know whether play improved social skills or the other way around.

It is also difficult to conduct experimental studies that perfectly isolate imaginative play and determine the causal forces. In one study, researchers randomly assigned six-year-olds into one of four thirty-six-week treatments: piano lessons, voice lessons, drama lessons, or a control condition with no lessons (Schellenberg, 2004). The intent of the study was to determine whether music (piano and voice) improved IQ, which it did, by about two points. A surprise finding was that the drama treatment improved the children's social competence based on a survey measure given to parents. The other treatments had no effect on social competence. Acting is a form of imaginative play. Was imaginative play responsible for the gains? It is hard to say, because the drama children also had higher degree of complex social interaction with the adult teachers, which may have been the source of the effect.

Human decency precludes separating the relative contributions of imaginative play and social interaction—we cannot lock children into closets and tell them to engage in imaginative play for the next month in absence of social contact. There is, however, a flourishing tradition of animal experimentation teasing apart play and social interaction. In one study (Pellis, Pellis, & Bell, 2010), researchers separated juvenile rats into a Social condition and a Play condition. In the Social condition, each juvenile spent eight hours a day with adult female rats. They engaged in grooming and other strongly social behaviors. However, adult females do not play much among themselves, let alone with juveniles, so these juveniles had a strong social experience but no play. The second group of juveniles stayed in relative isolation, except for one hour a day. During that hour, they were released into the same cage as another juvenile rat. They bolted into play fighting. The outcomes? The juveniles who only had one hour of play fighting, but little other social interaction, became more socially competent adults, less fearful, and quicker to recover from stress. Aggressive play, not social interaction, was responsible for social adjustment.

In case you were wondering, animals do not engage in imaginative play, so we cannot look to the animal research to clarify the role of imaginative play for learning and development.

I. How Imaginative Play Works

Children's early development involves tremendous cognitive changes to executive function. *Executive function* refers to abilities for cognitive control, including the ability to keep some things in mind, keep other things out, and switch from one idea to another. An important piece of this development is symbolic skills, such as knowing that one thing can stand for another. This requires holding two interpretations of the same thing at the same time. A stunning demonstration of how quickly this can change with development comes from a brilliant task designed by Judy DeLoache (1987). Children completed the task individually: They looked at a little toy room (Figure I.1). The researcher hid a Snoopy doll behind a piece of furniture, and the children saw the doll placement. The children then went to a full-size room that had an identical layout and were asked to find the doll hiding in the same place as in the little room. About 75 percent of three-year-olds went directly to the

I'm hiding Big Snoopy in the same place in his room. Can you find him?

I'm hiding Little Snoopy here.

Figure I.1. A task that children find difficult at thirty months of age but easy at thirty-six months: see the placement in a miniature room, and find the same placement when inside a full-size room.

hiding place, compared with about 20 percent of children two and one-half years old. What changed in just half a year?

The younger children did not understand the symbolic idea that the toy room could be like a map. To them, the toy room was exactly that—a toy to play with. It was not a representation of another room. To demonstrate this hypothesis, in a later study new children saw the doll being hidden in the toy room. A large curtain closed to hide the room. There were noises. The children were told that the noises were the toy room growing into a large room. The curtain opened to reveal the large room and children looked for the doll. Under these conditions, about 80 percent of the 2.5-year-olds went directly to the doll's hiding place. To solve this task they did not need the representational insight that the little room could also be representing something else—it was the same thing only bigger.

Imaginative play involves cognitive moves similar to those of the three-year-olds in the DeLoache studies. First, children need to inhibit a literal interpretation of the stimuli around them: a fork is not just a fork. Second, children need to construct another interpretation in their imagination: the fork is an airplane delivering food.

A second example of cognitive control comes from the classic "marshmallow" study by Walter Mischel and colleagues (see, e.g., Mischel et al., 2011). The question was whether children could resist stimulus control. A researcher shows a young child a marshmallow treat and says, "I have to leave the room now. If you can wait to eat the treat until I get back, I will give you a second marshmallow." Very few children resist the temptation to eat the treat. The question was how long they could resist the pull of the stimulus. Mischel and colleagues explored a variety of tricks to help children increase their delay of gratification. Telling the children to imagine how good the marshmallow would taste was one of the worst—it made them even more stimulus driven. One of the best was telling the children to imagine that the marshmallow was a picture of a marshmallow. Imagination helped the children switch from an appetitive response to a cognitive one.

II. How to Use Imaginative Play to Enhance Learning

There is a prevailing hypothesis that improving children's executive functioning, a major component of socioemotional functioning, will have cumulative effects on future learning. Children will be better able to control their attention, concentration, and impulsivity when learning and interacting with others. People have looked to play-centered curricula to strengthen executive functioning in four- and five-year-olds. The Tools of the Mind curriculum wraps executive function exercises around imaginative play (see http://www.

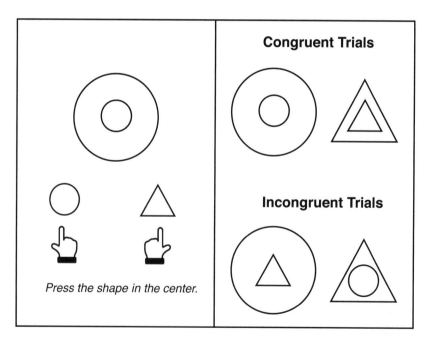

Figure I.2. The Eriksen flanker task. Young children have exceptional difficulty with the incongruent trials until their executive function develops.

toolsofthemind.org/). For example, children may be asked to play specific roles (e.g., doctors) and behave like doctors (and not patients). This differs from immature play where children do not try to play within rules. Rule-based behavior, by its very nature, is not stimulus driven.

In a randomized trial (Diamond, Barnett, Thomas, & Munro, 2007), five-year-olds from mostly low-income families were assigned to either the Tools of the Mind curriculum or their extant curriculum. At the end of the year, children completed an executive function test. Figure I.2 shows the Eriksen flanker task from the test. The children had to press a button indicating the shape in the center of the upper figure. The incongruent trials, where the outer shape (the flanker) is different from the center shape, tax executive function, because children must selectively inhibit the stimulus-driven response to the larger shape. For this measure, children in the Tools condition answered with about 90 percent accuracy, compared with 80 percent for the control children. In this example, engaging in imaginative play per se was not necessarily the cause of the executive function gains. Rather, activities to support executive function were instantiated through play, leading to positive gains.

Imaginative play is also a highly motivating way to deliver content and skills. Game play for learning has received increasing attention lately. For instance, the Quest to Learn schools in New York and Chicago frame a public school curriculum around games (see http://www.instituteofplay.org/work/projects/quest-schools/quest-to-learn/).

Many learning games simply add rewards to otherwise repetitive tasks (known as "chocolate-covered broccoli"). This borrows from an age-old form of play -- gambling. It has its uses; for example, using flash cards with points is more fun than flash cards without. It is also possible to design games that tap into imaginative play, for example, by creating strong narratives that help learners imagine they are on quests. A good rule of thumb is to have students anticipate (imagine) what will happen next so they can plan for it. In a board game, or even tic-tac-toe, some of the joy is anticipating what your opponent will do next. This drives deeper learning, because people need to learn the rules of the game (be they arithmetic or social rules) and use the rules generatively to imagine the possibilities.

III. The Outcomes of Imaginative Play

When considering the effects of play, or any other method of changing human behavior, it is useful to distinguish among development, learning, performance, and problem solving. *Development* refers to maturational changes that universally occur under normal conditions. They influence children's broad abilities to grasp and engage the world. Infants learn to focus their eyes regardless of specific experiences. *Learning* refers to adaptations to specific conditions that can vary greatly across individuals and cultures. In one culture, children learn to identify poisonous plants. In another, they learn the names of each Ninja Turtle. In schools, we try to deliver learning that is useful across many contexts. *Performance* refers to how well people complete designated tasks. Radiologists can quickly spot arthritis in an MRI scan of a knee, whereas novices would likely be clueless. *Problem solving* is a subset of performance. It refers to how people figure out solutions to challenges. For instance, children may have an effective strategy for finding hidden candy.

These distinctions are useful in considering applications of imaginative play. For instance, people often assume that successful problem solving guarantees learning, but problem solving and learning are different: *people can solve problems without learning what is most important to know; conversely, people may not solve a problem yet still learn a great deal* (see Chapter J). We can use these distinctions to help isolate imaginative play's most likely outcomes.

DEVELOPMENT

There is little consistent evidence that imaginative play itself drives cognitive development of executive function, social skills, or the ability to reason symbolically. Of course, the lack of evidence does not mean that play does not have a causal role—we simply do not know.

The social interactions around play give children opportunities to practice maturing social skills. For example, one of the authors frequently overhears her two young daughters practicing social negotiation. Sometimes they even succeed!

"I'm the mom. You be the dad."
"I don't want to be the dad. How about I'm little sister?"
"OK. You're little sister and we have to go to the store . . ."

Joint imaginative play requires cooperation and coordination. Practicing and experimenting with these skills surely must have some value. The costs of making mistakes during play are low, at least to the eyes of an adult, if not the eventually crying child.

LEARNING

Imaginative play, and play in general, can be an excellent vehicle for enhancing learning outcomes. Play is motivating, and being able to refashion lessons into a play format will increase engagement. Children will play a game for learning, and if the game is well designed, that learning will be useful outside the game. A good math game can improve math performance on nongame tasks.

PERFORMANCE

Under the umbrella of serious play, some companies have incorporated play elements into the work environment to foster more interest, team spirit, and effort. Making more sales for your team—increasing performance—might allow you to add a piece to a virtual team bridge in the company's video game. The purpose of play is to improve effort, on the assumption that it will increase performance.

PROBLEM SOLVING

For some classes of problems, a major challenge is letting go of old ideas to generate new creative solutions. Imaginative play can help with creativity, even if it does not help people learn to be more creative overall. For instance, Dansky and Silverman (1973) conducted a study where children received several objects (e.g., paper towels). In the Imaginative Play condition, children were told, "You may play with all of these things. Do whatever you would like to do with them." In the Imitate condition, children watched an experimenter use the materials in typical fashion (e.g., wiping wet cups with a paper towel). Afterward, children in both conditions tried to come up with alternate uses for the objects: how many different things can you do with a paper towel? Children who had played with the objects did better at this task. The study did not show that students learned to be creative generally. They may have simply learned how to solve the problem of coming up with ideas for using a paper towel.

IV. Can People Learn to Teach Themselves with Imaginative Play?

Imaginative play is a natural part of development. Adults can nurture it further, for example, by interacting with children in imaginative games and storytelling. Adults can also spark children's imaginations with very simple toys such as cardboard boxes and foam pool noodles. A pool noodle might be imagined into a fire hose, a kayak paddle, or the edge of a safe path across the crocodile-infested living room rug. On the other hand, a singing dancing toy robot will usually be used as a singing dancing toy robot.

V. Risks of Imaginative Play

Encouraging imaginative play does not pose any known risks, assuming children are not running with scissors or other crazy things. The primary source of risk involves adult attitudes toward play. For example, parents may become unnecessarily concerned that their young children do not engage in imaginative play, or conversely, they may believe children should not play in school.

Beliefs about play are strongly mediated by the narratives people construct rather than by empirical evidence (Fisher, Hirsh-Pasek, Golinkoff, & Gryfe, 2008). In this chapter, we have reviewed the evidence for the play-as-progress narrative or the idea that play leads to developmental growth. This should be familiar, as it has been a dominant western narrative for children's play for over a hundred years (Sutton-Smith, 2009). Other narratives include play as fantasy and play as fun. There is also a narrative involving play as fate, which suits games of chance. When thinking about the uses of play, it may be restrictive to only think of play as a catalyst for development. There are very many ways to use play as a vehicle for learning at all ages, for example, as a source of motivation or as a way for people to learn rules-of-the-game that are also useful rules-of-the-world.

VI. Examples of Good and Bad Use

One way to summarize the potential benefits of imaginative play is that it may help children become less stimulus driven and more thought driven. Rather than responding to the environment, children create a mental environment that guides their actions. With this in mind, maximize the thought-driven potential of play.

Bad: A child watches a blockbuster action movie. The people who made the movie exerted tremendous imagination. In contrast, the act of watching the movie is stimulus driven—there cannot be enough explosions, car chases, and high-end graphics (ditto for some video games). The child is being driven by the stimulus. (This is not to say there isn't a time for watching these movies; just don't expect action movies to develop people's executive functioning.)

Bad: An adult tells children exactly what to do. The child is being driven by the adult (a kind of stimulus) rather than exercising her own imagination.

Good: A mystery movie is thought driven, and the pleasure comes from constructing possible scenarios that might explain who did it. As an adult, make sure to help children realize that their task is to imagine the possibilities, whether reading or watching.

Good: A toy that suggests only part of the story. A playhouse requires children to construct a narrative. Blocks, rather than elaborate one-use toys, give children a chance to build and imagine forts, bridges, and more. Again, it is helpful if an adult offers tips without dominating the play. Introduce more opportunities for the child to imagine alternatives and map back and forth between the hard constraints of reality and the fancy of the imagination.

VII. References

Connolly, J. A., & Doyle, A. B. (1984). Relation of social fantasy play to social competence in preschoolers. *Developmental Psychology, 20*(5), 797–806.

Dansky, J. L., & Silverman, I. W. (1973). Effects of play on associative fluency in preschool-aged children. *Developmental Psychology, 9*, 38–43.

DeLoache, J. S. (1987). Rapid change in the symbolic functioning of very young children. *Science, 238*(4833), 1556–1557.

Diamond, A., Barnett, W. S., Thomas, J., & Munro, S. (2007). Preschool program improves cognitive control. *Science, 318*(5855), 1387–1388.

Fisher, K. R., Hirsh-Pasek, K., Golinkoff, R. M., & Gryfe, S. G. (2008). Conceptual split? Parents' and experts' perceptions of play in the 21st century. *Journal of Applied Developmental Psychology, 29*(4), 305–316.

Lévi-Strauss (1966). *The savage mind.* Chicago: University of Chicago Press.

Lillard, A. S., Lerner, M. D., Hopkins, E. J., Dore, R. A., Smith, E. D., & Palmquist, C. M. (2013). The impact of pretend play on children's development: A review of the evidence. *Psychological Bulletin, 139*(1), 1-34.

Mischel, W., Ayduk, O., Berman, M. G., Casey, B. J., Gotlib, I. H., Jonides, J., . . . Shoda, Y. (2011). "Willpower" over the life span: Decomposing self-regulation. *Social Cognitive and Affective Neuroscience, 6*, 252–256.

Pellis, S. M., Pellis, V. C., & Bell, H. C. (2010). The function of play in the development of the social brain. *American Journal of Play, 2*(3), 278–298.

Schellenberg, E. G. (2004). Music lessons enhance IQ. *Psychological Science, 15*(8), 511–514.

Sutton-Smith, B. (2009). *The ambiguity of play.* Cambridge, MA: Harvard University Press.

I IS FOR IMAGINATIVE PLAY

What is the core learning mechanic?
Imaginative play involves creating a story that is different from the world at hand. In pretend play, people let one thing stand for another.

What is an example, and what is it good for?
A child pretends a fork (a mother) is scolding a spoon (a child) for not eating all her peas. Theoretically, imaginative play should help children develop symbolic and social abilities, as well as cognitive control.

Why does it work?
Imaginative play involves two key moves. The first is that it requires preventing the stimulus from driving one's responses to the environment (a fork is not a fork). The second move is to construct an alternative, cognitively controlled interpretation (a fork is a mother). Exercising these core human abilities should spur their maturation. However, it has been difficult to develop definitive evidence about the causes and consequences of any form of play, despite its ubiquity across mammals. In the meantime, play, which is typically fun, can serve as a great vehicle for delivering activities known to support maturation and learning.

What problems does the core mechanic solve?
- Children do not think for themselves.
  - An overly prescriptive classroom tells students what to do and think.
- Children are driven by stimuli in the environment.
  - An action movie with high-end special effects does not engage the imagination, it replaces the need for one.
  - Children are impulsive.

Examples of how to use it
- Have students take on roles during their imaginative work.
  - Ask a child to imagine being a doctor and behave like a doctor and not a patient.
- Use adults to help encourage children's imaginations.
  - Have parents ask "what if" questions when reading a story with a child.

Risks

What counts as play and what it is good for are ambiguous. This creates room for strange beliefs, such as students cannot learn when playing, or imaginative play is the best way to advance the goal of producing more engineers. Educators need to avoid being drawn into one rhetoric or another.

J is for Just-in-Time Telling

Making lectures and readings work

JUST-IN-TIME TELLING ENABLES students to first experience problems before they hear or read the solutions and explanations. Lectures and readings are more effective when they address a problem students have experienced. This chapter considers how to provide those problem-solving experiences. When students appreciate the details of the problem, they learn the expository information more precisely, and they can use it to learn future material efficiently and solve novel problems effectively.

You probably remember sitting through a lecture in chemistry, history, or <insert least favorite class here>. The lecture slowly faded into a stream of separate words about an increasingly obscure topic. The amazing thing is that the topic was probably one of the most significant breakthroughs of its generation—that is why it was in the lecture. How is it possible that the greatest ideas can fade into a haze of words? Part of it could be a lousy lecture that goes on too long and packs in too much information. Breaking up lectures and providing opportunities for interaction can help with that problem. But maybe it was not all the lecturer's fault. You simply may not have been prepared to appreciate why the lecture's content was important, except that someone told you it was. You had never experienced the problems that the great ideas solved.

I. How Just-in-Time Telling Works

In business and military simulations, people engage complex scenarios. Afterward, a debriefing organizes those experiences together into a coherent framework. Without the experiences, the debriefing would be meaningless verbiage. Without the debriefing, the simulation would be just so many unique experiences that do not connect to a larger principle. The value of "telling" is that it puts things together, often joined by a single principle, framework, or solution. *Experience and explanation produce different types of knowledge, and they work very well together when the experience comes first.*

Effective knowledge has two components: an *if* and a *then*. The *then* is the action or response: "Add the numbers and divide by how many there are." The *if* comprises conditions under which one might take the action: "You need to find an average score." Unfortunately, most lectures and expository writings provide a very detailed explanation of the *then* but not an equally detailed *if.* They provide the output of expert reasoning, but not the conditions that make that reasoning relevant. The result is that people do not have sufficiently precise prior knowledge to match the precision of the lecture.

A nice example comes from trying to teach college students about human memory. Textbooks and lectures make very detailed distinctions among memory types and processes, such as associative and procedural, or encoding and retrieval. Even so, students seem to hear the coarser proposition, "People remember stuff." This is because they have not had a chance to appreciate the distinct memory phenomena that demand these precise distinctions.

Schwartz and Bransford (1998) tried to solve this problem by having college students notice memory phenomena on their own before a lecture. The students' task was to look at data from people trying to remember lists of words. They then had to graph the important patterns in the data. You can try the activity here by looking at the following example. See if you notice any interesting patterns in what people remembered.

> *Instructions:* Read the experimental background information and corresponding data. Graph the important patterns you see in the data.
> *Background information:* The data come from an experiment in which research participants tried to remember a list of words (below). Participants listened to one word per second. They did not see the list; they only listened to it. Afterward, the participants wrote down as many words as they could remember.
> *List of words (in the order heard):* car, sky, apple, book, cup, lock, coat, light, bush, iron, water, house, tape, file, glass, dog, cloud, hand, chair, bag

The data: What participants wrote down (in the order written):
Participant 1: bag, hand, chair, cloud, sky, light
Participant 2: bag, chair, hand, car, sky, book, house, bush
Participant 3: hand, bag, chair, cloud, car, lock, dog
Participant 4: bag, hand, chair, dog, car, apple, sky, water, glass
Participant 5: bag, chair, car, iron, apple, cup, water, light

If you did the activity (even half-heartedly), you probably recognized that many of the participants remembered bag, hand, and chair first and that they also mostly remembered car and sky. Relatedly, you likely noticed that these were the last and first items in the list of words, respectively. The data exemplify some key memory phenomena, such as the effects of *recency*, which refers to superior immediate memory for things one has just heard, and the effects of *primacy*, which refers to superior memory for the first things one hears.

The researchers examined whether the experience of analyzing the phenomena could lead to greater learning than some typical classroom learning techniques. In the study, one group of students graphed the interesting patterns from data, as in the activity above. A second group of students read a chapter that described the same experiments, showed graphs of the data, and described the theories that explained the results. These latter students did not see or analyze the original data; instead their task was to write a two-page summary of the chapter. Both groups of students required about the same amount of time overall to complete either the graphing activity or the summarizing activity. The next day students from both conditions attended a common lecture that presented the relevant theories of memory and explained how they accounted for the results of the experiments.

To find out what the students learned, they received two tests. A true-false test asked the students about simple declarative facts, for example, "Primacy is when people show superior memory for the last things they hear" (which is false). Students in both conditions did fine on this test—they had learned the *then* part of the theories. The difference showed up on a test a week later that asked students to apply, or transfer, their learning to new situations.

For the transfer test, students read a passage. Their task was to predict what people would remember from the passage. For example, they might predict, "People should exhibit good memory for the very first part of the passage." As shown in Figure J.1, the students who had graphed the data and heard the lecture predicted outcomes much better. By investigating and analyzing the data, these students had a chance to notice the different types of memory phenomena and the conditions that cause them. In turn, the lecture provided the explanation of the detailed phenomena they had

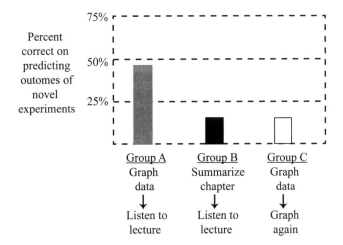

Figure J.1. The effects of creating a time for telling. Students had to predict the likely outcomes of a hypothetical study on memory after completing the activities shown beneath each group (data from Schwartz & Bransford, 1998).

noticed. In contrast, the students who summarized the chapter and then heard the lecture did not do very well on the prediction test. This is because they never had a chance to recognize where the theories apply. For example, they had read about primacy, and they even saw charts of the relevant data, but they never really engaged the phenomenon to understand the conditions under which it would occur. They could describe the theories, but they could not recognize when to use them.

Importantly, the researchers also included a third group of students, who graphed the data but, instead of hearing the lecture afterward, looked for more patterns a second time. These students did badly on both tests. They did not learn the names and theories for describing the phenomena they observed, so they did badly on the true-false test. Without the lecture, they also did not learn the principles behind the patterns they discovered, so they could not generalize to new situations that were somewhat different from what they had studied. For example, without the principles of recency and primacy, they had no way of knowing that patterns they found in the data also apply to reading a passage and not just lists of words.

To benefit from the accumulated wisdom of those who have come before, students need two things. They need to know the verbal explanations developed by experts who spent their lives figuring out those explanations, and they need to know the problems and situations that require those explanations. Telling people about those situations does not work very well, as shown by the students who had summarized the chapter. Instead, people learn explanations better when they have had some experience with the situations they address.

II. How to Use Just-in-Time Telling to Enhance Learning

People often refer to lecturing as the realization of a *transmission theory* of knowledge growth, where the instructor attempts to pour knowledge into the head of students. Who really believes it is possible to pour ideas into a mind? We have not met anybody yet. Instead, most people adopt some form of *constructivism*, whereby students need to connect and make sense of ideas on their own. Some people think constructivism needs to involve learning through discovery and hands-on activities—they think lectures are antithetical to constructivism. This is not true. The problem with lectures is not that they are anticonstructivist; people can construct knowledge when sitting quietly, if they have sufficient prior knowledge. The problem is that students often do not have the prior knowledge to construct knowledge from what they read or hear. Their only recourse is to memorize the words (or tune out) rather than understand the implications of those words.

To maximize the benefits of lectures and readings, instruction should first help students develop the prior knowledge that prepares them to construct knowledge from the expository materials. To create a time for telling, the most effective activities will help students confront the critical elements of a situation. We provide several examples below, which demonstrate that an effective activity requires two elements: the experience should be framed as a problem to be solved and the experience should be precise.

PROBLEM-SOLVING FRAME

One key ingredient is to engage students in the problem that needs to be solved, whether practical or theoretical. For instance, if one wants to prepare students to learn how to find their way in a forest using a compass and a map, do not have them just walk around a forest. Instead, have them try to solve the problem of how to navigate between two points using the compass and map.

Students do not always need to experience a problem firsthand. Instead, they need to experience trying to solve the problem, whether it is theirs or someone else's. As a thought experiment, take the case of preservice teachers, who have yet to teach and are just taking courses. Imagine that we want to prepare them for a lecture on how to handle classroom management issues. One approach might place the preservice teacher in charge of a rambunctious classroom for an hour. This would be a very compelling experience, and it would point out the desperate need for classroom management strategies. The difficulty is that the preservice teachers might not experience the types of classroom problems that the lecture addresses. For example, the lecture may address the challenge of ensuring students take turns, whereas the preservice teacher may have the experience of students playing with their cell phones during class. An alternative approach would employ authentic classroom videos that show the top ten classroom management problems. The preservice teachers could generate potential solutions. This experience would prepare them for the lecture, and it has the advantage of making sure the preservice teachers would engage the specific problems the lecture addresses.

PRECISE EXPERIENCES

The preceding example also highlights the second key ingredient—experiences should be precise and matched to the content to be learned. Imagine that you are giving a lecture on dam design. To prepare students for this lecture, you ask them to solve the problem of designing a dam for a river. This will activate their prior knowledge about dams. Unfortunately, it will not necessarily help them learn about the precise problems that dam design

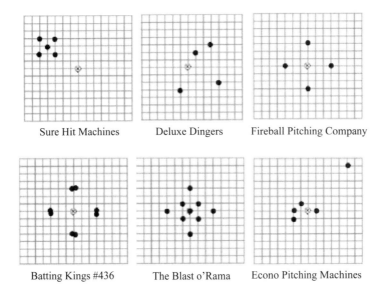

| Sure Hit Machines | Deluxe Dingers | Fireball Pitching Company |

| Batting Kings #436 | The Blast o'Rama | Econo Pitching Machines |

Figure J.2. An activity that prepared students for a lecture on measures of variability. Each grid presents the results from a different baseball-pitching machine. Each dot represents where a test pitch landed when aimed at the central target of the grid. The students' task is to come up with a single procedure that computes a reliability number for each machine. (People who are buying a machine for young children would want a very reliable machine.)

needs to solve, such as the relation of the center of water pressure to the dam's center of mass and the pitch of the dam wall. To prepare students to learn about these matters, they need an opportunity to confront problems that highlight issues of differential water pressure at different depths. Good problems give students a chance to confront the exact issues that the lecture or reading addresses.

As an illustration of a precise, problem-oriented activity, Figure J.2 shows contrasting cases (Chapter C) that students received in preparation for receiving an explanation and formula for computing variability (e.g., standard deviation). The students had to invent a way to characterize the reliability of the pitching machines, where each black dot represents where a pitch landed. The cases highlight a number of issues relevant to measures of variability. For instance, the contrast of Fireball Pitching and Blast o'Rama helps students notice that the density of the data, and not just the perimeter, matters for measures of variability. The comparison of Sure Hit Machines and Deluxe Dingers helps students notice the problem of different sample sizes (different n-values, in the parlance of statistics). Students who work on these cases are well prepared to understand the standard deviation formula afterward, because they have differentiated the features that the formula needs to account for. For instance, students who completed the cases and then heard a lecture were much better at explaining why the equation

$$\sigma = \sqrt{\frac{\Sigma(x - \bar{x})^2}{n}}$$

divides by n than were students who had not tried to solve the problem created by the contrasting cases (Schwartz & Martin, 2004). (Dividing by n solves the problem of different sample sizes because it is how one takes the average.)

Freely available science simulations (see, e.g., PhET Interactive Simulations at http://phet.colorado.edu) can also set the stage for just-in-time telling. If this is the intent, do not ask students to only explore a simulation on their own, because they may not experience a useful problem to be solved. Instead, let them explore for a few minutes, so they can learn the various controls and general simulation behavior and exhaust some of their initial "what does this button do?" curiosity. Then give them a specific problem relevant to the material to be explained, such as finding three different ways to achieve the same outcome in the simulation (e.g., find three different ways to adjust the velocity, height, and angle of a cannon shot to hit the same target). This should help them notice important characteristics of the simulation that are the topic of their reading or lecture.

III. The Outcomes of Just-in-Time Telling

Just-in-time telling can help people understand the purpose of the told knowledge. For example, after applying just-in-time telling, students will be better able to explain the purpose of an equation or a component of an equation (e.g., why divide by n), and they will be less likely to say, "Because, that's the way you're supposed to do it." They should also be able to answer, "Why is <X> important?" and to answer what-if questions.

A second outcome is more usable knowledge. Alfred Whitehead, a mathematician and philosopher, coined the phrase *inert knowledge*. People can have great stores of theoretical knowledge, but it remains inert if they cannot recognize when to use it. For instance, Michael, Klee, Bransford, and Warren (1993) found that early-career clinicians could describe all the syndromes they had been taught, but they could not diagnose patients on the floor. The reason is that they had not had a chance to observe the conditions that call for the diagnoses—they never learned the *if*. Providing learners a chance to experience the applicability conditions increases the chances they will recognize when to use what they know.

IV. Can People Learn to Teach Themselves with Just-in-Time Telling?

People are reasonably good at asking for an explanation when experiencing a problem they cannot solve. People are not as good at scouting out a problem in advance of a reading or lecture. To our knowledge, no studies have attempted to teach people to seek out appropriate experiences that create a personal time for telling. There are rare examples that come to mind. For instance, people may read a small portion of the rules for a new board game, play for a bit, and then read more of the rules. More generally, learning how to gain experiences ahead of an expository treatment is difficult, because one also needs to know which experiences to seek out.

Students sometimes resist engaging in problems before being taught the solution. It is useful to convince them of the benefits of these kinds of preparatory experiences, even if they cannot solve the problem (Kapur & Bielaczyc, 2012). For instance, we once asked college students in their physics recitation to engage in problems somewhat similar to those in Figure J.2 in advance of a lecture. Many complained that the problems did not look like the problems that would be on the test and that we had not yet taught them how to solve these problems. Their complaints made sense because these students had a lifetime of instruction that emphasized the routine of practicing what they had been told. It is too bad we never had a chance to tell these students that they ultimately did better on their next test compared with a group of students who had not engaged in the activities before the lecture.

V. Risks of Just-in-Time Telling

The first risk is that teachers want to share what they know, and it can be hard to withhold information long enough for students to engage a problem deeply. After all, what could be so bad about just telling students first? The risk of telling too soon has to do with a general principle of human cognition: *people often rely on what they know, instead of noticing what is new.* This has very direct, and somewhat unhappy, implications for instruction. If you show young children how to play with one feature of a toy, they will be less likely to explore other things the toy can do (Bonawitz et al., 2011). If you teach students a formula for solving a problem, they will pay attention to the formula you told them, instead of the situation it describes.

A study with eighth-graders shows the risk (Schwartz, Chase, Oppezzo, &

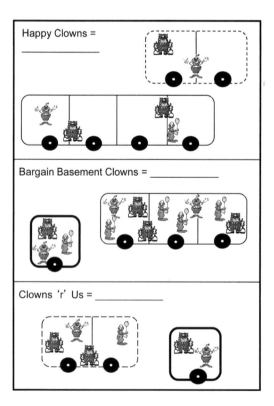

Figure J.3. A worksheet that exhibits proportionate ratios of clowns to bus compartments within each company. Students in a Tell-First condition were told the formula for density and then practiced applying it to determine the crowdedness of the clowns for each company. Other students did not hear about density but instead had to invent their own crowdedness index for each company. (From Schwartz, Chase, Oppezzo, and Chin, 2011.)

Chin, 2011). In a Tell-First condition, students received a brief lecture on density and how to use $d = m/v$ to compute it. Students then received the worksheet shown in Figure J.3. Their task was to figure out how much each company crowded its clowns into busses. For example, the answer for the company in the second row would be three clowns per compartment. Over 95 percent of the students correctly computed the density for each of the companies. Twenty-four hours later, the students had to redraw the worksheet from memory. Roughly 50 percent of the students redrew pairs of busses similar to those in Figure J.4A. The busses from the same company do not have the same ratio of clowns to compartments. This happened because, when students were solving the worksheet problems, they did not notice that a given density is defined by a common ratio of mass (clowns) to volume (compartments). Instead, they were simply doing what they had been told, dividing mass by volume. They overrelied on their knowledge of division, so they did not notice the significance of ratio.

To prove that this outcome was the result of telling too soon, the study included a second condition comprising students who had not been told about density. Their task was to invent a way to measure the crowdedness used by each company. When asked to redraw the worksheet the next day, 75 percent of these children's drawings looked similar to Figure J.4B—they had discovered the importance of ratio. This difference between the two conditions had a lasting impact on the children's ability to use ratio to learn

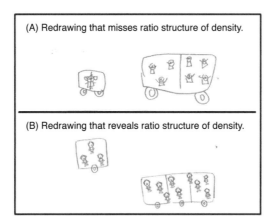

Figure J.4. Examples of what students remembered about the worksheet. (A) This drawing indicates the student did not notice that the density of clowns to bus compartments had the same ratio for a given company. (B) This drawing shows an appreciation that density is defined by a common ratio, in this case 3 to 1.

future topics several weeks later, with the "invent" students doing nearly four times better. Similar results have been found for primary school children learning to solve problems such as 3 + 4 = 5 + __, where letting them try first works better than telling them first and then having them practice (DeCaro & Rittle-Johnson, 2012). (Children who have little experience balancing equations often believe the answer is 12, because they think the task is to sum all the numbers into the final empty space.)

One implication of these studies involves "flipped" instruction, where students watch video lectures at home before doing problems in class. It may be better to have the students experience problems first, then watch the "telling" video, and only then practice executing what they have been taught. Just for fun, we dub our new instructional invention "double-flipped instruction."

A second risk is that people may discount compelling experiences, because they do not show an immediate benefit. For instance, Arena (2012) showed that commercial video games, such as *Civilization* and *Call of Duty*, prepare students to learn about World War II. Students who had played the games for several hours did not initially exhibit any more WWII knowledge than students who had not, so the games seemed useless. However, this would have been a premature conclusion. While the video games do not portray WWII history per se, students do engage in strategic and tactical problems that can prepare them to learn about those types of issues from a lecture on WWII. The video games revealed their value only when they were coupled with a subsequent explanation. Students who had played the games learned more from a lecture on WWII than those who had not. The benefit of many experiential activities is that they prepare people for future learning, and not that they are a complete lesson on their own.

This is an interesting result, particularly for those interested in games and learning. The point is not that playing war video games for hours is the most efficient (or politically correct) way to prepare students to learn about WWII. Rather, the point is that one can make effective games for learning without trying to cram expository material into the game: let the game provide the experience, and an expository text or lecture can provide the explanation afterward (Arena & Schwartz, 2013).

A third risk is that a telling may be poorly executed—weak examples, bad ordering of ideas, no statement of the big ideas, missing information, a monotone, and so forth. By far the most common problem is that lectures contain too much information. One count has it that an average engineering lecture introduces a new equation every 2.5 minutes and a new variable every 45 seconds (Blikstein & Wilensky, 2010). Imagine sitting through that for an hour! Perhaps instructors feel that they must cover the material, or maybe the material seems obvious (to them at least). The consequence is a warp-speed lecture that creates an overwhelming cognitive load. Listeners are trying to put together the new information, which takes time and effort to keep everything in mind. Even experts can fail to keep up when listening to an over-packed lecture in their general area of expertise. *Sometimes less is more—aim for the big idea, not every idea.*

VI. Examples of Good and Bad Use

Preparing people for a just-in-time telling about how sails and wind interact:
Bad: Have people imagine all the fun places they could go once they learn to windsurf. While this could be very motivating, it will not prepare them to understand the lecture.

Good: Make a fun little race where each person gets a miniature sailboat. They have to set the angle of the sail so they can blow from the side and still get the sailboat across a pool. This will help them experience the problem of sailing into the wind, which in turn will prepare them for a lecture on the topic.

VII. References

Arena, D. A. (2012). *Commercial video games as preparation for future learning.* (Unpublished doctoral dissertation). Stanford University, Palo Alto, CA.

Arena, D. A., & Schwartz, D. L. (2013). Experience and explanation: Using videogames to prepare students for formal instruction in statistics. *Journal of Science Education and Technology, 23*(4), 538-548.

Blikstein, P., & Wilensky, U. (2010). MaterialSim: A constructionist agent-based modeling approach to engineering education. In M. J. Jacobson & P. Reimann (Eds.), *Designs for learning environments of the future: International perspectives from the learning sciences* (pp. 17–60). New York: Springer.

Bonawitz, E., Shafto, P., Gweon, H., Goodman, N. D., Spelke, E., & Schulz, L. (2011). The double-edged sword of pedagogy: Instruction limits spontaneous exploration and discovery. *Cognition, 120*(3), 322–330.

DeCaro, M. S., & Rittle-Johnson, B. (2012). Exploring mathematics problems prepares children to learn from instruction. *Journal of Experimental Child Psychology, 113*(4), 552–568.

Kapur, M., & Bielaczyc, K. (2012). Designing for productive failure. *Journal of the Learning Sciences, 21*(1), 45–83.

Michael, A. L., Klee, T., Bransford, J. D., & Warren, S. (1993). The transition from theory to therapy: Test of two instructional methods. *Applied Cognitive Psychology, 7*(2), 139–154.

Schwartz, D. L., & Bransford, J. D. (1998). A time for telling. *Cognition and Instruction, 16*(4), 475–522.

Schwartz, D. L., Chase, C. C., Oppezzo, M. A., & Chin, D. B. (2011). Practicing versus inventing with contrasting cases: The effects of telling first on learning and transfer. *Journal of Educational Psychology, 103*(4), 759–775.

Schwartz, D. L., & Martin, T. (2004). Inventing to prepare for future learning: The hidden efficiency of original student production in statistics instruction. *Cognition and Instruction, 22*(2), 129–184.

J IS FOR JUST-IN-TIME TELLING

What is the core learning mechanic?
Enabling students to first experience problems before they hear or read the solutions.

What is an example, and what is it good for?
Students complete a simulated battle, and afterward there is a debriefing. The simulation provides students with rich experiences, and the debriefing provides an explanation or framework for organizing those experiences. Without the experience, the explanation would be too abstract. Without the explanation, the experiences would just be a collection of memories. Together, they produce usable knowledge.

Why does it work?
People learn from expository materials by integrating the explanations with their prior knowledge. Often, students do not have sufficient prior knowledge to integrate the explanations meaningfully. Providing learners an opportunity to develop prior knowledge of the problem helps make the lecture more meaningful, because students have experienced aspects of the problem that need to be solved.

What problems does the core mechanic solve?
- Students are bored or lost during a lecture.
  - A professor provides her finest lecture, but students cannot make sense of so many little details.
- Students exhibit coarse understanding.
  - A student reads about multiple types of memory phenomena but seems to have learned only that people remember stuff.
- Students fail to use what they have learned.
  - Students memorize the material fine, but they cannot figure out when they should apply it.

Examples of how to use it
- Have students gain experiences with a problem by trying to solve it.
  - Biology students try to think of how they would move twenty rubber ducks into the center of a pool without touching them. This prepares them for a lecture that explains how a cell collects material into the nucleus for cell division.

° Preservice teachers observe videos of several class management problems and try to generate possible solutions. This will prepare them to understand the details of the solutions presented in a lecture.

Risks

- Teachers may tell students solutions too soon.
- Students may resist trying to solve problems before being told how.

K is for Knowledge

*An essay on efficiency
and innovation in knowledge*

KNOWLEDGE INFUSES ALL of learning. Prior knowledge enables people to make sense of new information, and "post" knowledge enables people to imagine and achieve goals they previously could not. Because of knowledge's central importance, we decided to break form. Rather than presenting a chapter for the letter K in our usual style, we offer a brief essay on the broad outcomes of knowledge. Our goal is to help untangle a tacit dichotomy that leads to confusion about the design of educational experiences and desirable learning outcomes.

Learning scientists and educators often go beyond designing to pre-specified outcomes. They further need to decide which outcomes are worthwhile. This is ultimately a normative question to be decided by the stakeholders of education. Nevertheless, science can serve a clarifying role, particularly among competing proposals for learning.

Our proposed conceptual framework captures two major yet often competing goals of education (Schwartz, Bransford & Sears, 2005): (1) the development and use of efficient knowledge to solve recurrent classes of problems, and (2) the ability to adapt to novel conditions by innovating new knowledge. These two classes of outcomes show up in many debates within education, such as the relative value of training students to mastery versus asking students to discover new-to-them knowledge, as well as teacher-centered versus student-centered pedagogies. Are these goals mutually exclusive, or is there a framework that can help learners develop knowledge that supports both efficiency and innovation?

LEARNING FOR EFFICIENCY

A major, recurring theme in the science of learning is the knowledge-is-power thesis. The original phrase is often attributed to Francis Bacon. In learning, it refers to the idea that knowledge enables efficient control. In the 1950s, Newell and Simon (1972) began building the *General Problem Solver*, an intelligent computer program that used general problem-solving strategies, such as establishing subgoals, searching through alternatives, and making reasoned guesses. It was an intellectual tour-de-force. At the same time, the authors realized that general problem-solving techniques comprised *weak methods*—general strategies, but inefficient and laborious. In contrast, humans further engage in *strong methods*—knowledge-infused strategies tuned to specific applications. Novice chess players try to reason through all the possible responses and counterresponses for each move they might take. This is a weak method. In contrast, chess experts look for open columns, rows, and diagonals, because these often produce a major advantage. This is a strong method. Knowledge makes one more efficient and powerful.

Efficient knowledge is characterized by rapid retrieval, accurate application, and high consistency in performance. Doctors who have frequently performed a particular type of surgery have highly efficient knowledge. They can diagnose and treat a new patient quickly and effectively. When choosing a surgeon for a procedure, it is wise to ask, "How many of these have you performed previously?" The degree of practice is a better predictor of expertise than native intelligence (see Chapter D).

Efficient prior knowledge improves people's abilities to interpret new, related information, and it regularly predicts learning well beyond the method of instruction itself (see Chapter S). When assessing students' reading abilities, providing stories that are relevant to their experiences will improve test scores.

Knowledge even gives power over the effects of aging. As people age past their twenties, their abilities to hold, select, and switch among temporary sources of information decline (sorry, but it is true on average). Yet, knowledge trumps basic processing abilities. Hambrick and Engle (2002) had participants listen to several minutes of a baseball game. Afterward, the participants answered questions about what they had heard. Younger people who had the same amount of baseball knowledge as older people remembered the broadcast details better, because they were more able to hold on to the temporary information. But older people with baseball knowledge remembered more details than younger people who did not know much about baseball, despite the youths' superior working memories.

The science of learning has primarily focused on efficiency outcomes. This is especially true in America. Piagetian theorists have often expressed amusement when asked what they call the "American question" of "how do we get kids to progress through the developmental stages more rapidly?" This is an efficiency question that fits the American emphasis on pragmatism and "do it now."

By many accounts, it seems safe to say that the transition from novice to expert is characterized by increases in efficient knowledge. Most school-based assessments test for efficient knowledge, where there is a demonstrably single correct answer. The tests often take a sequestered problem-solving format (Bransford & Schwartz, 1999). Like a jury sequestered from contaminating influences, students need to solve problems without resources for learning or feedback. If they have built up an efficient store of prior knowledge, they can solve relatively familiar classes of problems correctly the first time and under time pressure.

LEARNING FOR INNOVATION

Efficient knowledge is ideal for stable, recurrent contexts. Reading occurs in a stable context, whether in a book or on a screen. In English, it is always the same twenty-six letters, they are always segmented into words, and the reading occurs from left to right. People develop automatic knowledge for decoding the visual stimuli of text, which is of great value. Efficient memories are far faster than problem solving anew. Without a body of efficient knowledge for recurrent tasks, people would have a difficult time in life.

Appropriate kinds of practice help people turn non-routine, difficult-to-solve problems into routine problems that can be solved quickly and easily. Phrased another way, efficiency-oriented practice is often about "problem elimination" rather than about in-depth, sustained problem solving. By preparing people so that the problems they will face in life are essentially routine problems—or, at worst, very "near transfer" problems—people reduce the needs for extensive problem solving and can perform quite effectively.

Yet—and this is the big *yet*—efficient knowledge is inadequate for variable environments and changing times, where what one knows is no longer fully applicable. In fact, highly efficient knowledge can interfere with effective performance. During the 2000 Summer Olympic Games, female gymnasts were crashing during their vaults. As it turned out, the vaulting horse had been set two inches lower than usual, which was enough to disrupt the high efficiency of these world-class athletes.

Knowledge is power; knowledge is also bias. Prior knowledge shapes how people interpret the world, and these interpretations can blind them to alternatives. As an example, tourists may believe that the locals "have culture" whereas their hometown is culture-free and simply the natural state of affairs.

People tend to seek evidence that their beliefs are true and neglect alternatives and evidence to the contrary (see Chapter U). Heckler and Scaife (2015) found that physics students' prior beliefs improved their abilities to find data consistent with their beliefs but blocked interpretations of opposing data.

Efficient knowledge seeps into problem posing, such that people presuppose the solution in their statement of a problem. Edwin Land, the inventor of the Polaroid camera, described insight as the sudden cessation of stupidity. The stupidity comes from one's initial framing of problems—framings that contain assumptions that were efficient in other contexts.

Adams (1979) provides the example of engineers who tried to design a mechanical tomato picker that did not bruise tomatoes. The engineers tried many creative solutions but had no breakthroughs. Later a group of botanists entered the picture. They helped the engineers reframe the problem. Instead of designing a mechanical picker that was less likely to bruise tomatoes, a better strategy might be to design a tomato that was less likely to be bruised. This reframing opened up new possibilities for thinking, and the group eventually engineered a new type of tomato with a thicker, less easily bruised skin (unfortunately, also less tasty). Interdisciplinary collaborations, at their best, help people realize that there are ways of thinking about a problem other than what their own efficient knowledge would tell them. Collaborations like these take time to nurture, because people have difficulty understanding why other people could possibly care about the details they do.

Highly efficient knowledge, in and of itself, seems inadequate for the task of innovation and discovery. Hatano and Inagaki (1986), in their discussion of abacus masters, generated a useful distinction between routine expertise and adaptive expertise. The abacus masters could do amazing feats of mental arithmetic by imagining they were manipulating an abacus (see Chapter D). However, the abacus masters did not use their skills to learn new kinds of mathematics, and they performed only in highly stable contexts of zero distraction. Hatano and Inagaki described the abacus masters as having a high degree of *routine expertise*. They could perform well-rehearsed routines in a stable environment to an astonishing degree of efficiency. The authors went on to propose a second kind of expertise, which they termed *adaptive expertise*. Unlike routine expertise, adaptive expertise depends on embracing variation and a willingness to adjust and learn new ways of doing things.

An example of routine expertise might be an engineer who is very good at designing a particular kind of bridge expansion joint that fits a common set of criteria. If a bridge plan falls outside those criteria, the engineer will not take the job. There is a natural gravity to stay within one's routine expertise, because taking on unfamiliar challenges requires leaving one's comfort zone and can lead to suboptimal performance, at least in the short run. In contrast, adaptive experts are willing to approach novel problems and flexibly generate new solutions. An adaptive engineer might embrace the chance to design a new kind of joint for a bridge.

Putting children on a trajectory of adaptive expertise seems especially important, because they have yet to commit to a professional trajectory. Three contextual features can be designed into an environment to protect people from becoming trapped by their routine success: (1) reduce the risk associated with suboptimal performance, so people do not retreat into the safety of the conventional; (2) provide situations that have sufficient variation, so that people develop general knowledge that can handle new situations; and (3) create a culture that embraces understanding and experimentation, not just short-term performance.

Often, student-centered curricula that emphasize abilities to adapt through inquiry and innovation inadvertently measure success with sequestered tests of efficiency. Sequestered tests of efficiency cannot evaluate whether people have become adaptive, and one often hears the comment, "Wouldn't it be more efficient if you just told them the answer instead of having them discover it?" A more sensitive measure, relevant to student abilities to adapt, would use assessments that provide students with an opportunity to learn information as part of the test (see Chapter P). Bransford and Schwartz (1999) described these assessments as testing students' preparation for future learning.

Preparation-for-future-learning assessments differ from measures of content-light problem-solving flexibility. Questions that test creative problem solving (e.g., Does there exist in New York City two people who have the same number of hairs on their head?) emphasize weak methods. They do not capture people's abilities to learn new information that helps them develop strong methods. (In case you're curious, the answer to the question is yes. Humans have about 100,000 hairs on their head on average. Given 8.5 million people in New York City with hair in the range of 0 to, say, 300,000 hairs, there have to be very many people with the same number of hairs.)

As a thought experiment on the perils of measuring adaptive expertise with measures of efficiency, consider an important educational experience for many young adults: college. Every few years a reporter interviews undergraduates on their graduation day. The reporter asks a question, maybe, "Why is the weather colder in winter than in summer?" The students sputter, because they do not know the answer. Based on this sequestered test, the reporter hints that a college education is not very special, because these students do not know about the tilt of the earth any better than high school students. This question misses the value of a liberal arts college education, which is the ability to learn and adapt to complex ideas in the future. If the reporter gave the students a day to learn the answer, the college students would probably do much better than high school students.

An example of the limitations of efficiency-driven exams comes from medical licensure. Medical exams do a poor job of predicting whether doctors have been prepared to learn on the job (Mylopoulos, Brydges, Woods, Manzone, & Schwartz, 2016). To measure whether instruction has put students on a trajectory to adaptive expertise, it is important to use measures of preparation for future learning that determine whether students adapt and learn from new information given the opportunity. For example, one might provide interning doctors, unbeknownst to them, a fake patient who has symptoms presenting a familiar diagnosis but also has an inexplicable symptom. One could evaluate whether the doctors pay attention to the discrepant symptom and spontaneously consult resources to help learn the true cause.

COMBINING INNOVATION AND EFFICIENCY

It is tempting to place efficiency and innovation at the opposite poles of a continuum, given that adaptation often requires letting go of previously efficient routines. This type of opposition shows up in arguments over entrainment pedagogies that emphasize efficiently transmitting correct ways of doing things and constructivist pedagogies that emphasize student-centered discovery. Our argument is that efficiency does not have to be the enemy of innovation. For example, it is well known that efficiency in some processes (e.g., driving a car, decoding written words and sentences) frees attentional capacity to do other things (e.g., talking while driving, reading for meaning). Similarly, if people confronted with a new complex problem have solved aspects of it before, this helps make these subproblems routine and easy to solve. This frees attentional bandwidth and enables people to concentrate on other aspects of the new situation that may require nonroutine adaptation.

Adaptive experts can resist the pull of early success and recognize needs for innovation. Wineburg (1998) compared history professors and college students. He asked historians who had expertise in a particular domain (e.g., Asian history) to solve history problems that, for them, were nonroutine because they came from an unfamiliar domain. The problems involved interpreting decisions made by Abraham Lincoln. The history experts were much more likely than college students to resist making assumptions that readily came to mind based on knowledge of their current culture. The experts realized that these assumptions were indeed coming from their current cultural context rather than from the context at the time of Lincoln. They therefore took the time to

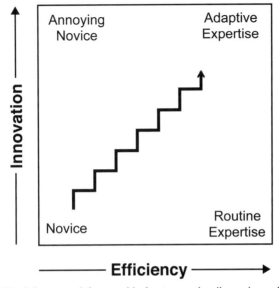

Figure K.1. A framework for considering two major dimensions of learning and outcomes (based on work by Schwartz, Bransford, and Sears, 2005).

research these issues to learn what they needed to know to solve the problem. In contrast, the college students went merrily on their way building confidently on a set of flawed assumptions that came from their current knowledge of the world.

Figure K.1 provides a possible framework for balancing experiences that promote efficiency and innovation. The lower left represents the starting point of a novice, who is low on both efficient knowledge and abilities to adapt intelligently. At the lower right is routine expertise, where people have developed a set of a highly efficient routines for handling familiar problems. At the upper right is adaptive expertise, where people have both highly efficient knowledge and foundational knowledge, as well as dispositions that enable them to innovate solutions and adapt to new situations. Finally, there is the annoying novice at the upper left. You probably know this guy—he's the one in the meeting who is happily brainstorming utterly unworkable solutions because he does not know anything of substance.

Training that is dedicated to routine expertise makes a great deal of sense for recurrent tasks that take a similar form each time. However, by itself, this training cannot lead people to adaptive expertise, because the lessons are tuned to specific problem conditions. On the other hand, instruction that emphasizes general, content-free skills of critical thinking and problem solving appear to provide a set of flexible weak methods that are too inefficient for the large problems surrounding many real-world tasks. This will not lead to adaptive expertise, and in the end, these methods are often taught and assessed as a set of routinized scripts. Educators have realized the importance of disciplinary ways of thinking (strong methods), rather than generalized methods (Star & Hammer, 2008).

Our reading of the literature suggests that it will not work to give students a course of efficiency-oriented, content-filled tasks that follow the horizontal axis of Figure K.1 and a separate set of strategy-training tasks that follow the vertical axis. It is not enough to expose students to content courses, on the one hand, and thinking courses, on the other, and then help students integrate them in a "capstone" course at the end of some educational program. This could be somewhat helpful, of course, but the conjecture is that it is far from ideal.

Our belief is that instruction needs to comingle efficiency and innovation opportunities if the goal is adaptive expertise. This leads to the question of whether experiences fostering innovation or efficiency should come first. Our claim, though the boundary conditions of this claim are unknown, is that students should first engage in disciplinary innovation, and then afterward learn the efficient solutions originally innovated by experts (see Chapter J). For instance, elementary students could be asked to invent a way to track how much money people owe one another before they learn about negative numbers. Exploring and innovating within a problem space can help students learn about the important variation and problems to be solved (see Chapter Q) as well as productive attitudes towards engaging challenging tasks without the expectation of getting the single right answer (see Chapter Y). In turn, this can set the stage for helping them understand the rationale for the efficient solution, which helps them learn the solution more quickly and use it more appropriately (see Chapter J).

The alternative ordering, where students learn the efficient solution first, can have the inadvertent side effect of overshadowing learner abilities to recognize the need to go beyond their efficient knowledge. For instance, in a study described in Chapter J, Schwartz, Chase, Oppezzo, and Chin (2011) showed that teaching students the density formula first interfered with their ability to recognize that density comprises a ratio (mass ÷ volume), as well as their ability to recognize ratio in other physical quantities (e.g., speed). Students who first tried to invent the density formula, and only then learned the efficient formula, did much better.

Our preferred ordering of experiences is tentative, because there is a shortage of relevant evidence. Most assessments of learning use sequestered tests that measure efficiency, which makes them a mismatch to the goals of adaptive expertise. Preparation for future learning measures are more suited to determining if students have learned to be innovative and learn new-to-them information. For example, Schwartz and Martin (2004) asked ninth-grade students to innovate their own ways to measure the variability (inconsistency) of different phenomena. Afterward, students received a lecture on a standard, efficient method for computing variability. Of particular interest was whether these learning experiences, which took a few hours, would prepare students to innovate solutions to highly novel problems. To find out, a subsequent test included a problem that required working with two variables, not just one. During instruction, students had learned about working only with univariate data, so determining the relation of two variables (covariance) would require innovation. At posttest, 34 percent of the students invented a way to measure covariance. Though this is far below 100 percent (it is a difficult task), it is a high level compared with the performance of students from a top public university who had recently completed a full semester of statistics: only 12 percent created a workable solution.

It seems unlikely that the high school freshmen had more sophisticated, content-free techniques for innovation than the college students did. And, it is also unlikely that they had more efficient knowledge of the statistical mathematics than the college students (who were, unsurprisingly, taught with an efficiency mind-set). Instead, the initial innovation task helped the high school students develop an understanding and stance toward the topic of variability that prepared them to be innovative later. Without a measure of their abilities to learn new solutions to a related problem, the hidden benefit of asking the high school students to invent their own solution first would have been missed. We suspect that the benefits of many methods of active learning have been missed due to mismeasurement.

EARLY LEARNING VERSUS LATER LEARNING

Researchers and instructional designers often use the same pedagogical moves for introductory and advanced learning in a topic. This is often the result of a natural desire for routines without qualification. By our analysis, early introductory learning should be dedicated to innovation opportunities, whereas later learning can be dedicated to efficiency. This proposal is reflected in the staircase structure of Figure K.1, where learners move upward on the innovation dimension before taking the turn to efficiency. Innovation activities provide learners a chance to:

- Explore and inquire into the structure and variation of the domain.
- Understand the problems that need to be solved and why.
- Participate in a learning culture that tolerates errors.
- Have a playful approach that fosters intrinsic satisfaction and minimizes ego threat.

- Learn to hold hypotheses lightly and seek feedback.
- Develop can-do attitudes that support adapting and innovating now and in the future.

Later learning, which can sometimes occur only a few minutes after early learning, should emphasize the development of efficient knowledge. This includes:

- Observe, read, or hear optimized solutions and theories.
- Develop a detailed understanding of why an idea works and under which conditions.
- Practice with an increasing press toward efficiency (e.g., time pressure, unaided retrieval).
- Engage in variation so that slightly different conditions will not be taken as new problems.
- Seek feedback that indicates how the execution of an idea or behavior can be refined.
- Feel the reward and self-efficacy of being able to do a thing well.

Of course, there will be exceptions. Sometimes it is important to give people a small bit of efficient knowledge so they can get started and avoid floundering. It is also more difficult to come up with good innovation tasks than efficiency tasks, because efficiency tasks are typically modified versions of well-known routines. Nevertheless, our simple framework may help people analyze and decide among different methods of learning. For instance, "flipped" classrooms often have an efficiency-only mind-set: teachers front-load learning of the relevant body of knowledge, and then classroom experiences involve refining and applying the knowledge more efficiently. This is appropriate for the goal of routine expertise. In contrast, many experiential pedagogies exhibit an innovation-only mind-set. Learners confront new scenarios and figure out solutions that are often idiosyncratic and partial. By our analysis, this will not lead to adaptive expertise. It would be better to combine experiential learning with subsequent opportunities to learn more efficient solutions and theories. If done well, the experiential activities help students learn to be innovative in the domain while also preparing them to learn the efficient solutions more effectively in the future.

References

Adams, J. L. (1979). *Conceptual blockbusting: A guide to better ideas.* New York: Norton.

Bransford, J. D., & Schwartz, D. L. (1999). Rethinking transfer: A simple proposal with multiple implications. *Review of Research in Education, 24*, 61–100.

Hambrick, D. Z., & Engle, R. W. (2002). Effects of domain knowledge, working memory capacity, and age on cognitive performance: An investigation of the knowledge-is-power hypothesis. *Cognitive Psychology, 44*, 339–387.

Hatano, G., & Inagaki, K. (1986). Two courses of expertise. In H. Stevenson, H. Azuma, & K. Hakuta (Eds.), *Child development and education in Japan* (pp. 262–272). New York: Freeman.

Heckler, A. F., & Scaife, T. M. (2015). Patterns of response times and response choices to science questions: The influence of relative processing time. *Cognitive Science, 39*(3), 496–537.

Mylopoulos, M., Brydges, R., Woods, N. N., Manzone, J., & Schwartz, D. L. (2016). Preparation for future learning: A missing competency in health professions education. *Medical Education, 50*(1), 115-123.

Newell, A., & Simon, H. (1972). *Human problem solving.* Englewood Cliffs, NJ: Prentice-Hall.

Schwartz, D. L., Bransford, J. D., & Sears, D. L. (2005). Efficiency and innovation in transfer. In J. Mestre (Ed.), *Transfer of learning from a modern multidisciplinary perspective* (pp. 1–51). Greenwich, CT: Information Age.

Schwartz, D. L., Chase, C. C., Oppezzo, M. A., & Chin, D. B. (2011). Practicing versus inventing with contrasting cases: The effects of telling first on learning and transfer. *Journal of Educational Psychology, 103*(4), 759–775.

Schwartz, D. L., & Martin, T. (2004). Inventing to prepare for future learning: The hidden efficiency of original student production in statistics instruction. *Cognition and Instruction, 22*(2), 129–184.

Star, C., & Hammer, S. (2008). Teaching generic skills: Eroding the higher purpose of universities, or an opportunity for renewal? *Oxford Review of Education, 34*(2), 237–251.

Wineburg, S. (1998). Reading Abraham Lincoln: An expert/expert study in the interpretation of historical texts. *Cognitive Science, 22*(3), 319–346.

L is for

Listening and Sharing

Learning more together than alone

WITH LISTENING AND sharing learners try to construct joint understandings. Listening and sharing are the cornerstones of collaborative learning. We can learn more working together than working alone.

A little history lesson: The study of cooperation arose after World War II as part of a research program on conflict resolution (Deutsch, 1977). Negotiation depends on cooperation, and negotiation is a preferable resolution to conflict than war. From this starting point, one reason to use cooperative learning is to help students develop better skills at cooperating (e.g., Johnson & Johnson, 1987). Subsequent research discovered a second reason to use cooperative learning: when students collaborate on class assignments, they learn the material better (we provide examples below). Ideally, small group work can yield both better abilities to cooperate and better learning of the content.

Simply putting students into small groups, however, does not guarantee desirable outcomes. Success depends on listening and sharing. Here is a description of students who did not collaborate well.

Sagging in his chair, Daryl gazed away, pointing his outstretched legs toward another group. Elizabeth, disgusted, looked down as she paged through the anthology. Across from them, Josh and Kara talked animatedly. When I stopped at their group, Kara told me the group had chosen Raymond Carver's poem "Gravy." Elizabeth complained that no one was listening to her and that she hated "the dumb poem they both want." . . . Finally came the day of their presentation. . . . Kara and Josh had taken over the presentation. The other two never really found their way into the project. (Cohen & Lotan, 2014, p. 25, citing Shulman et al., 1998)

Kara and Josh did the lion's share of the content work, and it may have been very good. Nevertheless, they did not listen to Elizabeth, and Daryl did not share any thoughts at all. The example resonates with people because most of us have been Daryl, Elizabeth, and Kara and Josh at some point. Fortunately, listening and sharing as cooperative techniques can alleviate frustration and, more importantly, allow group learning to surpass what would be possible by a single student (Slavin, 1995). Effective collaborative learning yields gains in motivation and conceptual understanding. Ideally, it also helps students learn how to cooperate in the future.

I. How Listening and Sharing Works

Everything is more fun with someone else!! Well, at least it should be. Many college students dislike group projects. Some of this is naïve egoism and an unwillingness to compromise—I can do this better alone than together. But more often than not, it is because one or more of five ingredients is missing: joint attention, listening, sharing, coordinating, and perspective taking.

JOINT ATTENTION

To collaborate, people need to pay attention to the same thing. If two children are building separate sand castles, they are not collaborating. They are engaged in parallel play. The abilities to maintain joint attention are foundational and emerge around the first year of life. Infants and parents can share attention to the same toy. Next, infants learn to follow the parents gaze to maintain joint visual attention. Finally, the infants learn to direct their parents' attention (Carpenter, Nagell, Tomasello, Butterworth, & Moore, 1998). Visual attention provides an index of what people are thinking about. If you are looking longingly at an ice-cold beer, it is a good bet that you are thinking about an ice-cold beer.

Using a common visual anchor (e.g., a common diagram) can help people maintain joint visual attention. In one study, Schneider and Pea (2013) had partners complete a circuit task, where participants had to figure out which circuit controlled which outcome in a simulation. They collaborated remotely over headsets. They saw the same image on their respective computers, so it was possible to maintain joint visual attention. In one condition, the authors used eye tracking: a moving dot showed each participant where the other was looking, so it was easier for them to maintain joint visual attention. These partners exhibited better collaboration, and they learned more from the task than did partners who did not have the eye-tracking dot to support joint attention.

LISTENING

Thoughts can be much more complex than an eye gaze. It also helps to hear what people are thinking. A common situation is that people refuse to listen to one another because they are too busy talking or they just discount other people's ideas. The How-To section describes a number of solutions.

SHARING

Sharing operates on two levels: sharing common goals and sharing ideas. First, if people do not share some level of common goal, they will collaborate to cross-purposes. Two professors of mathematics may agree to design homework together for a large class, but if one professor aims to increase students' interest in the field while the other aims to weed out the faint of heart, they will have a hard time reaching consensus. Second, if nobody shares ideas, collaboration will not go very far. In school, getting people to share can be difficult. Learners may be diffident, or they may not have good strategies for sharing. Children often do not know how to offer constructive criticism or build on an idea. It can be helpful to give templates for sharing, such as two likes and a wish, where the "wish" is a constructive criticism or a building idea.

COORDINATING

Have you ever had the experience of a group discussion, in which you just cannot seem to get your timing right? Either you always interrupt before the speaker is done, or someone else grabs the floor exactly when the other person finishes and before you jump in. Collaboration requires a great deal of turn-taking coordination. When the number of collaborators increases, it is also important to partition roles and opportunities to interact. You may hope coordination evolves organically, which it might. But it might turn into a *Lord of the Flies* scenario instead. It can be useful to establish collaborative structures and rules.

PERSPECTIVE TAKING

A primary reason for collaborating is that people bring different ideas to the table. The first four ingredients—joint attention, listening, sharing, and coordinating—support the exchange of information. The fifth ingredient is understanding why people are offering the information they do. This often goes beyond what speakers can possibly show and say (see Chapter S). People need to understand the point of view behind what others are saying, so they can interpret it more fully. This requires perspective taking. This is where important learning takes place, because learners can gain a new way to think about matters. It can also help differentiate and clarify one's own ideas. A conflict of opinions can enhance learning (Johnson & Johnson, 2009).

An interesting study on perspective taking (Kulkarni, Cambre, Kotturi, Bernstein, & Klemmer, 2015) occurred in a massive open online course (MOOC) with global participation. In their online discussions, learners were encouraged to review lecture content by relating it to their local context. The researchers placed people into low- or high-diversity groups based on the spread of geographic regions among participants. Students in the most geographically diverse discussion groups saw the highest learning gains, presumably because they had the opportunity to consider more different perspectives than geographically uniform groups did.

II. How to Use Listening and Sharing to Enhance Learning

One study found that children spent more time on task when they were engaged in group work than in individual work (Cohen & Lotan, 2014, citing Ahmadjian 1980). Was this luck? Not if you teach students how to be cooperative.

ESTABLISHING NORMS AND ROLES

Cooperation, like all social interaction, depends on norms of interaction (see Chapter N). For legislative cooperation, there are norms for trading favors. For collaborative learning, we need norms that support joint attention, listening, sharing, coordinating, and perspective taking. Here are some examples from Cohen and Lotan (2014):

- Pay attention to what group members need.
- No one is done until everyone is done.
- Explain by telling how (not doing for).
- Everyone gets a chance to speak.
- Find out what others think.
- Give reasons for ideas.
- Have a plan.

Cohen and Lotan suggest introducing activities specifically focused on learning the norms of cooperation *before* trying to introduce academic content.

The norms should be described as behaviors. This way a member of the group can act as an observer during norm-developing activities and record how well the group is following the behaviors. For example, the observer might tally how many times each person talks and how many times people give reasons for their opinions. Afterward, the observer can report back to the group for debriefing.

Multiperson cooperation can be difficult to coordinate for beginners. One solution is to assign people responsibility for learning different parts of the overall task and sharing what they have learned with the group (see Chapter T, Figure T.2). Another solution is to have explicit, rotating roles in the group process: facilitator, recorder, resource manager, and reporter. The facilitator can enforce behavioral norms. The recorder can take notes and keep a record of ideas and questions. The resource manager collects physical and informational materials for the group. The reporter synthesizes the group discussion and product in a presentation. (Be creative here; there are many possible roles.)

Students need practice and feedback with roles. In the online discussion component of an online course, some groups had one member play the role of facilitator, whereas other groups did not have a facilitator role. Students in the facilitated groups found the discussion marginally less motivating than did students in the unstructured groups, and they were less likely to join the same group given another opportunity (Kulkarni et al., 2015). One speculation is that the students who played the role of facilitator had not been prepared to do it well and did not receive useful feedback.

GROUP-WORTHY TASKS

Group synergy often depends on having a good task. Cohen and Lotan capture the point: "There is no particular advantage in giving groups a set of routine computational examples to complete. They will respond by doing the most sensible and expedient thing—copying the answers of the student who is perceived as best and probably fastest at computation" (2014, p. 10).

A group-worthy task is often one that no individual could complete alone, at least within the allotted time. This makes exchange among the group members necessary. Ideally, the task has room for multiple ideas, so everyone can contribute. Here is task adapted from Cohen and Lotan (2014), our heroes for this chapter:

> We have three tables. Each is 30 x 30 x 96 inches. How many guests can we invite to a fancy dinner?

This may seem like a typical math problem with one solution. Au contraire! Should the tables be arranged to maximize space or maximize conversation?

Will children be invited, and will they get their own table? And how much space do children and adults need anyway? Answering these questions, creating solutions, and justifying the solutions permit students to contribute in different ways depending on their preferences. There is space for honest collaboration, because there are opportunities for group decision making.

INTERDEPENDENCE AND ACCOUNTABILITY

The ideal collaborative arrangement occurs when there is (a) group member interdependence and (b) individual accountability. You and I need each other, and each of us needs to carry out our responsibilities. Norms and group-worthy tasks help establish both. Reward structures can also help.

An old approach that never worked very well was to randomly choose a single member of the group to take the test that determines all the group members' grades. Can you just imagine everyone cringing in anticipation of who gets chosen? Teachers who used this approach achieved good learning outcomes, but very few teachers wanted to use the scheme (Slavin, 1995). It is a recipe for blaming and the enemy of heterogeneity. Similarly, if only the group receives a grade, there will be a natural tendency to let the "best" student dominate the group.

A better approach is to give students some combination of their own grade and the group's grade. An approach that fits nicely in the college classroom starts with students taking a test individually. They then get to work in small groups to answer the same questions. The individuals then retake the test, and their grade is a combination of the first and second tests. This creates a natural need for interdependence, because the students want to know what each is thinking, and it maintains individual accountability because the test scores are the individual's alone.

Outcomes of Collaboration

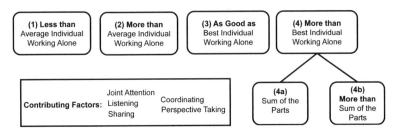

Figure L.1. Different levels of success in collaboration. The question is whether people working in a group do better than the average of individuals who work alone.

III. The Outcomes of Listening and Sharing

Are two heads really better than one? Not always. Researchers who study group performance determine the answer by comparing the performance of individuals (on average) with the performance of a group. Figure L.1 shows the range of possible outcomes. When group performance falls below the average individual, it is typically attributable to group dysfunction (see Section V in this chapter). The most typical outcome is that group members outperform the average individual. For instance, in a classic study of brainstorming, groups came up with more creative ideas than the average individual working alone. But the groups did not exceed the performance of the best individuals within their group when those individuals worked alone (Dunnette, Campbell, & Jaastad, 1963). The implication is that it is better to brainstorm separately and combine ideas afterward (perhaps using sticky notes) than it is to brainstorm in a group. People listen and share in a group, which leads people down the same brainstorming path.

One hopes that groups rise to the level of their most able members, and even exceed it. But this typically is not the case, because groups always have some degree of process loss. People may not listen and share perfectly, or maybe group members worry so much about taking turns that the most able member has insufficient opportunities to explain.

The tradition of comparing individual and group outcomes typically uses tasks and outcomes that can be completed by individuals. However, some tasks individuals cannot do alone, and groups will exceed the most able individual over the same period of time. These are group-worthy tasks. A simple example is building a house, where it is possible to partition tasks and then combine the results into a finished product. If there is minimal process loss, the outcome of a divide-and-conquer strategy is the sum of the individual efforts.

Finally, there is the holy grail of collaboration, where groups become more than the sum of their parts. This happens when the groups produce qualitatively different outcomes than individuals. For example, Schwartz (1995) looked at the visualizations created by seventh-grade students to help solve complex problems (see Chapter V). When working in pairs, 67 percent of students constructed abstract representations (e.g., matrices) that included important structural relationships in the problem. This was far above the 6 percent found for individuals working alone.. These results imply that something was happening in the group process that did not occur within individuals alone. When interviewing the students, one group pair stated, "He wanted to make rows, and I wanted to make columns." By listening and sharing, they integrated their points of view into something new—a matrix.

IV. Can People Learn to Teach Themselves with Listening and Sharing?

Does collaborative learning help students learn to cooperate later? Cohen and Lotan (2014, citing Morris, 1977) describe a study in which groups were trained on collaborative norms and processes while solving two similar problems on disaster preparation. Then participants received a new, unrelated problem without any group process instructions. Participants showed adherence to the collaborative norms they had learned earlier without explicit directives.

A more demanding question is whether students will cooperate when they move into a new group and a new setting. This fits the goal of the original proponents of cooperative learning, who wanted people to learn to avoid conflicts. Gillies (2002) conducted an impressive study that observed fifth-graders' cooperative behaviors two years after training. Trained students were more likely to show cooperative behaviors than otherwise equivalent students who did not receive training. For example, they were seven times less likely to interrupt and twice as likely to offer unsolicited explanations. They had learned to listen and share.

Determining whether students have learned to cooperate is daunting. Gillies (2002) recorded group member behaviors every 10 seconds—it is not an easily adopted methodology. People are working on more efficient solutions. Basketball has a solution. It is possible to measure the performance of teammates when player X is on the floor versus not. For example, do the teammates score more points when player X is on the floor? It is fun to think of how to do something similar for learning settings.

The Programme for the International Student Assessment (see http://www.oecd.org/pisa) is a common test taken by many nations (and causes consternation among officials when their country does poorly). The test makers are trying to measure cooperative skills in negotiation, consensus building, and divide-and-conquer tasks. In a fascinating sample item, a student interacts with three simulated team members in a computer-based task. The team is planning a welcoming activity for visitors. One of their tasks is to decide among several options offered by their simulated teacher, Ms. Cosmo. One of the simulated students, Brad, says, "Who cares? All these choices are boring. Let's take our visitors someplace they'll actually enjoy." The real student, the one being measured, has four choices:

1. You're right, Brad. If none of the choices are any good, let's go somewhere else.
2. Brad, you're right that we want them to enjoy themselves, but we should discuss Ms. Cosmo's options first.

3. Ms. Cosmo has no ideas what kids like. Rachel, George, do you agree?
4. Why don't we take a look at the Town Hall instead?

According to the creators of this item, choice 2 is the right answer because it is the only one that prompts the group to consider the options on the table. The idea of measuring cooperation is a good one, if only because it focuses our attention on an important set of skills. It will be interesting to see how this work evolves.

V. Risks of Listening and Sharing

One risk of groupwork is that students do not listen because they do not maintain joint attention. Barron (2003) videotaped groups solving a complex open-ended math problem. Successful and unsuccessful groups had an equal number of correct proposals for how to solve the problem. The difference was in how the group reacted to those proposals. In the successful groups, about two-thirds of correct proposals were discussed or accepted. In the unsuccessful groups, two-thirds of correct proposals were immediately rejected or ignored. In the unsuccessful groups, members talked past each other because they were attending to different parts of the problem. In the successful groups, almost all proposals were directly related to the previous conversation, and students discussed and built on one another's ideas.

Unequal status can also interfere with listening and sharing opportunities. Students of higher status dominate the discussion more, while the contributions of lower-status students are dismissed even when good. In one study, students were assigned bogus labels of "high" and "average" after taking a test. (Test results had no bearing on assignment of labels.) Those labeled as high showed greater participation in a subsequent group task, despite the fact that the label was objectively meaningless (Cohen & Lotan, 2014, citing Dembo & McAuliffe, 1987).

Unequal participation can cause a self-fueling cycle. Students perceived to have high competence dominate the discussion, cementing the perception that they are high competence, and vice versa for those ascribed low status. The risk of unequal participation is a primary reason to teach cooperation thoughtfully. (See Chapter P for designing activities for equal participation.)

VI. Examples of Good and Bad Use

Bad: College physics students are put in groups and asked to complete a problem set, which they will turn in for a grade at the end of class. The task could be completed by one competent individual just as easily as the group. Students receive no instruction on cooperation. Those who already know how to solve the problems take over to get answers expediently, garnering little advantage for learning.

Good: College physics again: "Consider a heavy truck ramming into a parked, unoccupied car. According to common sense, which force (if either) is larger during the collision: the force exerted by the truck on the car, or the force exerted by the car on the truck?" (University of Maryland Physics Education Research Group, 2004). The group members need to explain their intuitive reasoning. They then need to reconcile this with what they have learned about Newton's third law. (The forces are the same.) Group interdependence is established as all members are charged with explaining their own points of confusion or conflict to contribute to overall group understanding.

VII. References

Barron, B. (2003). When smart groups fail. *Journal of the Learning Sciences, 12*(3), 307–359.

Carpenter, M., Nagell, K., Tomasello, M., Butterworth, G., & Moore, C. (1998). Social cognition, joint attention, and communicative competence from 9 to 15 months of age. *Monographs of the Society for Research in Child Development, 63*(4), i–174.

Cohen, E. G., & Lotan, R. A. (2014). *Designing groupwork: Strategies for the heterogeneous classroom* (3rd ed.). New York, NY: Teachers College Press.

Deutsch, M. (1977). *The resolution of conflict: Constructive and destructive processes.* New Haven, CT: Yale University Press.

Dunnette, M. D., Campbell, J., & Jaastad, K. (1963). The effect of group participation on brainstorming effectiveness for 2 industrial samples. *Journal of Applied Psychology, 47*(1), 30-37.

Gillies, R. M. (2002). The residual effects of cooperative-learning experiences: A two-year follow-up. *Journal of Educational Research, 96*(1), 15–20.

Johnson, D. W., & Johnson, R. T. (1987). *Learning together and alone: Cooperative, competitive, and individualistic learning.* Englewood Cliffs, NJ: Prentice-Hall, Inc.

Johnson, D. W., & Johnson, R. T. (2009). Energizing learning: The instructional power of conflict. *Educational Researcher, 38*(1), 37–51.

Kulkarni, C., Cambre, J., Kotturi, Y., Bernstein, M. S., & Klemmer, S. R. (2015). Talkabout: Making distance matter with small groups in massive classes. In *Proceedings of the 18th ACM Conference on Computer Supported Cooperative Work and Social Computing* (pp. 1116–1128). New York, NY: Association for Computing Machinery.

Schneider, B., & Pea, R. (2013). Real-time mutual gaze perception enhances collaborative learning and collaboration quality. *International Journal of Computer-Supported Collaborative Learning, 8*(4), 375–397.

Schwartz, D. L. (1995). The emergence of abstract representations in dyad problem solving. *Journal of the Learning Sciences, 4*(3), 321–354.

Slavin, R. E. (1995). *Cooperative learning: Theory, research, and practice* (2ⁿᵈ Ed.). Boston: Allyn and Bacon.

University of Maryland Physics Education Research Group. (2004). Tutorial 4: Counterintuitive ideas: Newton's third law [Word document]. Retrieved August 1, 2015 from http://www.physics.umd.edu/perg/OSTutorials/04_Newton_Three/Tutorial_04_Newton3.doc

L IS FOR LISTENING AND SHARING

What is the core learning mechanic?
Listening and sharing are the cornerstones of collaborative learning, where students work together to complete projects, solve problems, and learn.

What is an example, and what is it good for?
Small groups of students collaborate on a class project to make a school system for fair decision making. With guidance, students can learn to cooperate more effectively, and they will learn about the topic of governance more deeply.

Why does it work?
Doing things with others can be very motivating, but it also takes cooperative skills. Done well, students maintain joint attention, listen, share, coordinate, and try to understand one another's points of view. This can help learners exchange information and develop a multifaceted understanding.

What problems does the core mechanic solve?
- Students are disengaged and bored with seat work.
  - A student distracts the class, partly because he does not know how to solve the problems and has no easy way of getting help.
- Students are trapped by their own thoughts.
  - A physics student knows how to procedurally solve problems involving Newton's third law but does not realize that there are holes in her conceptual understanding.
- Students do not know how to work together.
  - A difference of opinion escalates into conflict rather than negotiation.

Examples of how to use it
- Establish collaborative norms and expectations.
  - Have groups practice and reflect on their collaborative process.
- Use "group-worthy" tasks.
  - Leave some parts of the problem open for groups to decide on appropriate constraints. If asking students how many people could fit at three tables of a certain dimension, let groups discuss the best way to arrange the tables and how much space each person needs to be comfortable.

Risks

- Students perceived to have low status have unequal opportunity for participation. The group is less likely to engage with and take up their ideas.
- Learners fail to develop joint attention and end up talking past each other.

M is for Making

Producing interest and practical knowledge

MAKING MEANS CREATING shareable products, such as gardens, works of art, and computer programs. Making is motivating, yields practical knowledge, and may lead to sustained interest.

Being able to create things is both useful and satisfying. Dale Dougherty, who started *Make* magazine, claims, "The maker movement has come about in part because of people's need to engage passionately with objects in ways that make them more than just consumers" (2012, p. 12). Making starts with production, not consumption.

People make many things. Beer brewing is a fine example. A hobbyist brewer makes beer repeatedly. Each time, she produces the beer and tests it out, tasting it herself and sharing the product with others. She then uses the experience to lay plans for her next batch. The end result is, well, another brewing project! Because she enjoys making and sharing and making again, she is motivated learn more about beer and brewing. She gathers expertise on brewer tools and skills. For our brewer, the enjoyment of making is intertwined with the learning. This turns out to be true across many making-based hobbies.

In a survey of hundreds of hobbyists, such as model rocketeers, home brewers, motorcycle racers, and musicians, Pfaffman (2003) asked people to rate the

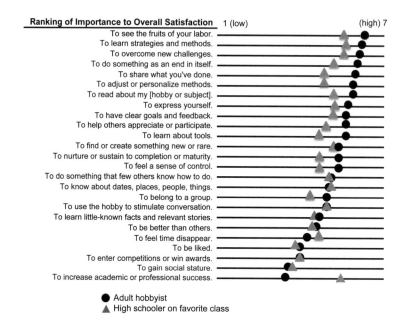

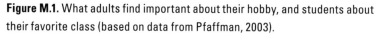

Figure M.1. What adults find important about their hobby, and students about their favorite class (based on data from Pfaffman, 2003).

importance of twenty-five different outcomes for their hobby satisfaction. Figure M.1 shows the results, ordered from most to least important. There are some interesting surprises. For example, belonging to a group falls in the bottom half of hobby satisfactions, despite being a basic motivational need (see Chapter B). The top-ranked satisfaction is most revealing.

The number one satisfaction is the chance to see the fruits of one's labor. Being able to experience one's creations was rated at or near the top for every single hobby. Seeing the fruits of labor was also near the top of what high school students found satisfying about their favorite class, be it music, English, history, or math. We label this motivation *productive agency* (Schwartz, 1999). People are highly motivated to see their ideas realized in the world. *Their goal is not to own ideas but, rather, to use ideas to produce.* Presumably, classes that emphasize single right answers to teacher-given questions do not generate a strong sense of productive agency, whereas classes that foster productive agency become students' favorite classes.

I. How Making Works

Karl Marx (yes, we really are bringing in Marx) wrote of two great forces that constitute a person. One is *appropriation*—we become what we are by taking

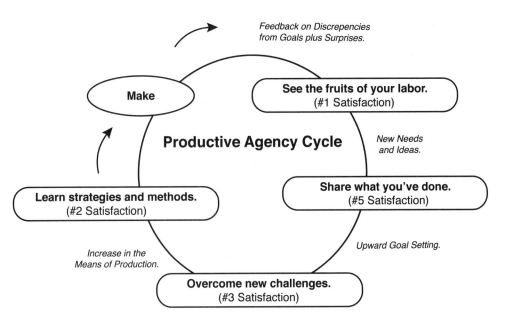

Figure M.2. The top satisfactions of hobbies create conditions that promote learning.

up the ideas and artifacts of those around us. The second is *production*. With Aristotle, he viewed humans quintessentially as builders. We want to produce and create ourselves in the world, whether through ideas or products. This way we can put our element in the social matrix, and other people may appropriate our ideas. Marx did not advocate for a welfare state in which people only had access to appropriation. He advocated for a productive state where people could contribute and impress themselves upon the world. For Marx, the critical political issue was always who owned the means of production, which is oddly consistent with arguments for student-centered classrooms. This does not imply that student-centered teachers are communists! But Marx did capture the essence of making and how it can contribute to learning.

PRODUCTIVE AGENCY

Making follows the idealized cycle shown in Figure M.2. The cycle comprises four of the top five motivations found in the Pfaffman survey. These are not just any motivations. They are motivations for more learning. People want to see the fruits of their labor. When people see their ideas rendered into practice, they receive feedback on what did and did not work, including surprising outcomes. People also like to share their creations, which in turn generates additional feedback about the features that others especially liked and disliked, along with suggestions for variations. These contribute to the appropriation of other people's ideas. The feedback further motivates makers to set new goals and challenges that create needs for new learning. This tilts the cycle into an upward spiral, because new challenges require new learning. Finally, given new goals, makers are motivated to seek out new methods that give them the means of production to achieve those goals. Who knew that hobbies were such a good play pattern for learning!

One reason the cycle is powerful is that people are exceptionally attentive to feedback that comes from their own productions. Okita and Schwartz (2013), for example, reported research in which high school students created a computer agent and taught it logical reasoning rules that would let it solve problems. Students either observed their agent solving problems or solved the same problems themselves, getting otherwise identical feedback about the answers. Those who watched their agent learned more from the feedback than those students who solved the problems themselves. They were better able to solve complex logic problems on a posttest. People pay special attention to feedback directed at their creations.

LEARNING AN INTEREST

A second powerful feature of the cycle is that it captures interest. There is an important distinction between situational interest and individual interest (Renninger, Hidi, & Krapp, 2014). *Situational interest* is driven by the immediate context. Museums are purveyors of situational interest—people become captured by an intriguing exhibit or activity. Situational interest is transient. When the situation is no longer there, the interest often is gone as well. Situational interest can eventually evolve into *individual interest* when there are sufficient resources, including expanding opportunities, access to expertise, and a community of sharing (see Chapter P). Ito and colleagues (2009) describe an interest trajectory for creating digital artifacts that graduate from hanging out and messing around to "geeking out." When people have individual interest, they seek relevant opportunities, and they show resilience in the face of temporary failures and even boring presentations (Renninger et al., 2014). People learn to be interested, and making helps.

II. How to Use Making to Enhance Learning

Making happens in clubs, museums, homes, and even school. One fun example is the SparkTruck (see http://sparktruck.org)—a big mobile truck carrying tools and materials that delivers maker projects to kids across the country, logging over 20,000 miles as of 2015.

At home, making typically does not have explicit learning principles that shape how the experience unfolds. In contrast, designed maker

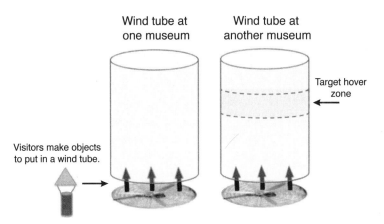

Figure M.3. Two variations of a maker exhibit. One museum provides visitors an optional goal, whereas the other leaves goal generation to visitors.

spaces often start from a set of principles. One principle involves the use of predefined goals. For example, some exploration-based museums use an exhibit called wind tubes (see Figure M.3). Visitors have access to consumable materials, such as baskets, paper rolls, and masking tape, to make an object that they put in the wind tube. In one museum we know of, learners are left to construct their own goals and questions as they watch what happens. Allowing learners to generate their own goals and questions is an important part of this museum's guiding principles. Another museum applies a slight variation: visitors receive the optional goal of making an object that hovers between two lines. This museum chose to build more structure into the learning activity. Which do you think is better?

While there is no (to our knowledge) empirical evidence about the effects of directed goal setting in museums, it has been studied in schools. In classrooms, making typically appears as project-based learning. Students learn skills and knowledge by engaging in an extended, often real-world, project (see Chapter Q). Petrosino (1998) showed that certain goals can facilitate project-based learning. He studied students building model rockets. He compared the outcomes of students doing a standard rocket task with those of students who received an additional goal statement at the start: create a design plan that NASA can use with its new model rocket kit. The students were asked to test several features of rockets, such as the number of fins and paint, to see their effect on flight. Later, students were asked the purpose of the rocket activity. Students with the standard curriculum said, "You know, to build them." Students who had received the NASA goal statement included additional information about which

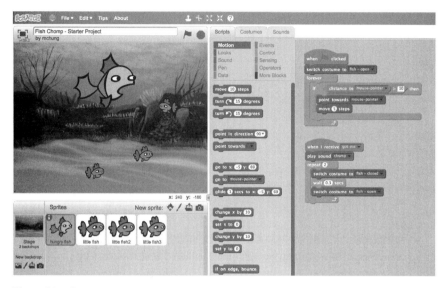

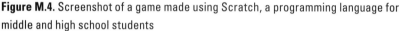

Figure M.4. Screenshot of a game made using Scratch, a programming language for middle and high school students

rocket features were important to flight and how flight elevation could be measured.

Whether making takes place in school or out, three elements should facilitate learning: increased access to means of production, built-in opportunities for feedback and appropriation, and ample resources for goal setting and learning.

We take the example of Scratch, a visual programming language developed at the MIT Media Lab (Resnick et al., 2009). Scratch includes the essential ingredients of productive agency. There are resources for making, namely, the learner-friendly programming language and media assets. Scratch enables people to create interactive media and games. This makes it easy for "Scratchers" to see the fruits of their labor. There is also an online Scratch community, where people can post their work and exchange comments (policed for inappropriate language). The postings and feedback provide Scratchers with ideas and inspirations for setting new, more advanced programming goals for their next project. There are also resources for learning new methods and skills. These resources include examples of code that Scratchers can modify, studios on specific topics, discussion forums, and more.

These ingredients are similar to the four elements Barron et al. (1998) suggested for good project-based learning in schools: (1) learning-appropriate goals; (2) learning resources; (3) multiple opportunities for feedback and revision; and (4) a social environment that supports original production and interaction.

III. The Outcomes of Making

Going to a concert is an end in itself. We do not need to justify concerts by claiming they improve math, human character, or the chances of getting into college. The same is true of hobbies and making. People find them satisfying in their own right. It seems unnecessary to justify them on any other grounds. But, if you need some ammunition, here are the learning benefits.

PRACTICAL KNOWLEDGE

Have you heard the story about the sinking college library? The architect failed to consider the weight of the books. The urban legend remains popular because it highlights how formal knowledge gets you only so far. Traditional school-based instruction emphasizes formal knowledge. In contrast, making emphasizes the hundreds of practical details, skills, tools, and dispositions needed for execution.

With enough experience, practical knowledge creates a network of facts and skills that Crowley and Jacobs (2002) term *islands of expertise*. Strong, precise knowledge supports further learning. People accrue new facts and skills to their islands of expertise. Doctors learn new medical terms and diseases more quickly once they have built up a strong library of prior knowledge.

Making can set the stage for formal knowledge. A science museum colleague relayed the story of a tightrope-walker exhibit, at which visitors tried to balance a toy acrobat. Children regularly extended the balancing pole of the tightrope walker, probably because they had seen this somewhere. Eventually, they stumbled upon an "aha moment": if the pole dipped below the walker on both sides, the system stabilized. These children discovered the self-correcting system when placing the center of mass below the tightrope walker. Of course, the children did not learn the concepts of a self-correcting system or center of mass, but they had experienced a compelling instantiation, which could conceivably set the stage for science instruction later (see Chapter J.) Early engineering opportunities in school may turn out to be pathways into science (and engineering, of course) because they start with the engagement and practical successes of making. Making engages many different ways of knowing that range from perception to rules, which permit success even without deep conceptual explanation (Azevedo, 2013).

INTEREST AND IDENTITY

Many see making as a way to cultivate individual interests. Interest is a good goal, because science interest in eighth grade predicts college majors in science better than test scores and grades (Tai, Liu, Maltese, & Fan, 2006). One can imagine the same phenomenon occuring in other domains; for example, an interest in rap lyrics evolves into the pursuit of creative writing. The opportunity to make is surely a pathway into individual interests and disciplinary identities for some people. For how many people and under what conditions, however, is unknown.

DISPOSITIONS TOWARD FAILURE

Making may help students develop dispositions to embrace failure, or at least not fear it as much (Martin, 2015). Failing is often seen as a constructive part of the process rather than something to be avoided. Maker competitions sometimes have a "Most Spectacular Failure" award.

Design-based learning relies on making. Students create a product to solve a problem, often with a real or hypothetical client. Students might have the challenge of designing a better cafeteria layout for the students in their class (Carroll et al., 2010). A significant part of the design process is trying out prototypes of the design and getting feedback from stakeholders about what works and what could be better. Several educators we have talked to have said the thing they like best about design-based learning is that it helps students not be afraid of failure and negative feedback—they are just part of the process.

While we do not know of empirical evidence showing changes in attitude toward failure, we have found changes in attitudes toward constructive criticism. In one study (Conlin, Chin, Blair, Cutumisu, & Schwartz, 2015), sixth-grade students completed design units in math, social studies, and science over several weeks. In one condition, the children followed a stakeholder design methodology, where they had to get feedback from their potential clients. In a subsequent computerized assessment (see Chapter F, Figure F.3), these children were more likely to seek constructive criticism than students who had followed a different design methodology that did not emphasize seeking feedback.

IV. Can People Learn to Teach Themselves with Making?

Making is highly motivating. Given the right resources and communities of practice, people will naturally teach themselves through the productive agency cycle, if they advance from situational to individual interest. For instance, Barron (2006) describes Jamal, a high school student who became interested in making websites after a computer science class in school. He bought books, started a web design business, and got tips on website making by contacting the maker of a website he liked. Jamal, like the other students Barron interviewed, sought out different learning sources on his own, with peripheral support from his parents. He took the lead on finding the expertise he needed to continue growing and learning. Jamal is an exceptional case.

More often, situational interest requires nurturing to advance to individual interest, and novices may not be able to arrange that nurturing on their own. Currently, a tried-and-true method to spark enduring individual interest is beyond the state of the art in learning theory, but the idea of using making as an interest catalyst certainly shows promise.

V. Risks of Making

Making tends to generate highly situated knowledge and attitudes that may not generalize. A child who does perfuming at home may not spontaneously apply her inquiry and experimentation strategies in science class (Tzou, Zimmerman, Bell, & Learning in Informal and Formal Environments Center, 2007). Papert (1980) developed a simple visual programming language called Logo. The startup costs for making a Logo program were very low. Children could direct a computerized turtle to draw a box using commands: "go 5 steps, turn left, repeat." Papert famously claimed that children were learning to plan in general by using Logo, and almost as famously, Pea and Kurland (1984) demonstrated that in noncomputer tasks children did not use whatever planning skills they may have learned. Helping learners generalize can take extra steps, such as a follow-up explanation of how to broadly apply what they learned. Ideally, teachers could support sudents to generalize not just situational maker experiences, but also their existing islands of expertise and interests.

For informal pursuits, a common challenge is reaching a performance plateau or, worse, having insufficient resources or preparation. A bad computer science textbook can crush an incipient interest in creating web pages. Providing multiple pathways that support and encourage evolving interests can help. Online cooking sites feature recipes to fire the imagination at all levels of ability, along with techniques to achieve them and a virtual community of opinions and suggested variations. Some educators are experimenting with making connected learning environments so that adolescents can follow pathways from one experience to another, for example, from one internship to another (Ito et al., 2013).

In school, the primary challenge is balancing student agency in choosing projects while still ensuring that the projects feed into instructional objectives. The lab sections that accompany college courses usually tilt too far away from productive agency to count as making: students are told exactly what to make, along with the expected outcome. There is a common confusion worth rectifying: *while many making activities have a hands-on component, being hands on does not entail a making activity* (see Chapter H).

A useful task is to think of instructional goals that can serve as project constraints without throttling originality. These goals may not be identical to the academic content of the course. For instance, one might require students to use a 3-D printer, whatever their project of choice. This goal targets the methods and tools of the trade, rather than the abstract content. It is a natural fit for the primary outcome of making, which is to learn the means of production.

VI. Examples of Good and Bad Use

Grade F: Students are shown exactly what to make and how, and they receive a grade. Rather than cultivating a sense of agency, this cultivates a sense of compliance.

Grade D: Middle schoolers receive strips of paper and glue. They can make anything they like out of papier-mâché without any help, support, or direction. The complete liberty of choice may promote agency for experienced students, but without knowing the means of production, beginners will be incapable of expressing any agency.

Grade C: A touch-screen game where users make and test Rube Goldberg machines and then share their creations with others in an online community. To encourage continued engagement, new levels unlock new items and techniques to build the machine.

Grade B: A two-week tinkering camp includes supplies, example projects, a set of optional goals, places to display final products, and a plan with multiple built-in maker projects. Students in this setting can make with agency, get feedback when they see their final product in action, see other people's creations, and use what they learn to inform their next project.

Grade A: Capitalizing on an early passion topic by lending expertise for where to take it next.

VII. References

Azevedo, F. S. (2013). Lines of practice: A practice-centered theory of interest relationships. *Cognition and Instruction, 29*(2), 147–184.

Barron, B. (2006). Interest and self-sustained learning as catalysts of development: A learning ecology perspective. *Human Development, 49*(4), 193-224.

Barron, B. J., Schwartz, D. L., Vye, N. J., Moore, A., Petrosino, A., Zech, L., & Bransford, J. D. (1998). Doing with understanding: Lessons from research on problem- and project-based learning. *Journal of the Learning Sciences, 7*(3–4), 271–311.

Carroll, M., Goldman, S., Britos, L., Koh, J., Royalty, A., & M. Hornstein. (2010).

Destination, imagination, and the fires within: Design thinking in a middle school classroom. *International Journal of Art and Design Education, 29*(1), 37–53.

Conlin, L.D., Chin, D.B., Blair, K.P., Cutumisu, M., & Schwartz, D.L. (2015). Guardian angels of our better nature: Finding evidence of the benefits of design thinking. *Proceedings of the 2015 meeting of the American Society of Engineering Education*, Seattle, WA.

Crowley, K., & Jacobs, M. (2002). Building islands of expertise in everyday family activity. In G. Leinhardt, K. Crowley, & K. Knutson (Eds.), *Learning conversations in museums* (pp. 333–356). Mahwah, NJ: Erlbaum.

Dougherty, D. (2012). The maker movement. *Innovations, 7*(3), 11–14.

Ito, M., Antin, J., Finn, M., Law, A., Manion, A., Mitnick, S., . . . Horst, H. A. (2009). *Hanging out, messing around, and geeking out: Kids living and learning with new media*. Cambridge, MA: MIT Press.

Ito, M., Gutierrez, K., Livingstone, S., Penuel, B., Rhodes, J., Salen, K., . . . Watkins, S. C. (2013). *Connected learning: An agenda for research and design*. Irvine, CA: Digital Media and Learning Research Hub.

Martin, L. (2015). The promise of the maker movement for education. *Journal of Pre-college Engineering Education Research, 5*(1), 30-39.

Michael. (2013, February 9). Benefits of teaching kids to code that no one is talking about. *Inspired to Educate* (blog). Retrieved December 1, 2014, from http://inspiredtoeducate.net/inspiredtoeducate/benefits-of-teaching-kids-to-code-that-no-one-is-talking-about/

Okita, S. Y., & Schwartz, D. L. (2013). Learning by teaching human pupils and teachable agents: The importance of recursive feedback. *Journal of the Learning Sciences, 22*(3), 375–412.

Papert, S. (1980). *Mindstorms: Children, computers, and powerful ideas*. New York: Basic Books.

Pea, R. D., & Kurland, D. M. (1984). On the cognitive effects of learning computer programming. *New Ideas in Psychology, 2*(2), 137–168.

Petrosino, A. J. (1998). *The use of reflection and revision in hands-on experimental activities by at-risk children*. (Unpublished doctoral dissertation). Vanderbilt University, Nashville, TN.

Pfaffman, J. A. (2003). *Manipulating and measuring student engagement in computer-based instruction*. (Unpublished doctoral dissertation). Vanderbilt University, Nashville, TN.

Renninger, A., Hidi, S., & Krapp, A. (2014). *The role of interest in learning and development*. New York: Psychology Press.

Resnick, M., Maloney, J., Monroy-Hernández, A., Rusk, N., Eastmond, E., Brennan, K., . . . Kafai, Y. (2009). Scratch: Programming for all. *Communications of the ACM, 52*(11), 60–67.

Schwartz, D. L. (1999). The productive agency that drives collaborative learning. In P. Dillenbourg (Ed.), *Collaborative learning: Cognitive and computational approaches* (pp. 197–218). New York: Elsevier.

Tai, R. H., Liu, C. Q., Maltese, A. V., & Fan, X. (2006). Career choice: Planning early for careers in science. *Science, 312*(5777), 1143–1144.

Tzou, C., Zimmerman, H. T., Bell, P., & Learning in Informal and Formal Environments Center. (2007, April). Bringing students' activity structures into the classroom: Curriculum design implications from an ethnographic study of fifth graders' images of science. Paper presented at the annual meeting of the National Association of Research in Science Teaching, New Orleans, LA.

M IS FOR MAKING

What is the core learning mechanic?
Producing an artifact or performance and taking up feedback and setting new goals.

What is an example, and what is it good for?
Brewing beer at home and tasting it; writing a poem to perform at the local spoken-word festival. Makers learn practical knowledge and interest.

Why does it work?
Making has motivations that naturally produce a learning cycle that expands one's means of production. Motivations include the desire for feedback on the realization of one's ideas, and the creation of new challenges that motivate makers to learn more skills and methods. With support, making can evolve from a situational interest driven by the environment to an individual interest where people independently pursue making opportunities.

What problems does the core mechanic solve?
- Learners have little interest in a topic.
  - Students do not see the point of learning literature.
- Students are unmotivated to get feedback on their work and set new learning goals.
  - A student says, "The point is to get a good grade on a test."
- People do not pursue learning on their own.
  - An adult just watches television in his free time.

Examples of how to use it
- Kick off the science unit about electricity with a project where students construct electrical circuits.
- Start an after-school maker club, where students do several related maker projects over the year and share the products with one another.
- Create an online community for people making video game modules, where they can share what they've created—getting and giving tips and feedback.

Risks
- Too little structure or support: novice makers will abandon their efforts early.
- Maker knowledge is highly situated. It may not contribute to any other activity.

N is for Norms

Cultivating the rules of the game

NORMS ARE RULES of social interaction. They are often culture specific and can vary by intellectual tradition and setting. Good norms enable productive learning interactions. Norms of intellectual engagement shape what people learn and what they value.

Norms do not regulate behavior; they regulate conduct. Riding a bike without falling involves behavior. Riding a bike down a crowded sidewalk involves conduct. Bike riding on a crowded sidewalk violates a norm, and violating a norm brings social sanctions.

Erving Goffman, who introduced the study of norms, proposed that people are compelled to follow norms due to a universal rule: "The rule of behavior that seems common to all situations . . . is the rule obliging participants to 'fit in'" (1966, p. 11). Society needs people to fit in to operate smoothly, and psychologically people often want to fit in (see Chapter B).

Figure N.1 shows an example of norms developed by students in a teacher preparation class at Stanford University. The large words, Safe Place, Team, Equity, and Person, actually refer to values, not norms. Values are beliefs about what is important. Norms are prescriptions of conduct, and in the figure they appear in the text for each of the values. For instance, for Safe Place, a norm states "Challenge the idea, not the person."

Figure N.1 offers norms for general classroom participation. Different

Figure N.1. Values and norms displayed in a program to support teacher education. The large words refer to values, and the secondary text gives norms relevant to those values.

communities can have different norms, so norms can differ across classrooms. Moreover, different topics or practices may have different norms of engagement. For dangerous activities that depend on precise coordination among people (e.g., a military operation), the norm may be to follow authority without question. For the science laboratory, the norm may be to rely on evidence and logic over authority. If people engage a new situation following an undesired norm—for instance, children coming to school believing they should acquiesce to bigger people regardless of their own beliefs—teaching them a new norm can take work. An important task of instruction is to help novices learn the norms appropriate to a particular topic of learning.

Here is a paraphrased transcript from a mathematics teacher who is working to help a young girl, Donna, learn that the correctness of an answer is not determined by the status of the person who gives the answer (Yackel & Cobb, 1996). Earlier in the class, Donna proposes the answer "six," and the teacher Mr. K responds by asking the class whether she is correct. Donna assumes this response means she is wrong, and she promptly changes her answer. Later, Mr. K appears to accept the answer "six" from other students, which leads to the following exchange.

> *Donna:* (*protesting*) I said the six, but you said, "no."
> *Mr. K.:* Wait, wait, listen. What is your name?

Donna: Donna Walters

Mr. K.: What's your name?

Donna: Donna Walters

Mr. K.: If I were to ask you again, would you tell me your name is Mary?

Donna: No

Mr. K.: Why wouldn't you?

Donna: Because my name is not Mary.

Mr. K.: And you know your name. Donna. And I can't make you say your name is Mary. So you should have said, "Mr. K. Six. And I can prove it to you." I've tried to teach you that.

The teacher uses Donna's comment as an opportunity to teach a social norm for discussing mathematical ideas in his class. He explicitly confronts a norm the student had imported to class and substitutes it with a different one. The teacher's norm suits the value of intellectual autonomy in mathematics, where conclusions and understanding can be achieved through axiomatic reasoning. This teacher is particularly aware of the influence that norms have on how students will come to think of mathematical activity.

I. How Norms Work

A world without regularity would be a world that few humans could tolerate. Regularity can be physical: humans achieve impressive feats of engineering because they use the regular laws of physics to their advantage. For the social world, rules are socially constructed: people invent social norms and rules to create regularity. The monetary system is an elaborate system of social rules of exchange. The stability of the rules enables the invention of many forms of commerce, some for good and some for bad.

Socially constructed rules, unlike physical laws, can be broken. To enforce dependable social interactions, social rules come with incentives for compliance and sanctions for noncompliance. Critical rules become codified and enforced by governments as laws. Norms can vary from one cultural group to another—Mrs. B's students greet each other with handshakes, Mr. C's class uses friendly insults. Most norms do not rise to the level of governmental laws. Even so, norms that fall short of laws still come with incentives and sanctions, sometimes as simple as a glare of disapproval at a person riding a bike down a busy sidewalk.

Norms that fall short of codified laws can still have large societal consequences, even norms about learning. While it remains unproven, an influential argument by Jean Anyon (1980) shows how norms of learning might serve to maintain an inequitable social order. Anyon proposed that classrooms of working-class children have norms that reflect working-class job norms— unquestioning obedience, efficiency, and silence. These become associated with success in students' minds and thus adopted as strategies to succeed. If the students later take jobs on assembly lines—following their working class roots—then these behaviors create successful employees. However, in a boardroom of a large company, obedience and silence are the opposite of what one needs, and students steeped in the norms of a working-class classroom would have a hard time succeeding in such an environment. In contrast, high-income schools full of the nation's elite children espouse norms more befitting a power player on the world stage. These students are rewarded for synthesizing and communicating ideas, thinking far outside of the box, and reasoning intellectually. With so much practice with these norms, it is no surprise to see these students flourish in high-power positions later in life. According to Anyon's theory, school norms perpetuate the class structure of America.

Sometimes, people do not recognize the norms that regulate their lives. As the saying goes, "The fish is the last to know it is in water." For instance, the young child of one of the authors used to attempt to take off his shoes when he entered a shop, not understanding that shoe removal is a norm for his family home but inappropriate for American grocery stores. Fortunately, unintended norm violation usually sparks a reaction from witnesses, allowing swift changes to realign the social order. Harold Garfinkel (1967) studied norm repair with an obnoxious methodology called a breaching experiment. His researchers intentionally used inappropriate social norms to reveal the social forces that would rush in to repair the tear in the social fabric. For example, student researchers behaved like hotel patrons when they returned home for a family visit. (Mom must have loved that.) Unsurprisingly, the students reported reactions of astonishment, anger, and embarrassment from their family members.

On the assumption that people know a norm, people will follow a norm to the extent that (a) they believe their social group expects them to and (b) they expect their social group to follow the norm (Bicchieri & Chavez 2010). Evidence to the latter point comes from New York City in the 1990s. The mayor created a task force to fix broken windows across the city, to clean graffiti, to get rid of abandoned cars, and to remove other signs of vandalism and social deviance. The year after the clean-streets effort began, misdemeanor crimes dropped significantly, and not because more criminals were behind bars. The theory behind the plan—the broken windows theory (Wilson & Kelling, 1982)—is that visible vandalism and social deviance make people decide nobody else is following the recommended norm, so they do not need to either. The simple take-home message is that if you want to introduce norms for learning, make sure that everyone follows them, including you.

II. How to Use Norms to Enhance Learning

Culture does not surround people; it weaves them together. Social norms are the thread. Formal education has the responsibility to introduce many new social norms for successful learning arrangements. For example, kindergarten teaches children to raise their hands. Here are some broad suggestions for helping people to learn norms.

IMPLEMENTING NORMS

Through simple participation, people often learn norms without explicit instruction: they observe and imitate how people behave, they receive rewards or punishments depending on their norm-relevant behaviors, and they draw analogies between different situations to find the underlying consistencies. Norms are important and recruit many different learning mechanisms. Even so, people can misapprehend the extent of a norm. For example, researchers gave a poll on alcohol use to Princeton undergraduate students (Prentice & Miller, 1993). Students overwhelmingly reported that their own comfort with alcohol was lower than the average comfort level on campus. This was a misperception, as not everyone can be below the average. The bigger the perceived gap between a student's own views on alcohol and his or her perception of the norm, the more alienated from the school the student felt in general, reporting less likelihood to donate money in the future or attend the college reunion. Extra steps can be useful for making norms known. This is especially true for environments designed to achieve specific purposes, such as classrooms and workplaces.

When introducing a new norm to an established practice, one can use motivating and modeling. Suppose a company is trying to establish a norm of extended paternity leave for new fathers. At the time of writing this book, paid paternity leave is beginning to gain traction in company policy books, especially in the tech sector. However, employees have been slow to take advantage. Many comments come to mind about the gender norms that underlie this reluctance to take paid leave from work, but we defer. The point is to say that companies can help their employees embrace the new policy by motivating and modeling. For motivating, company leaders can explain the reasoning behind a policy (to attract top talent who want gender equity in the workplace). For modeling, setting the example in upper management is especially effective at spreading paternity leave practices (Dahl, Loken, Mogstad, 2012). The CEO of social media giant Facebook, Inc., for instance, announced he would soon take two months of paternity leave to bond with his first baby. We expect his decision to go a long way toward the uptake of paternity leave as a norm throughout his company.

When introducing a new person to the norms of an established practice, one can focus on relationship building. A poll of new engineers at a large American company showed that they learned about "the way things work here" from coworkers around 80 percent of the time (Korte, 2009). These norm-learning events grew from official mentorship relationships and from getting to know coworkers personally. The poll's recommendation was to facilitate socialization for newcomers by fostering relationships between new and existing employees.

The preceding examples describe introducing a new norm or person to an existing organization. Now, imagine creating a new social order from scratch. This is what teachers need to do. (Online social environments confront the same challenge.) In classrooms, there are twenty-plus students who eventually comprise the social order, and a lone teacher who needs to orchestrate a social fabric of norms. And each student likely enters a new class with an assumed set of norms already, with more or less consciousness about how those can change.

Making the norms explicit, for example, on a poster, and explaining the expectations for each one is helpful for the community. Equally important, learners need to believe there is social consistency. Consistency, at least in the early stages, depends on explicit enforcement. Once norms take hold, the community will enforce the norms with spontaneous responses to normed behaviors. Until that time, it is up to the teacher.

Armadillo Technical Institute, a sixth- through twelfth-grade school in Oregon, has implemented an unusual norm where all students are responsible for cleaning the school. Professional staff handle only dangerous or difficult cleaning tasks, while students have rotating, team-based duties, such as scrubbing toilets and sweeping. Students may have balked at the idea at first, but keeping a clean school quickly became a norm that was enforced as much by the students as by the school leaders. Students police each other to ensure they throw out their own garbage.

Discourse norms are exceptionally important in classrooms. Cazden (2001) identified the ubiquitous initiate–response–evaluate (IRE) sequence. A teacher initiates a question, a student responds, and the teacher evaluates with a brief response, such as "yes, very good" or "not quite." With this rhetorical norm, the teacher is in full intellectual control of the conversation. It is a reasonable inference that students internalize the norm that learning means being able to answer a given question with an approved answer, which fits Cazden's proposal that language use defines what counts as knowing and learning. Many scholars, including Cazden, prefer other conversational norms, where students can initiate their own questions, evaluate answers, and address one another directly. The assumption is that students will develop norms of intellectual autonomy, and perhaps gain identities as producers of knowledge, not just receptacles. One simple addition to the familiar IRE pattern is to adopt an IRE-F pattern, where F stands for *follow-up*. Students have an opportunity to follow up with their own thoughts about good and bad responses to the initial question. Ideally, they will also begin to pose their own questions. Of course, this will depend on establishing norms for open conversation, which is probably one reason that teachers so often rely on IRE. IRE is simple and easily controlled, effective for learning or not.

IDENTIFYING NORMS

An incalculable number of norms concern generally acceptable conduct, hence the existence of *Dear Abby* and *Miss Manners* columns. Classrooms and learning environments also have general norms of engagement useful for creating a learning community, such as "no insulting." Because norms can be difficult to see, teachers often do not realize they embrace a specific norm until a student breaches it. It is good to be proactive rather than reactive when establishing a learning community. Many classes start the year by establishing a set of classroom norms (often called *classroom rules*—a Google image search provides many examples to draw from). Sometimes these come directly from the teacher. Other times, the teacher and students jointly construct the rules, based on a vision of how their learning environment should be. Engaging students in rule construction can help increase student buy-in and their sense of connection with their classroom community.

More subtle norms involve productive disciplinary engagement (Engle & Conant, 2002). These are discipline-specific rules of engagement. For example, in science, there is a norm to defend conclusions with evidence; in logic, there is a norm to defend conclusions with deduction. Identifying norms for a specific community of scholarship is difficult if one is not part of that intellectual tradition. One helpful resource is lists of standards developed by disciplinary experts that specifically identify what students should learn. Contemporary education standards increasingly incorporate norms of intellectual engagement and not just factual knowledge and skills. For example, the Next Generation Science Standards (see http://www.nextgenscience.org) suggest the following practices (norms of disciplinary behaviors):

1. Asking questions (for science) and defining problems (for engineering)
2. Developing and using models
3. Planning and carrying out investigations

4. Analyzing and interpreting data
5. Using mathematics and computational thinking
6. Constructing explanations (for science) and designing solutions (for engineering)
7. Engaging in argument from evidence
8. Obtaining, evaluating, and communicating information (National Research Council, 2012)

Notably, the recommended norms often run counter to what children actually experience (or think they experience) in school. For example, in science class many students come to believe that doing science means memorizing facts and following instructions. They may be in for a surprise when asked to engage in science the way disciplinary experts do. On the other hand, perhaps memorization and following instructions are important prerequisites for future productive disciplinary engagement. It is an open question how the norms of domain experts should be reflected or adapted for children's classroom learning.

III. Outcomes of Using Norms Successfully

As Richard Posner put it, "If you don't play chess by the rules, you're not playing it at all" (1997, p. 365). Norms allow people to play the game of social life. If players have different rules of the game, it is a recipe for frustration and no game play at all. In a learning setting, productive norms increase the effective exchange of information and ideas. Shared goals and methods of interaction ensure that learners are playing the same game, smoothing out the process of learning and problem solving together. Shared norms reduce the need to enforce rules of engagement.

At the individual level, norms yield several psychological outcomes. First, norms can become values. A norm of giving up a bus seat for the elderly can become a belief about how the elderly should be treated. For disciplinary norms, checking scientific claims against evidence can eventually become a belief that ideas should be checked against evidence. Second, norms can produce a sense of belonging, if one shares in the norms of the group. In a society where people greet each other with a handshake, giving a peck on each cheek is a way to feel like an outsider. Third, norms contribute to identity development. Different cultures have different norms, so partaking in a set of norms increases identification with the given culture. Inversely, if one wants to maintain an exclusive identity with one cultural group, then take an oppositional stance to other norms.

IV. Can People Learn to Teach Themselves Norms?

The best way to learn norms in a new environment is to start with simple awareness. Many people fail to recognize they are using default norms in a new situation. For instance, in Korea an American businessperson may greet new colleagues by first name, only to find out later that the norm is to address even longtime colleagues as Mr. or Ms. Last-name-goes-here. Lack of awareness can lead to many mistakes, as norms are ubiquitous. Worse yet, some people are opposed to adopting local norms at all. (Think of the ugly tourist who complains about the way local people do things.) Once awareness is established, the process of learning norms can begin. *Assume there are reasons people like their norms, and your job is to figure them out.* Think, "OK, I'm in this new situation with unfamiliar ways. What are they, why do people follow them, and do I want to follow them?" If permissible, establish a relationship with a veteran of the situation who can help. There are also commercial enterprises that prepare students and businesspeople for international travel, and taking these courses might help prevent an egregious faux pas while figuring out the more subtle norms.

V. Risks of Norms

Not all norms are productive for learning. Moreover, the strictness of a norm and the associated sanctions may be too severe or too lax. Here, we consider a different risk of norms, which occurs when cultures meet and there are conflicting norms. Classrooms are a major site of normative work. Does the dominant culture of a society force its norms on a minority group (even if most of the class is from the minority group)? How can we respect the norms of the minority group while still preparing students for a life of success in a world currently dominated by another culture? The following example from Martha Crago captures the challenges facing schools where cultures meet:

> A speech pathologist working in an Inuit school (in northern Canada) asked a principal—who was not an Inuit—to compile a list of children who had speech and language problems in the school. The list contained a third of the students in the school, and next to several names the principal wrote, "Does not talk in class." The speech-language pathologist consulted a local Inuit teacher for help determining how each child functioned in his or her native language. She looked at the names and said, "Well-raised Inuit children should not talk in class. They should be learning by looking and listening." . . . [W]hen the pathologist asked that teacher about one toddler she was studying who was very talkative and

seemed to the non-Inuit researcher to be very bright, the teacher said: "Do you think he might have a learning problem? Some of these children who don't have such high intelligence have trouble stopping themselves. They don't know when to stop talking." (Crago as cited in Bransford, Brown, & Cocking, 1999, p. 146.)

Cultures will always collide, whether at the level of nations or the level of schools with high racial and ethnic diversity. This is a good thing, because a homogeneous world of identical norms would lack the diversity needed for healthy social systems. Nevertheless, handling diversity is challenging because of conflicting norms. Heath (1983) and Delpit (1988) explain that in elementary classrooms run by middle-class American teachers, the norm is that certain questions be interpreted as directives—"Are you ready to line up?" really means "Line up now." If a student who has been accustomed to a different norm assumes it really is a question—"No, I'm not ready to line up. I'm staying here"—teachers may misinterpret the student's response as defiance. The failure to acknowledge disparate norms may be one factor behind the disproportionate number of disciplinary actions directed toward African American children in elementary schools.

Where cultures meet, there are issues of power. Multiple scholars, concerned with the oppression of minority cultures and races, have proposed solutions that respect and advance the norms of the minority while recognizing the significance of the norms of the dominant culture. These include proposals for culturally appropriate (Au, 1980), culturally relevant (Ladson-Billings, 1995), and culturally sustaining (Paris, 2012) norms of discourse, as well as norms that take advantage of cultural funds of knowledge (Moll, Amanti, Neff, & Gonzalez, 1992). One general proposal is that incorporating ethnic forms of discourse (and knowledge) enables minority students to engage the content more naturally and equitably and without denigrating the culture from which they come. This leads to better learning and reduces threats to identity formation. Ideally, it should also be possible to feather in dominant norms of discourse, so that students can thrive within the academic criteria of the dominant culture if they choose to do so.

An original example comes from Kathryn Au's (1980) study with native Hawaiian primary school children. Au was concerned with the general finding that Native American students did not respond well to typical IRE discourse structures, and they were underperforming in reading skills. These children were very familiar with a local conversational norm of "talk story." By this norm, speakers riff off of one another when speaking, and there is careful attention to whose turn it is. Talk story strongly contrasts with IRE, where the teacher is the pivot point of a conversational norm that is as much evaluative as it is instructional. Au chronicles how one teacher masterfully orchestrated the classroom discourse about class readings so it moved seamlessly between talk story, where children directly addressed one another, and IRE, where the teacher emphasized key points. Au points out that the students from this teacher's classroom regularly outperformed other students in reading skills.

VI. Examples of Good and Bad Use

Good: In a public speaking class, students introduce themselves in one sentence before beginning their speech, even though the class already knows them. Because this is something that speakers do in a real-life public speaking engagement, setting it as a norm in the class helps students stay in the mindset of performing for a real audience, which helps them learn to speak for a real audience.

Bad: A teacher tells his class that critical thinking is an important norm in his class, but his quizzes include only memorization questions. For norms to take hold, they need to be demonstrated through consistent actions, not just stated.

VII. References and Additional Readings

Anyon, J. (1980). Social class and the hidden curriculum of work. *Journal of Education, 162*(1), 67–92.

Au, K. H. P., (1980). Participation structures in a reading lesson with Hawaiian children: Analysis of a culturally appropriate instructional event. *Anthropology and Education Quarterly, 11*(2), 91–115.

Bicchieri, C., & Chavez, A. (2010). Behaving as expected: Public information and fairness norms. *Journal of Behavioral Decision Making, 23*(2), 161-178.

Bransford, J. D., Brown, A. L., & Cocking, R. R. (Eds.) (1999). *How people learn: Brain, mind, experience, and school.* Washington, DC: National Academy Press.

Cazden, C. B. (2001). *Classroom discourse: The language of teaching and learning.* Portsmouth, NH: Heinemann.

Dahl, Gordon B.; Løken, Katrine V.; Mogstad, Magne (2012) : Peer effects in program participation, Discussion Paper series, Forschungsinstitut zur Zukunft der Arbeit, No. 6681

Delpit, L. D. (1988). The silenced dialogue: Power and pedagogy in educating other people's children. *Harvard Educational Review, 58*(3), 280–299.

Engle, R. A., & Conant, F. R. (2002). Guiding principles for fostering productive disciplinary engagement: Explaining an emergent argument in a community of learners classroom. *Cognition and Instruction, 20*(4), 399–483.

Garfinkel, H. (1967). *Studies in ethnomethodology.* New Jersey: Prentice Hall.

Goffman, E. (1966). *Behavior in public places: Notes on the social organization of gatherings.* New York: Free Press.

Heath, S. B. (1983). *Ways with words: Language, life and work in communities and classrooms.* Cambridge, UK: Cambridge University Press.

Korte, R. F. (2009). How newcomers learn the social norms of an organization: A case study of the socialization of newly hired engineers. *Human Resource Development Quarterly, 20*(3), 285–306.

Ladson-Billings, G. (1995). Toward a theory of culturally relevant pedagogy. *American Educational Research Journal, 32*(3), 465-491.

Moll, L. C., Amanti, C., Neff, D., & Gonzalez, N. (1992). Funds of knowledge for teaching: Using a qualitative approach to connect homes and classrooms. *Theory into Practice, 31*(2), 132–141.

National Research Council. (2012). Dimension 1: Scientific and engineering practices: Practices for K-12 science classrooms. In *A framework for K-12 science education: Practices, crosscutting concepts, and core ideas.* Retrieved October 29, 2015, from http://www.nap.edu/read/13165/chapter/7

Paris, D. (2012). Culturally sustaining pedagogy a needed change in stance, terminology, and practice. *Educational Researcher, 41*(3), 93–97.

Posner, R. A. (1997). Social norms and the law: An economic approach. *American Economic Review, 87*(2), 365–369.

Prentice, D. A., & Miller, D. T. (1993). Pluralistic ignorance and alcohol use on campus: Some consequences of misperceiving the social norm. *Journal of Personality and Social Psychology, 64*(2), 243-256.

Wilson, J. Q., & Kelling, G. L. (1982, March). Broken windows. *Atlantic Monthly, 249*, 29–38.

Yackel, E., & Cobb, P. (1996). Sociomathematical norms, argumentation, and autonomy in mathematics. *Journal for Research in Mathematics Education, 27*(4), 458–477.

N IS FOR NORMS

What is the core learning mechanic?
Social norms are informal rules that regulate social interaction. Social interaction determines what and how people learn.

What is an example, and what is it good for?
An elementary math class adopts the norm of class discussions in which ideas and answers need to be justified with mathematical arguments, rather than just saying an answer and letting the teacher evaluate. This norm helps students learn what it means to do math and think mathematically.

Why does it work?
People want to fit in, and following social norms is the way. People are likely to follow a social norm when they believe society expects them to, and they believe other people also follow the norm. Good norms help coordinate learning interactions, both at the level of good behaviors and at the level of the way different disciplines engage their topics.

What problems does the core mechanic solve?
- People are unprepared to fit in.
  - A recent college graduate thinks that turning in assignments on time is the most important part of doing well at his new consulting job.
- People are making the wrong choices in a social learning setting.
  - A new PhD student spends his time participating in social events when he should really be reading research papers.
  - A new business student spends her time reading research papers when she should really be participating in social events.
- People do not carry their weight in the learning community.
  - A student does not do his share in a small-group activity.

Examples of how to use it
- At the start of the school year, host a class discussion in which students generate and agree upon norms of conduct for the year.
- In a chef apprenticeship program, create norms that mimic the practices of successful chefs, such as keeping an immaculate kitchen.

Risks
- Not acknowledging that norms exist—this can lead to misunderstandings between people who are accidentally following different sets of norms.

- Establishing norms that set people down the wrong path; for example, a norm of unquestioning obedience in a school leads people down the wrong path if later success requires free thought.
- A clash of cultural norms can lead to poorer learning. Children from a nondominant culture may appear to misbehave when expected to follow the dominant culture's norms in school.

is for
Observation

Imitating feelings and procedures

PEOPLE LEARN BY watching other people's attitudes and behaviors. Learning by watching is called *observational learning*. It is especially effective for overt procedural skills, affective responses, and social values. Observational learning occurs naturally without explicit instruction—people learn to imitate both good and bad behaviors by watching those around them.

Here is an excerpt about a Mayan factory worker learning to use a loom:

[A girl] watched the operator go through the motions of running the loom [for five weeks]. She neither asked questions nor was given advice. . . . [A]t the end of this time, she announced that she was ready to run a loom. . . . [T]he machine was turned over to her and she operated it, not quite as rapidly as the girl who had just left it, but with skill and assurance. What went on in the "training" period? . . . She observes and internally rehearses the set of operations until she feels able to perform. (Gaskins and Paradise, 2010, p. 85, citing Nash, 1958)

This is an impressive example of learning by observation. No coaching, no explanations, no trial and error, no positive reinforcement, yet she figured it out. Mayan culture relies heavily on observational learning. It may be hard to imagine a typical American teenager having the patience to learn so

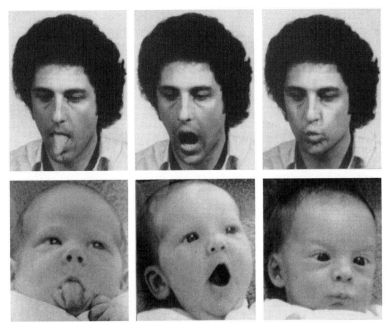

Figure O.1. Infants 2 and 3 weeks old observe and imitate adult facial motions. (From Meltzoff and Moore, 1977.)

much this way. Nevertheless, all humans are born to learn from observation. Figure O.1 provides a lovely example of a newborn spontaneously imitating the facial expressions of an adult (Meltzoff & Moore, 1977).

Observation is critical for learning affective responses. It is hard to tell people that they should be sad about a situation in a way that they can feel. However, if they see you crying in that situation, they will observe, and even feel, your emotion, and they will learn that sadness is an emotion they should feel in similar situations. Observation is also effective for learning overt behaviors. Try writing a paragraph that describes how to use chopsticks. There are many tiny details about the angle of the wrist, the placement of the thumb, the amount of pressure, the angle of approach. It is much easier to show people and allow their powers of observation to take over.

I. How Observation Works

During instruction, people often pair observable demonstrations and verbal explanations (see Chapter W). Here, we focus on the basic mechanisms that make observational learning so powerful, even without accompanying explanations. How is it possible that humans can learn complex behaviors and emotional reactions just by watching others?

The imitation story has two parts: mirroring and theory of mind. Part 1 has an evolutionary starting point. Primates have mirror neurons—a type of brain cell that activates when the primate takes an action herself or observes another primate perform the same action. Mirror neurons blur the line between "I" and "thou." Human brains can mirror complex behaviors that require millions of neurons. The mirroring capability is present in human infants. Researchers can study baby brains using electroencephalograms (EEGs). Harmless electrodes are set on the scalp, and the brain's electrical signals show a similar pattern when an infant sits still and watches someone else grasp an object and when the infant moves his own arm to grasp the object (Southgate, Johnson, Osborne, & Csibra, 2009). Adults are no different. Ballet dancers who observe dance moves show activation in similar parts of the brain as when they perform those dance moves themselves (Calvo-Merino, Glaser, Grezes, Passingham, & Haggard, 2005).

Our brain's ability to resonate to other people's behaviors is amazing, but it is finite. People need some familiarity with the observed behaviors to make sense of them. Ballet dancers exhibit greater activation than do non-ballet dancers when observing ballet movements.

With observation, one does not merely see a behavior; one experiences the behavior—albeit in a muted form. It is why you involuntarily cringe when you see another person's finger pinched by a car door. When observing other people cry, the experience resonates with you, stimulating the sense of sadness that comes with a downturned mouth and tears. Mirroring yields empathy; reasoning yields sympathy. People with autism spectrum disorder often have a hard time sensing emotions by mirroring and resonance (Begeer, Koot, Rieffe, Terwogt, & Stegge, 2008). Instead, they may use reasoning to figure out emotional situations: "The girl's eyes are wide, she just jumped out of her seat, and a loud noise just sounded. She must be surprised."

Mirroring helps learning because people map the actions and feelings of others onto patterns for their own bodies and feelings. People can replay these patterns to enable physical action and feelings or to simulate those actions and feelings in their mind. We are so good at mirroring that we even covertly experience the reward another person receives. A teacher who praises a preschooler for putting her toys away can spur the rest of the class to do so as well. Conversely, observed punishment reduces the chances that others will imitate the offending behaviors. Think of the office where the boss screams at an employee for disagreeing. People will be unlikely to imitate disagreement behaviors.

Part 2 of the imitation story involves *theory of mind*, which refers to people's abilities to think about other people's mental states. Humans are the only primate that has pronounced whites in their eyes. One explanation is that the

Figure O.2. False belief task. Children younger than four years often say that Sally will look for the marble in the white box in panel 5. The children know the marble is in the white box, and they do not consider that Sally will have a different representation of the marble's location. (From Byom and Mutlu, 2013.)

whites make it easier to see where other humans are looking, which provides a window into what others are thinking about. Unlike animals, humans know that other people have their own thoughts. As demonstrated by Figure O.2, the ability to represent other people's thoughts develops during early childhood. The ability to think, "I know that you know that I know . . . " is a nontrivial accomplishment of child maturation.

Theory of mind enables people to infer the goals of another person. This is important for observational learning. It helps the observer figure out which parts of a behavior to imitate and how to make useful variations. Imagine a young child's first visit to the bowling alley. His mom says, "Do it like this." She runs to the line, flings the ball with her right arm, and coughs. Because the child assumes the intent is to roll the ball down the alley, he knows to skip the cough. He also figures it is OK to push the ball with two hands instead of flinging it with one. Now, if the child could not figure out the goal of mom's behaviors, for example, if she were practicing her form in the living room without a ball or alley, he would try to imitate all her behaviors exactly.

Theory of mind and mirroring work together. In fact, the mirroring system appears to be especially active when observing someone engaged in goal-directed actions, compared with observing random movements. The human capacity to imagine other people's goals helps constrain the features of the activity they should mirror.

II. How to Use Observation to Enhance Learning

Albert Bandura conducted the original research on learning by observation to develop his social learning theory. The research occurred at a time when behaviorism, the dominant theory of learning, proposed that people could learn only through reinforcement (see Chapter R). Showing that people could also learn by observation was a major contribution to the science of learning. Bandura and colleagues proposed several ways to enhance learning by observation. We present each with examples of where they work for desirable and undesirable outcomes. Observational learning is occurring all the time, and it is important to consider what people are having an opportunity to observe.

INCREASE LEARNERS' ATTENTION TOWARD THE MODEL

Many people flow in and out of one's daily life. How can we help learners pay attention to the right people and behaviors? One answer is that people naturally imitate people of high status. If you want to help people pay attention, ask someone of high status to model the behaviors.

- *Happy version:* A celebrity donates time and money to a charity.
- *Unhappy version:* A popular student smokes in public.

People also pay more attention to the behaviors of people like themselves. It is one important reason to provide role models with whom people can identify. For example, seeing people like yourself fulfill roles of high status (e.g., an African American president) can be very compelling (e.g., to African American children).

- *Happy version:* A child sees another child receive a vaccine shot without crying.
- *Unhappy version:* A kindergarten girl sees her female teacher exhibit math anxiety.

Interacting with a social model further enhances learning. Kuhl, Tsao, and Liu (2003) found that nine-month-olds developed sensitivity to the sounds of a foreign language when they interacted with a live speaker, for example, by looking at each other. However, when equivalent infants watched an identical speaker shown on an audiovisual recording, they did not learn. One speculation is that the infants paid more attention to the model during the live interaction. Another possibility is that the coordinated timing of speech and social interaction helped the infants segment the flow of sound into speech units.

Helping people decompose complex behaviors is a major way to improve observational learning.

IMPROVE LEARNER ABILITIES TO OBSERVE AND ENCODE ASPECTS OF THE BEHAVIOR

Behaviors can be complex, and people may not be able to follow or remember all the moves. Perhaps you have heard people speak a foreign language quickly, and you could not tell where one word ended and another began. The same challenge confronts novices observing complex behaviors, where they cannot determine where one action ends and another begins. Segmenting the behaviors into a series of steps can help.

- *Happy version 1:* Watching someone change the printer toner can be verbally coded: "Push the yellow button, open the drawer, remove the cartridge . . ."
- *Happy version 2:* A ballet dancer can mentally rehearse a series of complex steps broken down and demonstrated by a coach.
- *Unhappy version:* A child watches a vibrant cartoon character beat up a foe with a clear "wham" for each blow.

Knowing the purpose of a complex behavior also helps learners encode the relevant aspects of the subbehaviors and the situation.

- *Happy version:* While pulling out weeds, a gardener explains that the goal is to give the vegetables space.
- *Unhappy version:* While cheating on homework, an older brother explains the goal is to avoid getting caught.

INCREASE LEARNER MOTIVATION TO IMITATE THE BEHAVIORS

Attaching a value to a behavior makes people more motivated to imitate that behavior later. When someone coughs at a theater, other people often cough (an annoying form of automatic imitation). Fortunately, people do not attach positive value to the coughing, and they will not voluntarily repeat it later. However, if people observe a behavior that results in a positive outcome, people will be more likely to imitate it later. Observing other people receive positive reinforcement for a behavior is called *vicarious reward*, because people vicariously project into the positive reinforcement (see Chapter R).

- *Happy version:* A medical resident sees a patient's demeanor improve after the attending doctor shows empathy.

- *Unhappy version:* A student sees his peers respond positively to a class-mate who skips class.

The trustworthiness or competence of a model also influences the likelihood of imitation. Even infants are less likely to imitate models that appear incompetent (Williamson, Meltzoff, & Markman, 2008).

- *Happy version:* A person observes two different models perform a task and imitates the successful one.
- *Unhappy version:* Children mistakenly conclude their teacher is incompetent, so they do not imitate useful behaviors modeled by the teacher.

Observing a behavior without a chance to imitate the behavior makes it more difficult to remember. Giving people an opportunity to enact the behavior and experience its positive consequences increases the chances of latter use.

- *Happy version:* A student tries a soccer move she observed. She practices it a few times and sees that it gets the ball around an opponent, which makes her more likely to use it in the future.
- *Unhappy version:* A teenager practices using foul language that he saw on television and sees that it gets him attention.

III. The Outcomes of Observation for Learning

A unique outcome of observation is affective learning. Providing a human model is an exceptionally effective way to teach people how they should feel about an event, a situation, or other people. Learning affective responses through observation comes naturally. One example comes from social referencing (Walden & Ogan, 1988). When an infant falls, he may look to his mother to see her reaction: if the mother laughs, the child will laugh about the fall; if the mother shows alarm, the child will cry about the fall. Social referencing is a powerful way that children learn how to feel about strangers and novelty. The reactions of an adult (or even a video game character) to children's failure should be an important consideration when designing instruction.

For procedural activities, the outcome of observing is overt imitation: a learner observes steps 1, 2, and 3; the learner does steps 1, 2, and 3. For conceptual material, imitation can be a difficult way to learn. Imitating a teacher writing $A = \pi r^2$ does not help the student understand $A = \pi r^2$. Simple imitation is not good evidence of understanding. Pure observation works best for content that primarily involves perceptible body movements and affective states. However, when combined with verbal explanations, people can learn the conceptual underpinnings of a behavior (see Chapter W).

IV. Can People Learn to Teach Themselves through Observation?

Yes! People teach themselves through observation all the time. For example, you may learn how a subway ticket machine works in a new city by watching the customers in front of you.

People can also learn to rely on observation as a function of the culture in which they live. Rogoff, Paradise, Arauz, Correa-Chávez, and Angelillo (2003) found that observational learning is more prominent in many indigenous American cultures than in industrialized Western cultures. For example, parents may quietly point children to observe competent others rather than providing explanations. In cultures where children participate in the activities of adults going about their business, such as child rearing and animal husbandry, this makes a great deal of sense. This is in contrast to Western school environments that sequester children from ongoing adult activities, and children often learn through child-focused lessons, verbal instruction, and asking questions. To change an instructional context to promote more observational learning, it may be useful to establish observational learning as a social norm (see Chapter N): rather than always expecting explicit instruction, learners realize they should sometimes learn by quietly observing others.

V. Risks of Observation

There are two key risks of observational learning: that people do not learn what you want, and that they learn what you do not want.

People may not know what aspects of a complex behavior are crucial and may miss key components. This is especially prevalent when people do not understand the goal or purpose of the modeled behavior. As an example, the toddler son of one of the authors observed his parents using potholders, and he wanted to use them too. However, he did not yet understand the goals or important features of the behavior he observed. As he imitated the action during play, he (appropriately) used a potholder to hold the handle of a toy pot but then placed his bare hand on the bottom of the pot to help carry it.

People may also learn unwanted behaviors and attitudes that they observe in their environment. In a classic series of studies with preschool children, Bandura, Ross, and Ross (1961) studied what children learned from observing aggressive adult behaviors. In one study, a group of preschool children saw an adult act aggressively toward a Bobo doll. A second group of children saw the adult quietly assemble toys with the Bobo doll in the background. Later, to

Figure O.3. The Bobo doll experiments. A child who observed an adult behave aggressively toward a large inflatable doll subsequently beat up the doll when left alone with the doll. (From Bandura, 1963.)

build up the children's frustration in both conditions, the experimenter gave the children toys and then took them away while saying they were actually meant for other children. The children then entered a room with the Bobo doll and other objects to play with. Compared with the children who had seen the adult quietly playing with toys, children who had seen the adult aggression were more likely to imitate those aggressive behaviors toward the Bobo doll and even add in new verbal and physical abuses (see Figure O.3).

Subsequent studies examined whether viewing media aggression would have similar effects. Children watched a video or cartoon of a model showing aggression. Figure O.4 shows the average number of subsequent aggressive

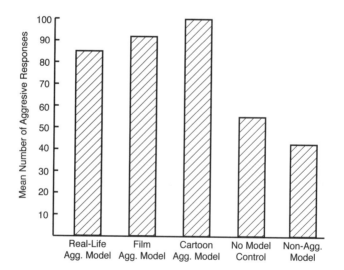

Figure O.4. Mean number of aggressive responses performed by children under different modeling conditions. (From Bandura, 1963.)

behaviors (Bandura, 1963). Whether the aggression was live, taped, or in a cartoon, children engaged in more aggressive acts than otherwise equivalent children who saw an adult playing quietly or who never saw an adult take any behavior at all. Interestingly, revealing the effect of vicarious reinforcement, if children saw the model punished for aggressive behaviors, they were less likely to imitate the behaviors (Bandura, 1965).

VI. Examples of Good and Bad Use

In a moment of chagrin, you may have uttered, "Do as I say, not as I do"— good luck with that! The most likely outcome is that the observers will eventually do as you do *and* say as you say—they will imitate the whole of it. When teaching through observation, it is important to model the desired behaviors. Ideally, the learner understands the goals of the behavior and can parse the components of the behaviors. A good cooking show explains the purpose of each step and executes them slowly enough to follow. To further help, the model cook may offer alternative behaviors to achieve the same goal, for example, by showing how to whip eggs with a fork if there is no whisk available. A bad cooking show moves quickly without indicating the purposes of the substeps. This makes imitation very difficult, especially if one's kitchen does not have a sous chef who has already prepared all the ingredients for you.

VII. References and Additional Readings

Bandura, A. (1963). The role of imitation in personality development. *Journal of Nursery Education, 18*(3), 207-215.

Bandura, A. (1965). Influence of models' reinforcement contingencies on the acquisition of imitative responses. *Journal of Personality and Social Psychology, 1*(6), 589–595.

Bandura, A., Ross, D., & Ross, S. A. (1961). Transmission of aggression through imitation of aggressive models. *Journal of Abnormal and Social Psychology, 3,* 575–582.

Begeer, S., Koot, H. M., Rieffe, C., Terwogt, M. M., & Stegge, H. (2008). Emotional competence in children with autism: Diagnostic criteria and empirical evidence. *Developmental Review, 28*(3), 342–369.

Calvo-Merino, B., Glaser, D. E., Grezes, J., Passingham, R. E., & Haggard, P. (2005). Action observation and acquired motor skills: An fMRI study with expert dancers. *Cerebral Cortex, 15,* 1243–1249.

Gaskins, S., & Paradise, R. (2010). Learning through observation in daily life. In D. F. Lancy, J. Bock, & S. Gaskins (Eds.), *The anthropology of learning in childhood* (85-118). Lanham, MD: AltaMira Press.

Kuhl, P. K., Tsao, F. M., & Liu, H. M. (2003). Foreign-language experience in infancy: Effects of short-term exposure and social interaction on phonetic learning. *Proceedings of the National Academy of Sciences of the USA, 100*(15), 9096–9101.

Meltzoff, A. N., & Moore, M. K. (1977). Imitation of facial and manual gestures by human neonates. *Science, 198*(4312), 75–78.

Byom, L. J., & B. Mutlu. (2013). Theory of mind: Mechanisms, methods, and new directions. *Frontiers in Human Neuroscience, 7, Article 413, 1-12.*

Rogoff, B., Paradise, R., Arauz, R. M., Correa-Chávez, M., & Angelillo, C. (2003). Firsthand learning through intent participation. *Annual Review of Psychology, 54*(1), 175–203.

Southgate, V., Johnson, M. H., Osborne, T., & Csibra, G. (2009). Predictive motor activation during action observation in human infants. *Biology Letters, 5*(6), 769–772.

Walden, T. A., & Ogan, T. A. (1988). The development of social referencing. *Child Development*, 59(5), 1230–1240.

Williamson, R. A., Meltzoff, A. N., & Markman, E. M. (2008). Prior experiences and perceived efficacy influence 3-year-olds' imitation. *Developmental Psychology, 44*(1), 275-285.

O IS FOR OBSERVATION

What is the core learning mechanic?
Learning by observation involves watching and imitating other people's behaviors and affective responses, as well as vicariously seeing the consequences of other people's behaviors.

What is an example, and what is it good for?
A child is not sure how to play a game on the playground. She stands on the sideline and watches the other children play for several minutes, until she figures out the rules and decides to join in.

Learning by observation is especially good for learning overt behaviors. It is also a powerful way in which people learn affective responses.

Why does it work?
Human brains are wired to learn by observing others. The brain shows similar patterns of activation when people observe others as when acting themselves. People can learn physical skills or emotional reactions by imitating the behaviors they observe in others. Additionally, seeing the consequences of other people's actions allows learners to determine which behaviors should be favored or avoided.

What problems does the core mechanic solve?
- Trial and error is too slow or impossible.
  - A salesperson at a clothing store does not know how to fold shirts neatly.
- A behavior is too complex to explain verbally.
  - A novice mountaineer needs to tie climbing knots in ropes.
- Learners are not sure how to act or feel.
  - A child stumbles and does not know whether to laugh or cry.

Examples of how to use it
- Have a new employee tag along with an experienced employee for a few days, learning job skills and how to interact with customers.
- As a teacher, let students see you experience failure (e.g., not knowing how to solve a problem) and model resilience (using it as an opportunity to learn).

Risks
- Students may learn to imitate a behavior at a shallow level.

- Learners may display the behavior in inappropriate contexts.
- People may not learn the purpose of the steps of a behavior, leaving them unable to adjust to new situations. If a teen learns that laundry involves detergent and fabric softener, but does not learn why, the teen may not know how to clean the clothes when the fabric softener runs out.
- Students may learn unintended or antisocial behaviors.
  - Students learn aggressive behaviors by seeing them modeled.
  - A student sees other students being praised for getting good grades and concludes that getting an A is more important than understanding the content.

P is for Participation

Getting into the game

I. What Is Participation?

PARTICIPATION REFERS TO engaging in an existing cultural activity. The major benefit of learning through participation is that it involves a rich and purposeful social context, often with a trajectory of continued participation and growth.

Many of the chapters in this book describe research on psychological processes. A different kind of analysis considers the role of culture in shaping how we interpret and engage the world. Some scholars define culture as that which remains as people come and go. (Chapter N offers a different characterization.) People learn by participating in and perpetuating culture. A major challenge is how to help beginners start participating. Once you can get a child to swim a little bit, she can start to figure out why people like to swim, learn how to swim better, develop relevant vocabulary, swim to play games, and perhaps even aspire to much greater participation through swimming competitions. To get all those potential benefits, however, the child needs to get started, and getting started is not easy on one's own—the pool is deep and the child is scared, so she stands on the deck looking at the pool.

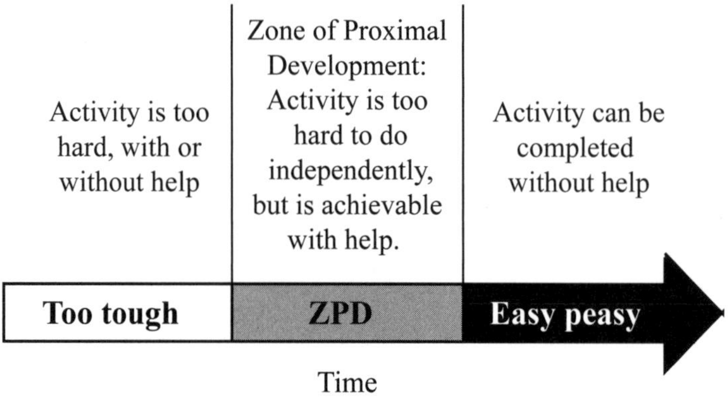

Activity is too hard, with or without help	Zone of Proximal Development: Activity is too hard to do independently, but is achievable with help.	Activity can be completed without help
Too tough	**ZPD**	**Easy peasy**

Time

Figure P.1. The zone of proximal development. The center region indicates a zone of difficulty where students can accomplish an activity with help but not alone.

Developmental psychologist Lev Vygotsky stated, "What a child is able to do in collaboration today he will be able to do independently tomorrow" (1934/1987, p. 211). This thought undergirds his most influential idea, the zone of proximal development (the ZPD, as it is fondly called), a region along a trajectory of growth where, with a little social help, learners can begin participating in an activity. Participating, in turn, further drives the processes of development and learning so that eventually the learner can participate without help.

Figure P.1 summarizes three possible stages. The left side represents learners prior to entering a ZPD, when they cannot learn an activity. Consider as an example children learning to ride a bike. Very young children cannot learn to ride a bike no matter how much parents help, and many parents frustrate themselves by expecting too much too early. The ZPD in the center of the figure indicates that an appropriate combination of social and material supports can help the child. For instance, training wheels help children ride a bike by solving the problem of keeping balanced. During this time, children also need to learn to brake, steer, and look where they are going. Training wheels do not directly teach any of these tasks, but children can begin to learn them while pedaling around. Once those abilities develop, the child can learn to balance without the training wheels. This learning trajectory is characteristic of learning through participation. Early on, learners do not grasp the fullness of an activity. This grasp is what participation brings them. Finally, at the right of the figure the learner has exited the ZPD and can complete the activity without supports—there is no more need for training wheels. After exiting one ZPD, another one may open up. For instance, the children may be ready to learn to ride a unicycle with some help. The ZPD identifies the "Goldilocks zone" for instruction—not too hard, not too easy, just right given a little help. (Some suggest that Vygotsky meant for the ZPD to characterize a child's development more broadly, rather than referring to individual skills, e.g., Chaiklin, 2003. We find the ideas of the ZPD useful for both.)

The ZPD and deliberate practice (see Chapter D) are in some ways opposites. The ZPD is relevant to helping people learn when they *start participating* in an activity (ride a bike). In contrast, deliberate practice helps with learning at a more expert level and often requires people to *stop participating* in the short term, so they can exercise decontextualized aspects of the performance (lift weights to improve at cycling).

I. How Participation Works

It is a safe guess that you have heard (or even said) some variation of the following: "Trust me! You will need to know this in the future." Now that is a desperate way to motivate learning! It would be much better if students could experience the context that renders the knowledge meaningful (see Chapter J). As a thought experiment, imagine a child building a fire with her family on a camping trip. She is fully immersed in the purposes for building the fire (light, warmth, marshmallows). Important details and consequences are ready at hand to support learning. There are strong social values for collaborating to achieve the best results possible, and parents are keen to guide her participation. In contrast, imagine a child who has never gone camping and is memorizing how to build a campfire from a manual. It creates a much thinner experience, and there is no trajectory to continued learning.

People can be eager to start participating, but there may be skill barriers. For instance, young children may see their parents and other family members reading books. They want to be readers too, but they cannot decipher words yet. Picture books enable children to start taking part in some of the activities of reading, such as turning the pages and guessing what will happen next in a story. Going to storytime at the library allows them to join a community of readers. Children can start participating in many of the practices of reading long before they can actually read on their own.

The ZPD was intended to describe child development and the role that social and cultural supports play in shaping thought. The premiere example is that young children learn to talk by interacting with others, and eventually, they internalize this speech into inner-speech and can discuss matters in their heads. You may have noticed that even adults sometimes talk to themselves softly when working out a tough problem. This may reflect the idea that thought starts externally before being internalized. Interestingly, deaf children learn to "inner sign" and imagine hand gestures instead of word sounds, when thinking things through. Language does not emerge fully formed from a genetic blue print; social forces drive its development.

Though developmental in spirit, ideas from the ZPD can apply to adults as well. For example, beginning skiers of all ages can learn faster if they start with short skis, which are easier to maneuver (Burton, Brown, & Fischer, 1984). With short skis, the novice can participate in the act of skiing and learn how to stop, start, and turn more easily. After grasping the basics, skiers move to longer skis to gain power and speed.

This brings up an important point. *Good learning environments provide a trajectory for continued learning and deeper involvement.* Sports provide an impressive example: children can begin in little leagues and move through clubs of increasing abilities until they become professional athletes. The best video games make extensive use of the ZPD to create trajectories for more complex participation (Gee, 2003). At early levels, the computer accomplishes many of the tasks of the game, such as maneuvering additional players and offering a lax opposition. Players have a chance to experience why one would play such a game while also learning some of the basic game mechanics. As the player moves up in skill level, the game reveals more complexity along a "Goldilocks" ramp that is neither too hard nor too easy. (See Chapter R for why this is also very motivating.)

II. How to Use Participation to Enhance Learning

We focus on three key elements for supporting early participation: a community of practice, social mediation, and scaffolding.

COMMUNITY OF PRACTICE

Most pursuits—hobbies, jobs, or families—comprise a network of interlocking, purposeful people and activities. The larger context provides constraints on what is worth knowing and doing and why. Environments where learners can produce artifacts, contribute meaningfully, and envision their future selves are especially effective in helping students develop an identity within a community. In contrast, school tasks are often decontextualized relative to the practical contexts where students might use what they learn. To help students learn through participation in the context of school, one needs to create a broader context that reveals the meaning and goals of the activity at hand. One solution is to situate learning activities within a larger community purpose.

To illustrate, here is an example of when a larger community purpose helped a good teaching technique become even better. Palincsar and Brown (1984) created a method of reading instruction called reciprocal teaching.

The instructor scaffolds early readers by asking them questions when reading (e.g., what will happen next?). Over time, the teacher puts students into the role of the teacher, so they need to ask the questions, hence the name *reciprocal teaching*. By participating as a teacher, children will ideally internalize these questions so that they ask themselves similar questions when reading on their own. Reciprocal teaching is a good idea and broadly adopted. However, the researchers also noticed some fatal mutations. Sometimes the question asking became robotic: a child, playing the role of teacher, asks what will happen next, and another student gives an absurd answer; the child teacher then dutifully moves to the next question—the purpose of asking the question was lost. To solve this problem, researchers created a larger purpose for reading (Brown & Campione, 1994). They had children create a collaborative research project (with teacher support, of course). Given their self-selected research context, there was a reason for children to learn from the texts, and they could intelligently monitor question and answer quality by reference to whether they were helping address their community's research question. (Chapters Q and L have further examples of tasks with enough substance that they can be used to help develop a community of practice.)

SOCIAL MEDIATION

Social mediation is support from a knowledgeable person who selects tasks, provides interpretations, and points to the larger social context to lend significance to what one is learning. Apprenticeship, or guided participation, is an age-old model for social mediation. Rogoff (1990) describes how young Mayan children in Guatemala learn to make tortillas: A mother gives a young girl a small piece of dough and helps her flatten it. The mother cooks the tortilla, and the family eats it with their meal. The young girl experiences tortilla making and her contribution to the family. As the child becomes more skillful, the mother begins to add pointers while working side by side, and the child takes on more responsibility.

Establishing an apprenticeship is not always possible. Still, teachers and parents can enact roles that help students continue on a trajectory of learning. Barron, Martin, Takeuchi, and Fithian (2009) examined the ways that parents nurtured their children's interests in technology. They identified the following possible roles: teacher, collaborator, learning broker, resource provider, nontechnical consultant, employer, and learner. When designing a role for social support in an instructional design, it is useful to go beyond the standard classroom roles and think of other ways that teachers, older peers, and parents can provide support for participation. For example, an older peer who serves as a social broker for a new student can greatly increase the community's embrace of the newcomer.

When designing a participation structure, it is important to find ways to encourage equitable participation. This does not mean everyone does the same thing; it means that everyone can contribute. One of the characteristics of many participation structures is that there are different roles that people can adopt to help accomplish an activity—a newsroom, for example, has reporters, editors, people responsible for layouts, and more. Compare this to many classrooms, where there are only two roles—student and teacher. In traditional classrooms, where children can only take a single role, status characteristics, incuding perceived ability, race, gender, and popularity, can affect whether students are seen (by themselves or others) as effective contributors, and lead to inequalities in participation. A good participation structure can create equal opportunities for participation by relying on the existence of multiple roles—for a classroom magazine, a student can take on the role of scribe, interviewer, or copy editor.

In studying small group interactions in classrooms, Cohen and Lotan (1995) found that certain kinds of status treatments helped increase participation rates for low status students, while exhibiting no deleterious effect on high status students. These treatments focused on increasing expectations of competence for low status students, for example by calling attention to their contributions, and by discussing the multiple kinds of important contributions and roles that a task requires, decreasing the perception that there is a single dimension of ability that will lead to success. (See Chapter L for additional discussion.)

SCAFFOLDING

Scaffolding is a wonderful term used to describe the material and social supports that help learners begin to participate (Pea, 2004; Wood, Bruner, & Ross, 1976). Scaffolds are temporary structures that can come down once the building (child) can stand on its (her) own. Material scaffolds tend to be task specific—short skis, batting tees, training wheels. The trick is to figure out the skill barrier that blocks participation and then invent a way to reduce the demands needed for that skill. Early readers, for example, know the meaning of many words they have heard, but they cannot read them yet. One might scaffold their reading by using simpler words or pictorial cues or by including a way for them to hear written words (e.g., by clicking on the word).

A common barrier to beginners is the sheer complexity of orchestrating multiple novel subskills simultaneously. Reducing the cognitive burden for one task can help. For beginning guitar players, it can help to place stickers on the frets as a reminder of where to place their fingers. If your grandmother is learning the computer for the first time, you can have her work on mastering the mouse while you indicate what to click on.

When you do manage to think of a good scaffold, make sure there is a way to have it fade, lest it become a crutch. Cash registers that compute exact change are a powerful aid for sales clerks. However, these cash registers are not going away anytime soon—they have become part of a system of distributed cognition, where the clerk and cash register share in the overall intelligent behavior of making change. Clerks are unlikely to get better at subtraction as long as the cash register is doing all the work for them.

III. The Outcomes of Learning through Participation

"Where before there was a spectator, let there now be a participant" (Bruner, 1983, p. 60). By definition, the outcome of a just-right ZPD and a just-right scaffold is that learners can eventually participate without any special support. "Hey look, Johnny is riding his bike without training wheels!" On a longer view, the desired outcome is usually that learners continue on a trajectory toward more advanced participation. As the saying goes, "The reward for a job well done is . . . more work." One way to tell people are learning through participation is that they take on more responsibility in the central tasks of the practice (Lave & Wenger, 1991). A classic example is starting in the mailroom and working one's way up to the board room.

A second outcome of a participation framework is that it can change how educators think about tests. Vygotsky offered the following analogy:

> Like a gardener who in appraising species for yield would proceed incorrectly if he considered only the ripe fruit in the orchard and did not know how to evaluate the condition of the trees that had not yet produced mature fruit, the psychologist who is limited to ascertaining what has matured, leaving what is maturing aside, will never be able to obtain any kind of true and complete representation of the internal state of the whole development. (1934/1987, p. 200)

Most tests measure mature knowledge (e.g., mastery). Can the person solve the problem or not? These summative assessments look to see if a person is in the far right of Figure P.1. Here is the novel part: it may also be useful to measure whether someone is in a ZPD for learning. Doing so requires dynamic assessments that evaluate whether a person can learn, given opportunities and resources. Reuven Feuerstein (1979) used a dynamic assessment approach in his work with cognitively challenged children. As part of an IQ test, he tried to teach the children how to solve the problems to determine if they could benefit from reasoning instruction. His dynamic assessment approach was much more sensitive to the children's potential than simply giving them an

IQ test. More generally, providing students an opportunity to learn as part of a test gives a better indication of whether their prior instruction has expanded their ZPD so they are prepared to learn new material on their own, a major goal of instruction. (Chapter K provides more discussion and examples of dynamic assessments.)

IV. Can People Learn to Teach Themselves through Participation?

People learn all sorts of ways to scaffold their own participation. A favorite example comes from a study of learning to play dominoes (Nasir, 2002). A young novice, David, selects a tile to play, but asks his partner to put it on the board. David pretends he cannot reach the board. In reality, he does not know where to play the piece. His partner plays the tile and the game continues. This allows David to participate and learn without interrupting the game play.

There are also specific self-scaffolding techniques that one can teach. A generic strategy involves modifying components of a completed work, also known as remixing. For example, when learning to make websites, some people directly copy the programming code behind their favorite site and then choose one section to recreate in their own fashion. They employ the existing code as scaffolding.

V. Risks of Learning through Participation

Risk 1: Participatory structure is missing, so there is nothing to participate in. Say you want disadvantaged youth to learn about producing digital media and computer programming. You choose participation as the learning method, because it provides a richer set of learning supports than textbook treatments, and it creates a nourishing sense of purpose and a potential identity as a maker. You look around, and you realize there are no suitable participatory structures for digital literacy—no relevant internship opportunities, no relevant school clubs, no local youth media groups (such as Youth Radio, based in Oakland, CA). This means it is up to you to make a context for learning through participation, which is a daunting task, but doable (Barron, Gomez, Pinkard, & Martin, 2014).

Risk 2: The learning does not transfer. Learning from participation is tuned to specific experiences and participation structures. It takes extra steps to help learners lift out the generalizable aspects of what they have learned so they know how to use it elsewhere. One solution is to provide a debriefing that explains the generalizable aspects of the practice (see Chapter J).

Risk 3: Misestimating the ZPD. It is easy to misestimate when people are ready for help and when they are ready for independent action. It appears to be a ubiquitous failing of parents that they buy too advanced toys for infants, who have yet to discover their hands, let alone push around a toy truck. On the other side, nobody likes help when they can do something themselves. For nondangerous pursuits, a simple solution is to offer minimal help at start and then build up as needed. For dangerous pursuits, such as back flips on a balance beam, it may be better to overhelp at first and then dial it down as appropriate.

Risk 4: A scaffold inadvertently becomes a crutch. Parents should feel sheepish if helping their sixth-grade son write a persuasive essay eventually leads to writing his college admissions essay, too. When planning to use scaffolds, have a plan for fading them.

Risk 5: Throwing out the baby with the bathwater—it is possible to provide support that completely removes the key thing students need to learn. This happens when people try to simplify tasks without thinking about the learning outcomes. For instance, students may receive a complex mathematics problem intended to approximate real-world practices outside the classroom. A major point of this type of problem is to help students learn to formulate the mathematics buried in the situation. However, teachers may try to simplify the problem, for example, by formulating the buried mathematics into formal expressions. The result is that students only need to plug-and-chug, which they could practice without an elaborate problem.

VI. Examples of Good and Bad Use

A paint-by-number kit is a nice thought experiment. It allows nonpainters to paint pretty images, but is painting by numbers an example of good scaffolding? First, we can consider whether it supports participation in a broader social activity. If the paint-by-numbers activity occurs within the context of an art studio, where others also regularly paint, then the paint-by-numbers kit can support learning to participate in the group, for instance, by gaining an affinity for and identity as a member of the painting community. In some sense, it does not matter if children learn to paint better with paint-by-numbers kits, because they are finding a way to begin participating in the group. If there is no larger art community, then painting by numbers cannot support a trajectory into sustained participation and further learning. Second, we can consider whether paint-by-numbers kits scaffold the skill of painting, regardless of group membership. Painting by numbers helps children perform at a level they could not do without help. It should help children develop fine motor skills. On the other hand, the kit is unlikely to improve one's painting skills beyond what one could do before using the kit, and despite what the kit says on the cover, it is unlikely to help children become more creative. As in all things educational, it is worth trying to be precise about the intended outcomes as a way to backward map to good and bad uses of an instructional strategy.

VII. References

Barron, B. J., Gomez, K., Pinkard, M., & Martin, C. K. (2014). *The digital youth network: Cultivating digital media citizenship in urban communities.* Cambridge, MA: MIT Press.

Barron, B. J., Martin, C. K., Takeuchi, L., & Fithian, R. (2009). Parents as learning partners in the development of technological fluency. *International Journal of Learning and Media, 1*(2), 55–77.

Brown, A. L., & Campione, J. C. (1994). Guided discovery in a community of learners. In K. McGilly (Ed.), *Classroom lessons: Integrating cognitive theory and classroom practice* (pp. 229-270). Cambridge, MA: MIT Press/Bradford Books.

Bruner, J. S. (1983). *Child's talk: Learning to use language.* New York: Norton.

Burton, R. R., Brown, J. S., & Fischer, G. (1984). Skiing as a model of instruction. In B.Rogoff and J. Lave *(Eds.). Everyday cognition: Its development in social context* (pp. 139-150). Cambridge, MA: Harvard University Press.

Chaiklin, S. (2003). The zone of proximal development in Vygotsky's analysis of learning and instruction. In A. Kozulin (Ed) *Vygotsky's Educational Theory in Cultural Context.* (pp. 39-64). Cambridge, MA: Cambridge University Press,

Cohen, E. G., & Lotan, R. A. (1995). Producing equal-status interaction in the heterogeneous classroom. *American Educational Research Journal, 32*(1), 99-120.

Feuerstein, R. (1979). *The dynamic assessment of retarded performers: The learning potential assessment device, theory, instruments, and techniques.* Baltimore, MD: University Park Press.

Gee, J. (2003). *What video games have to teach us about learning and literacy.* New York: Palgrave Macmillan.

Lave, J., & Wenger, E. (1991). *Situated learning: Legitimate peripheral participation.* Cambridge, UK: Cambridge University Press.

Nasir, N. S. (2002). Identity, goals, and learning: Mathematics in cultural practice. *Mathematical Thinking and Learning, 4*(2–3), 213–247.

Palincsar, A. S., & Brown, A. (1984). Reciprocal teaching of comprehension-fostering and comprehension monitoring activities. *Cognition and Instruction, 1*(2), 117–175.

Pea, R. D. (2004). The social and technological dimensions of scaffolding and related theoretical concepts for learning, education, and human activity. *Journal of the Learning Sciences, 13*(3), 423–451.

Rogoff, B. (1990). *Apprenticeship in thinking: Cognitive development in social context.* New York: Oxford University Press.

Vygotsky, L. S. (1934/1987). *The collected works of L. S. Vygotsky.* (Eds). R. Rieber & A. Carton. NY: Plenum.

Wood, D., Bruner, J. S., & Ross, G. (1976). The role of tutoring in problem solving. *Journal of child psychology and psychiatry, 17*(2), 89-100.

P IS FOR PARTICIPATION

What is the core learning mechanic?
Participating in a socially contextualized activity provides learners with access to the goals, consequences, methods, and interpretations that render learning meaningful. The challenge involves finding a way to help beginners to start participating.

What is an example, and what is it good for?
Learning to surf: The instructor tows the beginner out to sea and pushes the surfboard at the right moment to catch the wave. Meanwhile, the surfer can focus on balancing and experiencing what it means to surf. With improvement, the instructor can fade the support, and the beginner can participate in other aspects of surfing such as being very cool.

Why does it work?
With just the right amount of social or physical supports, beginners can start to participate in an activity that they could not engage in on their own. Over time, learners come to manage the complexity of the activity and no longer need special supports.

What problems does the core mechanic solve?
- An activity is beyond a person's skill level.
  - A child cannot hit a baseball pitch but wants to play.
- Students do not understand why they have to learn the class material.
  - Students complain that learning the quadratic equation is stupid.
- Tests underestimate student potential or the value of compelling experiences.
  - Students show no gain on standard achievement tests but have experienced valuable lessons elsewhere that prepare them to learn in the future.

Examples of how to use it
- A parent assumes responsibility for some parts of an activity.
  - In a piano piece, the parent plays the left-hand notes and keeps the beat.
- A teacher creates a broader participation context to situate classroom activities.
  - A teacher turns the class into a research team that needs to solve a challenge.

Risks

- Scaffolds become crutches.
- Students fail to apply what they have learned to a new participation structure.
- The level of support provided is inappropriate (too much or too little).
- Oversimplifying a task to enable participation inadvertently displaces a key feature of the activity.

Q is for
Question Driven

Creating a reason to inquire

QUESTION-DRIVEN LEARNING IS undertaken in the service of answering a question, whether yours or someone else's. Done well, question-driven learning increases curiosity, purpose, attention, and well-connected memories. Complex questions may further boost problem-solving skills and strategies.

Question-driven learning starts early in life. An infant drops a bowl of peas from her high chair, waiting to learn what happens next. A young child asks innumerable why questions. Adults search the web for answers to health problems. A criticism of many school environments is that they distort question asking. Ben Stein, in the movie *Ferris Beuller's Day Off*, ad-libbed a great sendup of bad classroom instruction:

> In 1930, the Republican-controlled House of Representatives, in an effort to alleviate the effects of the . . . Anyone? Anyone? . . . the Great Depression, passed the . . . Anyone? Anyone? The tariff bill? The Hawley-Smoot Tariff Act? Which, anyone? Raised or lowered? . . . raised tariffs, in an effort to collect more revenue for the federal government. Did it work? Anyone? Anyone know the effects? It did not work, and the United States sank deeper into the Great Depression. (http://www.filmsite.org/best-speeches38.html)

These rhetorical questions do not help anything. Instead, students (well, maybe not those students) could have been engaged with a more open-ended and complex question: "What do you think the House of Representatives should have done differently in 1930, and what might have been the outcome?" Good question-driven learning creates a context of sustained inquiry, not just one-shot factual answers.

I. How Question-Driven Learning Works

Question-driven learning taps into very basic mechanisms that support learning. It also provides opportunities to learn to solve complex problems. We begin with the basic mechanisms of curiosity.

MECHANISMS OF CURIOSITY

> In 1923, Sir Francis Walshe, a British neurologist, noticed something interesting while testing the reflexes of patients who were paralyzed on one side of their bodies. When they yawned, they would spontaneously regain their motor functions. In case after case, the same thing happened; it was as if, for the six or so seconds the yawn lasted, the patients were no longer paralyzed. (Konnikova, 2014)

Do you want to know why? Curiosity is a powerful mechanism. When piqued, curiosity sidesteps the question, "Why am I learning this?" Curiosity activates the brain's reward and memory systems (see Chapter X). People will expend resources (time, money, energy) to learn answers to questions they are curious about, despite the lack of external reward (Kang et al., 2009). People are also more likely to remember those answers and use them to solve problems later. Try the following insight problem:

> Uriah Fuller, the famous superpsychic, can tell you the score of any baseball game before the game starts. What is his secret?

Adams and colleagues (1988) used a series of insight questions like this to examine how two types of initial learning influence subsequent problem solving. In the Fact-Oriented condition, participants first read a list of facts. Among them:

> Before any game is played, the score is zero to zero.

Afterward, they received the Uriah Fuller problem. They were surprisingly unsuccessful at applying the list of facts they read earlier. The theory is that having acquired the information in a fact orientation, participants did not spontaneously see its relevance to problem solving.

In the Problem-Oriented condition, participants also first read a list of facts, except they were presented as answers to implied questions. A problematic phrase was stated, followed by a pause, and then the fact:

> You can tell the score of any game before it is played [two-second pause] because the score is zero to zero.

These participants were much more likely to spontaneously apply the information to solve the subsequent insight problems. Acquiring information as an answer to a question made it more likely that participants would apply that information in a problem-solving context.

MECHANISMS OF COMPLEX QUESTION ANSWERING

Most question-driven lessons use meaty questions. They require multiple ideas to work together to create a solution. "Can we harness the energy of the northern lights?" The central focus of the question binds information into a network of ideas rather than isolated facts. Connected ideas improve understanding and memory (see Chapters S and E, respectively).

Complex questions encourage the exercise of important problem-solving skills, such as goal decomposition. People determine subgoals that need solving. For example, given the broader question of how to make a viable funfair booth, students need to learn to create and solve the subgoals of determining expenses and likely income. In turn, subgoal decomposition often suits collaborative learning, where team members take on subgoals and learn to communicate and negotiate with one another.

Many of the high-level skills required for question-driven learning occur on lists of twenty-first-century competencies, including formulating questions, evaluating evidence, thinking critically, and seeking feedback and resources. Assessments that can determine whether question-driven learning achieves these outcomes are only starting to appear, so it is currently unknown how to maximize these outcomes for question-driven learning (Schwartz & Arena, 2013).

II. How to Use Question-Driven Approaches to Improve Learning

Question-driven learning often occurs under the rubrics of problem-based learning, project-based learning, case-based learning, and inquiry-based learning. There appear to be three key elements the teacher can introduce to facilitate question-driven learning, in addition to teaching students how to collaborate (discussed in Chapter L): developing a good question, taking on a coaching role, and scaffolding the inquiry process.

DEVELOPING A GOOD QUESTION

If learning is question driven, the question had better be a good one. But good for what? There is a useful distinction here between well-structured and ill-structured problems. Well-structured problems have a clear goal and a set of steps or rules for moving towards that goal. Sometimes, well-structured problems have a guaranteed best solution that can be obtained by applying an appropriate procedure or algorithm: "A car is traveling at 50 mph. How long . . ." Well-structured problems are good practice for untangling and automating skills and concepts one has already learned. In contrast, ill-structured problems do not have a single correct solution: "How can we solve global warming?" There are many ways to approach the problem, and different solutions satisfy different constraints. Ill-structured problems are better suited for making learners dive deep.

Questions should be (or become) meaningful to the learner and create a "need to know." There are a few ways to make this more likely. One is to set the stage so learners can generate their own questions. Science museums use exhibits that encourage learners to formulate their own how-is-that-possible questions. When there is specific content that needs to be learned, such as the concept of percentages in math class, it can be helpful to present a question that is specifically designed to address that content yet still authentically engaging to the leaner. How can something be "authentically engaging" if students did not generate the question? Create a compelling context.

In the Adventures of Jasper Woodbury series, students start a mathematics unit by watching a video narrative that develops a complex problem (Cognition and Technology Group at Vanderbilt, 1992). This serves as an anchor for subsequent problem solving, which led to the name *anchored instruction*. In one episode of the series, students view a twenty-minute video in which an eagle is shot in the wing and needs to be rescued in a remote area. Various constraints and possibilities for the rescue are presented as the story unfolds, including distances, available people, transportation options, rate of travel, and fuel availability. Over a week, students rewatch the video as needed to build a rescue solution that can meet the constraints with the available resources. There are multiple workable solutions, although there is one optimal solution that teachers often explain after students have developed their own.

The Jasper Woodbury videos are carefully constructed problem-based learning activities with two key features: they introduce a rich and compelling video-based problem-solving context that does not handicap children with poor reading skills, and they are self-contained and provide sufficient information to address the question. This latter feature is in contrast to more open-ended, project-based approaches that have students work on real-world problems, such as, "How can we increase the percentage of students who recycle at school?" This is more authentic, in the sense that it has a potential impact on people's lives. Projects can be very rewarding, but they are also more demanding for the instructor, because the space of subproblems and possible relevant resources can become unruly.

In the middle ground, some educators use constructed problems, but ones that are similar to what students will encounter in the real world. Problem-based learning (PBL), which originated in medical schools in the 1960s, is a good example. Often, when choosing a medical school, students will choose which kind of training they want—traditional or PBL. Traditional instruction involves two years of lectures and seminars covering basic science subjects, such as anatomy, pathology, and chemistry. This is followed by two years of clinical instruction. In contrast, PBL integrates multiple subjects together from the start through case studies that model the kinds of reasoning doctors might have to do in practice. For instance, small groups of students might receive the following:

> On a nice day in the summer Henry (5 years old) returns from school and would like to have a cup of tea. The tea is soon made and poured, but by accident Henry gets the hot tea over his bare leg. Although his mother immediately holds the screaming Henry under a gentle jet of cold running water, his leg looks badly affected; he has burst blisters and the entire anterior side of his thigh is quite red. The doctor takes care of the wound and asks Henry to come to surgery the next day. Because the wound is patchy and locally covered with a whitish coating, Henry is then referred to the hospital. Despite optimal care, part of the wound (10cm x 10cm) has still not healed completely after three weeks. (Schmidt, 1993, p. 427)

In their groups, students discuss what they know about the problem, bringing in their prior knowledge and generating initial hypotheses. They also discuss what they do not know and need to learn, setting their own learning goals with the help of a facilitator. Students then study and research on their own. When the group reconvenes, they discuss what they have learned, refining their hypotheses and understanding of the initial problem, sometimes through a few cycles. Finally, they reflect on their learning process. For an elaborate example of this process with a facilitator's guide related to drug abuse, see Barone and Sattar (2009).

COACH-ON-THE-SIDE, NOT SAGE-ON-THE-STAGE

If you think of a teacher's role as primarily imparting accumulated knowledge, question-driven instruction will require a dramatic shift. The teacher's role here is to help students construct knowledge themselves by seeking, evaluating, and integrating different sources of information. The teacher should model good strategies for reasoning and learning, but without stealing students' opportunities to engage in those strategies. Good teachers ask good questions at the right time. For example, they might ask students to justify their claims with evidence or explain their reasoning (Hmelo-Silver, 2004). The teacher may also bring up additional points or questions, to ensure that important content is being covered. They might, for example, ask how bias could play into a medical diagnosis, if a group had not considered the issue. (Case-based lessons in law schools are similar, except the professor is on the stage, and playing a stronger hand in guiding student reasoning through a Socratic dialog, the mother of all question-asking pedagogies.)

Teaching a question-driven lesson is demanding because of the continual pedagogical decision making, often in real time. It is also exhilarating, like being a good basketball coach—you need to help your players do their best, but you cannot play the game yourself. You need to prepare them to work together and solve their own problems on the field. You can always provide a debriefing after, where you get to be the sage-on-the-stage again (see Chapter J).

SCAFFOLDING THE INQUIRY PROCESS

In professional endeavors that are open-ended and question driven, there are often explicit stages tuned to the nature of the profession. Design studios execute the stages of their design process, whereas scientists hypothesize, test, and revise. Experts are not slaves to these stages, and they can jump around as needed. However, novices, who are just learning to engage in the complexity of question-driven activities, may get lost and fail to see how the pieces fit together. It can help to scaffold the inquiry process itself.

One useful method is to offer an explicit representation of the idealized process, so students know where they are. Figure Q.1A shows one inquiry cycle (Sharples et al., 2014). It starts with finding a topic of inquiry and deciding on a specific question to address within that topic (with the help of the teacher). For example, one group of students wanted to know about noise pollution and focused their question on how it affected bird feeding. Students plan how they will approach the question and collect evidence (e.g., compare amount of food eaten on noisy and quiet days). After analyzing the evidence, students determine what they learned about their question and then share and reflect on the outcomes. The explicit cuing of the separate stages can be

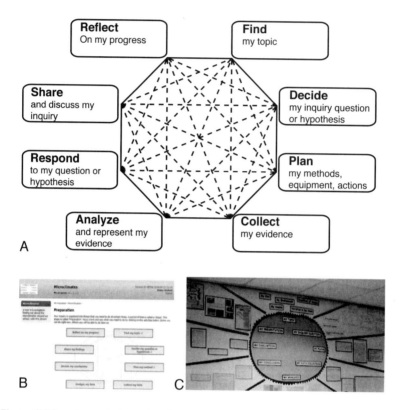

Figure Q.1. Inquiry cycle from the nQuire project. (A) The basic cycle. (B) A version in a computerized inquiry environment. (C) An interesting way to share and map student work products back to the cycle. (From Sharples, et al., 2014.)

annoying to experts, because the stages and moves have become obvious to them—does Figure Q1a really need to show all the intersecting lines to indicate that people can deviate from the implied sequence? For novices explicit visual support can be quite useful.

Some additional examples of K-12 question-driven cycles are the Web-Based Inquiry Science Environment (WISE; see http://wise.berkeley.edu) and the STAR.Legacy software (Schwartz, Brophy, Lin, & Bransford, 1999). Simpler visual organizations can also be helpful. Consider a whiteboard with the following columns (Hmelo-Silver, 2004).

FACTS	IDEAS	LEARNING ISSUES	ACTION PLAN

Imagine you were addressing the question of how to get more students to recycle. What kind of information do you think would go beneath each of the labels?

III. The Outcomes of Question-Based Learning

Evidence from medical education that compares PBL and traditional instruction suggests that both approaches lead students to perform at about the same level on tests of factual knowledge, though some studies show that the traditional approaches do slightly better on basic science content. The benefit of PBL shows up on applied problems that are more similar to what students will experience on the job (Hmelo-Silver, 2004). A problem-solving orientation during learning leads to improved abilities to solve related problems.

Medical students are high performing, which is how they get into medical school. They are also adults. To see how question-driven learning would influence typical children, researchers taught a diverse group of sixth graders about groupthink, a type of dysfunctional decision making that occurs in groups with low cognitive diversity and a tendency toward conformity. There were three conditions: Lecture, Problem-Based Learning in a Group, and Problem-Based Learning Individually (Wirkala & Kuhn, 2011). As can be guessed, the Lecture condition (ever the patsy) used lectures and class discussion to learn about groupthink. The two problem-based conditions used a central problem to drive the learning—a letter from a fictional NASA manager asking why a management team disregarded evidence in the *Columbia* space shuttle disaster and how to avoid similar problems in the future. Students first thought about the problem using their prior knowledge, then heard a condensed lecture describing groupthink, and then continued to solve the problem given the new information they had learned. The individual and group conditions differed in whether students worked alone or in small groups.

About nine weeks after the instruction, students completed an assessment. Below is one item:

> You are President Obama's head diplomat to Iran. Iran has a nuclear energy program and it's possible that they already have a nuclear bomb. Iran's president has expressed hostility toward the US, so diplomatic efforts must be handled with maximum competence and intelligence. Obama has made you director of a committee to plan negotiations with Iran. How would you select and run your committee, to make sure it is successful? Give as detailed an answer as you can. (p.1169)

The researchers wanted to see whether students would spontaneously apply what they had learned about groupthink (e.g., "…you want to make sure there is no Group Think … which is bad because you never really get to look at all the sides of an argument"). Other more traditional assessment items asked students to define and explain terms. On all assessments, students in the two problem-based conditions performed better than those in the Lecture condition. The Problem-Based Group and Individual conditions did not show any differences, which was surprising, given that many people take small group interaction as an important element in problem-based learning.

In addition to the transfer of content knowledge, do students also transfer high-level problem-solving skills from question-driven lessons to new contexts? There is some, though limited, evidence that the answer can be 'yes.' Hmelo-Silver (2004) points to studies of medical students, showing that they spontaneously applied a learned hypothesis-driven strategy when confronted with new problems. Research on anchored instruction found that students who went through the Jasper Woodbury curriculum were better able to break down complex problems into manageable subgoals (Cognition and Technology Group at Vanderbilt, 1992). They also showed improved attitudes toward mathematics, something that has also been seen in other studies of question-driven learning (Boaler, 2002). They were more likely to agree with statements like, "I see lots of uses for math outside of school," and "I like the challenge of solving complex problems that involve mathematics." They were less likely to agree with the statement, "Math tests scare me." These are promising findings. In contrast, students in control classrooms showed decreased affinity for math over time.

IV. Can People Learn to Teach Themselves with Question-Driven Learning?

It is rumored that Albert Einstein once said, "If I had an hour to solve a problem and my life depended on the solution, I would spend the first 55 minutes determining the proper question to ask, for once I know the proper question, I could solve the problem in less than five minutes." Learning to pose productive questions and then make the effort to answer those questions is a major goal of liberal arts education (see Chapter K). It is one of the reasons for all of those open-ended essays, where it is up to the student to generate the question and fashion the answer.

V. Risks of Question-Driven Approaches

Some scholars are concerned that question-driven learning is ineffective for early learning, because people do not have sufficient prior knowledge, and the problem-solving process is a drain on cognitive resources that could be used for learning instead. For instance, Kirschner, Sweller, and Clark (2006) highlight studies showing that minimally guided instruction is not as effective as worked examples. However, the minimally guided instruction studies used to make this argument did not include scaffolding and supports, such as skilled facilitators and cycles of inquiry, that are crucial to many forms of question-driven learning (Hmelo-Silver, Duncan, & Chinn, 2007). Nevertheless, without appropriate supports, early learners may choose poor questions, flounder and become overwhelmed, and fail to learn the intended content.

A second issue involves curricular coverage. Question-based learning takes time and offers less structured coverage because it unfolds based on student inquiry rather than a top-down organization. This can be mitigated by well-designed question-posing activities and resources. An additional solution is to use question-driven learning selectively rather than for everything.

A final issue is that an instructor needs to walk a narrow path to do question-driven learning well. With too little direction, students will not receive sufficient guidance. Solving problems is a good way to learn how to apply what one knows, but for students to gain new knowledge it is important to have resources to learn from. With too much direction, the teacher may undermine the point of question-asking lessons. A teacher may simplify a problem, telling his students the key questions and information they need.

VI. Examples of Good and Bad Use

Project-based learning shares many of the same characteristics as *problem*-based learning, except it emphasizes producing something. (Because of this, project-based learning also appears in Chapter M on making.) The Buck Institute for Education has gathered great examples of project-based learning that you can search for by grade and topic (see http://bie.org/project_search). Here is a project statement for an eleventh-grade economics class:

> Given new federal laws outlining "Smart Snacks" in schools, students need to reinvent the vending machines in order to make a profit to help support student extras, such as field trips, dances, & student events. Students will identify products that qualify under the new law, survey the student body for possible demand, analyze price points, contact vendors, and pitch the top 5 products they believe will post the most profit. (Baer, 2014)

Bad (too little support): The teacher gives students the project without providing additional supports or learning resources. Students rely exclusively on what they already know.

Bad (too much support): The teacher lays out all the steps students need to take to solve the problem in a worksheet. Students fill in the blanks with correct answers.

Good (just right support): The teacher provides support and learning resources to help students understand the core concepts, such as supply and demand, government regulation, and consumer behavior, as they address the driving question. Students determine the important constraints and how to seek and integrate information.

VII. References

Adams, L. T., Kasserman, J. E., Yearwood, A. A., Perfetto, G. A., Bransford, J. D., & Franks, J. J. (1988). Memory access: The effects of fact-oriented versus problem-oriented acquisition. *Memory and Cognition, 16*(2), 167–175.

Baer, M. (2014). Sample project: Are you buying what I'm vending? Buck Institute for Education. Retrieved February 1, 2015, from http://bie.org/object/document/are_you_buying_what_im_vending

Barone, E., & Sattar, P. (2009, November 8). Two problem-based learning cases: Methamphetamine. Creighton University School of Medicine. Retrieved February 1, 2015, from http://www.drugabuse.gov/sites/default/files/methamphetamine_0.pdf

Boaler, J. (2002). *Experiencing school mathematics: Traditional and reform approaches to teaching and their impact on student learning.* Mahwah, NJ: Erlbaum.

Cognition and Technology Group at Vanderbilt. (1992). The Jasper series as an example of anchored instruction: Theory, program description, and assessment data. *Educational Psychologist, 27*(3), 291–315.

Hmelo-Silver, C. E. (2004). Problem-based learning: What and how do students learn? *Educational Psychology Review, 16*(3), 235–266.

Hmelo-Silver, C. E., Duncan, R. G., & Chinn, C. A. (2007). Scaffolding and achievement in problem-based and inquiry learning: A response to Kirschner, Sweller, and Clark (2006). *Educational Psychologist, 42*(2), 99–107.

Kang, M. J., Hsu, M., Krajbich, I. M., Loewenstein, G., McClure, S. M., Wang, J. T. Y., & Camerer, C. F. (2009). The wick in the candle of learning: Epistemic curiosity activates reward circuitry and enhances memory. *Psychological Science, 20*(8), 963–973.

Kirschner, P. A., Sweller, J., & Clark, R. E. (2006). Why minimal guidance during instruction does not work: An analysis of the failure of constructivist, discovery, problem-based, experiential, and inquiry-based teaching. *Educational Psychologist, 41*(2), 75–86.

Konnikova, M. (2014, April 14). The surprising science of yawning. *New Yorker.*

Retrieved February 1, 2015, from http://www.newyorker.com/science/maria-konnikova/the-surprising-science-of-yawning

Schmidt, H. G. (1993). Foundations of problem⊠based learning: Some explanatory notes. *Medical Education, 27*(5), 422–432.

Schwartz, D. L., Brophy, S., Lin, X. D., & Bransford, J. D. (1999). Software for managing complex learning: An example from an educational psychology course. *Educational Technology Research and Development, 47*, 39–59.

Sharples, M., Scanlon, E., Ainsworth, S., Anastopoulou, S., Collins, T., Crook, C., . . . O'Malley, C. (2015). Personal inquiry: Orchestrating science investigations within and beyond the classroom. *Journal of the Learning Sciences, 24*(2), 308-341.

Wirkala, C., & Kuhn, D. (2011). Problem-based learning in K-12 education: Is it effective and how does it achieve its effects? *American Educational Research Journal, 48*(5), 1157–1186.

Q IS FOR QUESTION DRIVEN

What is the core learning mechanic?
Learning in the service of answering a driving question increases curiosity, purpose, attention, and well-connected memories and may develop problem-solving skills.

What is an example, and what is it good for?
As part of a unit on humans and the environment, a class investigates how noise pollution is affecting the wildlife around their school. The teacher supports students in constructing an answerable question, figuring out what they know and what they need to find out, and deciding how to evaluate and integrate different sources of information. Students are engaged with learning content from various disciplines, including science, math, and social studies.

Why does it work?
Question-driven learning draws on several useful mechanisms. Curiosity drives reward and motivation systems. Learning with a problem-solving orientation can help students apply what they have learned to solve problems in the future. A focusing question allows disparate information to build into a network of related ideas, which should support memory retrieval.

What problems does the core mechanic solve?
- Learners do not apply what they know.
  - A learner knows a lot of facts but does not realize they are relevant to solving problems.
  - Learners do not have effective strategies for approaching complex questions.
- Students are disengaged from class content.
  - A student thinks the purpose of learning in school is to do well on exams.
  - A student asks, "Why do I need to learn this?"
- Students are unable to inquire for themselves.
  - A student complains that he has not been told how to solve a novel problem.

Examples of how to use it
- Learners construct their own driving questions.
  - A science museum provides engaging materials for patrons to experiment with. A docent supports their question asking.

- Instructors organize learning around a driving question.
  - A government and economics class tries to solve a problem relevant to their town, such as how to lobby for reducing the speed limit in front of the school.
  - A medical school curriculum is organized around diagnosing patient cases.

Risks

- Learners can become overwhelmed and flounder in the problem-solving process.
- Instructors provide too much or too little support.
- Time constraints and the scope of curriculum make it challenging to fit in.

R
is for Reward

Motivating behavior

A REWARD IS a desirable outcome received in response to behavior. As might be expected, rewarding a behavior drives people to adopt that behavior. Punishing a behavior leads to the opposite. People often think about learning in terms of improved understanding. Another important outcome of learning involves simply taking on good behaviors. If only parents could get their teenagers to do homework instead of playing video games all the time!

Thorndike's law of effect summarizes the basic reinforcement story. People will repeat a behavior that leads to a desirable effect. People will not repeat a behavior that leads to an undesirable effect. The law of effect works regardless of rational processes. If you need some compelling evidence for the latter point, think of all the crazy superstitions in baseball. Aubrey Huff, a baseball player on the San Francisco Giants, wore a red thong to relieve the clubhouse stress of a pennant run. The team won and kept winning, so Huff wore the same red thong under his uniform for months.

A progression of appropriately applied rewards can produce complex behaviors. B. F. Skinner (1986), a major proponent of behaviorism, tells the story of nurturing art appreciation. Two undergraduates wanted to place a painting on their dormitory wall, but their roommate wanted to put up his sports awards. The undergraduates decided to change their roommate's behavior by rewarding pro-art behaviors surreptitiously. During a party, they paid a young woman to ask the roommate about art and to hang on his every word. They later took him to a museum and covertly dropped a $5 bill on the floor next to a painting he was observing. They also paid more attention to him when he discussed art. As the story goes, a month later the roommate had bought his first painting for the dorm room.

I. How Reward Works

There is a distinction between extrinsic and intrinsic rewards. *Extrinsic rewards* are not integral to a behavior and come after completion. Musicians do not play instruments using money, yet good musicians may receive money as a reward. In contrast, *intrinsic rewards* are integral to an activity and self-re-inforcing. Musicians can find that playing a piece of music is very rewarding, even if they do not receive any money.

SHAPING BEHAVIOR WITH EXTRINSIC REWARD

The major educational application of extrinsic reward involves shaping behavior. Shaping brings learners to the target behavior, so that the behavior can be reinforced. Suppose we want a chick to learn to face away from a fence. (The reason for this is immaterial; extrinsic reward will work regardless.) Our stubborn chick is unlikely to face away from the fence on its own. We need to shape or move its behavior toward the target, so we can finally reinforce the exact behavior we want. Figure R.1 shows the progression of shaping the behavior.

Shaping 1: A chick will peck the ground with natural variation. Whenever the chick pecks to the right, we deliver immediate positive reinforcement (e.g., food). We make the reinforcement immediate so we do not accidentally

Training a chick to keep its back to a fence.

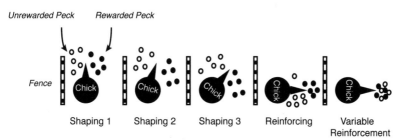

Figure R.1. Shaping behavior.

reward a behavior that could slip in during a delay. Proximal rewards work better for shaping behavior than delayed rewards.

Shaping 2: The chick now faces a little farther to the right on average. It randomly pecks around its new set point. Again, we reward pecks to the right. When it turns to the left, we do nothing. We could punish the chick for turning left, but it is unnecessary and stressful. Moreover, a punishing shock does not indicate the behavior the chick should do instead. It might just as well jump into the air as turn to the right. The same is true for people: punishment can stop a very specific behavior, but it does not help to replace it with a preferable behavior.

Shaping 3: We keep shaping the behavior, steering the chick rightward, until the chick finally faces the desired direction.

Reinforcing: Finally, we can reward the behavior we wanted all along. This period of reward further helps the chick differentiate whether the rewarded behavior is turning to the right or facing away from the fence. To stop the chick from turning in circles, the reinforcement only occurs directly ahead.

Variable Reinforcement: This part is nonintuitive. We do not reward the target behavior every time. Instead, we use variable reinforcement. By using occasional rewards, the chick learns that even if it does not get a reward for the behavior one time, continued behavior will eventually lead to reward. Variable reinforcement helps prevent the extinction of a behavior when it goes unrewarded. Surprisingly, variable reinforcement also leads to more vigorous behavior than steady reinforcement. Need proof? Think of people sitting at slot machines for hours.

SUSTAINING ENGAGEMENT THROUGH INTRINSIC REWARD

Intrinsic reward leads to intrinsic motivation, such that people pursue activities that produce enjoyable mental states. They pursue activities because of the enjoyment of the activity itself, not because of the promise of external reward. Different people find different things intrinsically rewarding. A cook likes making a good meal, whereas a sports fan likes cheering a good game. One ideal is personalizing instruction to match each student's individual interests. This is a good idea, but can be hard to achieve when there are many different students, each of whom finds personal relevance and interest in different things. Fortunately, we can rely on situations that nearly everyone finds intrinsically motivating. Ryan and Deci (2000) have proposed three foundational intrinsic motivators: autonomy, competence, and social relatedness. *Autonomy* relates to a feeling of control over your own decisions and actions. The authors found that classrooms where students had more autonomy showed higher levels of curiosity, desire for challenge, and sustained motivation than did classrooms where teachers were very directive and con-

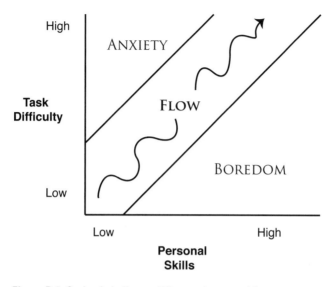

Figure R.2. Optimal challenge. When tasks are neither too easy nor too hard, people reach a peak state of intrinsic motivation called "flow."

trolling. *Competence* relates to the feeling that one is capable of achieving desired goals and gaining mastery. Positive feedback that one's free-throw percentage is improving can motivate further practice. *Social relatedness* taps into the human desire to connect with others (see Chapter B). While relatedness is not necessary for intrinsic motivation (many solitary activities are inherently motivating), it can help support motivation. For example, many hobbyists find the opportunity to share the fruits of their labor, such as a painting or a brewed beer, a strong source of motivation (see Chapter M). Activities that foster any or all of these feelings will be highly motivating because they tap into human psychological needs.

Optimal challenge is an especially important intrinsic motivator, because it leads people to engage in increasingly difficult tasks from which they can learn. As shown in Figure R.2, tasks that are too far away from people's abilities cause anxiety, whereas tasks that are too easy become boring. (This is not to say that all easy tasks are boring—knitting a familiar pattern over and over can be a satisfying activity in the context of a good chat with friends.) Tasks that require current skills but are also just ahead of one's skills are exceptionally engaging. Optimal challenge leads to a state that Csikszentmihalyi (1990) has labeled *flow*, characterized by complete absorption in the task at hand, during which people often lose a sense of time. Rock climbers famously enter flow states, but we all have experienced pockets of locked-in concentration where we suddenly discover that thirty minutes somehow disappeared. There is little evidence that the flow state improves learning, but the thirst for optimal challenge will drive people to new challenges from which they can learn.

Other things people generally find intrinsically motivating include good stories, fantasy, and the opportunity to make choices, such as customizing one's character in a video game (Malone, 1981). Giving students a choice of which activity to work on first can provide a little motivational boost.

II. How to Use Reward to Enhance Learning

Creating learning experiences that are intrinsically rewarding is a desirable goal. However, in some cases extrinsic reward may be more effective. *Where reason and internal motivation fail, reward can work.* You may believe that you can reason with your new puppy, but you cannot—rewards work better. Even when you *do* understand the reasons for a behavior, such as exercising, you may be unable to motivate yourself. The prudent application of reinforcement can work wonders for driving behavior change.

ACHIEVABLE GOALS

The tenets for shaping behavior and for sustaining flow converge on the same insight: provide learners a ramp of small incremental tasks that are slightly ahead of their current behaviors. Skinner (1986) introduced the concept of programmed instruction: a computer presents problems in a sequence of incremental difficulty, with reinforcement for succeeding at each step. This format is still in great use among educational computer games, where students answer problems at one level, and when they begin to exhibit mastery, the computer introduces a slightly new set of problems. Games like these can help students to master key behaviors, for example, saying "ten" when seeing 2 x 5. (Of course, reinforcement, in and of itself, does not help students learn why 10 is the right answer.) The importance of small achievable goals also applies to lifestyle changes. The goal of losing ten pounds is admirable, but one needs behaviors to reward along the way, such as walking ten more minutes each day. It is important to establish proximal, achievable goals that merit reward and that contribute to a path toward the final goal.

REWARD THE RIGHT BEHAVIORS

Reward is very specific in its action, so it is important to reward exactly the right behavior. Imagine a lesson in Spanish, where students receive the English word *four* and receive points or other rewards when they choose the corresponding Spanish word from a list: (a) cuatro, (b) uno, (c) tres, (d) dos.

Selecting the word from a list is not really the behavior of interest, but that is what we would be rewarding. We want students to be able to state or write *cuatro*, not pick it from a list, so we should arrange conditions where learners can produce the precise behavior of interest, not a proxy for that behavior. In this regard, open response items are better than selection items, unless the ultimate behavioral goal is to make selections (e.g., in preparation for a standardized test).

Open response items can be more difficult for students. In this case, it is OK to show or tell a student how to give the right answer early on. Skinner claimed, "We do not learn by doing, as Aristotle maintained; we learn when what we do has reinforcing consequence. To teach is to arrange such consequences" (1986, p. 107). You want students to do the behavior so you can reward it; later you can withdraw the supports for producing the right behavior.

USE THE RIGHT REWARDS

The most powerful rewards are *primary reinforcers* (also known as unconditioned reinforcers, because people do not need to learn that they are rewards—they instinctively experience reward). Among other things, they include food, drink, and affection. These basic rewards were presumably evolutionarily important to survival. Educators should not use primary reinforcers, because they can be coercive. Researchers, for example, are not allowed to use primary reinforcements with children; they cannot reward with food or punish by withdrawing affection.

Instead, it is more ethical to apply *secondary reinforcers*, such as grades, points, and badges. Secondary reinforcers (also known as conditioned reinforcers) become rewarding because of their association with other reward experiences. "Good dog!" can become a conditioned reinforcer for a dog if the expression was originally associated with the delivery of food shortly after. In the opening example, art became rewarding for the undergraduate because of its association with other rewards (money and attention).

An advantage of secondary reinforcers is that they are cheap, easily delivered, and nondisruptive. One simple strategy is to create a token economy. Learners receive a token, such as points or stars, upon completing a desirable behavior. Later, when the learners have accrued sufficient tokens, they can be exchanged for desirable rewards, such as extra time on the playground or more powerful characters in a video game. Frequent flyer programs create highly effective token economies. People pay more and take less desirable flights to gain more program miles—miles that often have less cash-in value than the financial and misery burden required to gain them in the first place.

Behavior change programs often rely on rewards to help people stop smoking, lose weight, and change other damaging behaviors. An important caution is to avoid short-term solutions that inadvertently reinforce the undesirable behavior. If you stop a young child from crying with candy, you have inadvertently just rewarded crying, so it will occur again later. If you use candy now and again, you are providing variable reinforcement—the crying will become more vigorous and even more difficult to stop in the future. A more complex version of this story involves classroom management. Paying extra attention to misbehaving children inadvertently rewards them for their misbehavior, because receiving attention is very rewarding. Wielkiewicz offers a golden rule of behavior management in classrooms: "Ignore, as much as possible, all minor annoyances and misbehavior, and spend as much time as possible giving positive attention to students who are behaving correctly" (1995, p. 5).

ENTICING ENVIRONMENTS

Good video games are a wonder of reward. They employ multiple extrinsic reinforcement schemes. These include several simultaneous point schemes, juicy graphics, and rewards of new powers and levels. They further use variable reinforcement so that players sometimes lose but eventually always win. If that were not enough, they also include multiple intrinsic reward schemes, including narrative, fantasy, customization (choice), and optimal challenges. The powerful motivation schemes of video games have led to the idea of "gamifying" otherwise unappealing tasks (Reeves & Read, 2009). For instance, call centers have a terrible employee turnover problem—nobody wants a job where strangers yell at them on the phone. One solution could be a rich video game where answering calls is part of the game. Employees receive points, complete quests, and advance levels by effectively answering calls.

It is worth noting that a gamification strategy may not be sufficient for academic learning. Reinforcement is an evolutionarily old learning mechanism that applies to animals, including humans. It drives behavior, not understanding, and an education composed solely of reinforced behaviors may yield narrower results than desired. Even so, creating an environment that is rich in opportunities for extrinsic and intrinsic reward creates a good context for incorporating the techniques from other chapters of this book. For instance, one might make a fun game that involves rewarding analogies (see Chapter A).

III. The Outcomes of Reward

The prospect of reward is motivating—it leads people to approach an activity and remain engaged. The very fact that people are engaged in a new activity is evidence of behavioral learning because their behavior has changed (they are engaged in a new activity). By using variable reinforcement, rewards can lead to the repetition of desirable behaviors, even in the absence of regular reward.

The action of reward is very specific. It creates an association between a specific behavior and a specific situation of reward. These types of associations tend not to generalize, so rewarded behavior does not transfer very well to new situations. Returning to our chick in Figure R.1, when the chick sees a different fence, it may not turn its back to it, and the chick will definitely not turn its back to a fire hydrant.

To appreciate the specificity of the association between behavior and the rewarding context, consider extinguishing an acquired habit. People who quit smoking need to break the association of the smoking reward with each situation in which they regularly smoked. For instance, people may have a habit of smoking after their morning coffee. They manage to break this association, so they no longer feel the urge to smoke immediately after morning coffee. Next, they need to break the association between smoking and their mid-morning work break, and then their lunchtime smoke, and so on. With concerted effort, they may break each of the associations between daily situations and the reward of smoking. They will declare themselves free of smoking. Alas, when they go visit their family, suddenly the smoking urge comes back full force, because they always used to smoke on the porch. One does not quit smoking in general—one quits smoking for each context. Returning to using reward to form a new behavior, the implication is that *you often need to reward the behavior in each context where you would like it to occur.*

IV. Can People Learn to Teach Themselves with Reward?

People can create environments that shape their own behaviors. For example, early in his career, an author of this book could not motivate himself to write, which he desperately needed to do to keep his job. To solve the problem, he set aside three hours each Friday evening to write. After working for those three hours, whether or not he wrote anything useful, he had a scotch and a steak, which he found fabulously rewarding. Fast forward twenty years, and the author is writing a book.

Most people know self-talk strategies for maintaining their will power: "I can make positive choices about my eating." Alas, it is exactly at those times when temptation is greatest that rationality is weakest. Establishing reinforcement systems in the environment beforehand may be more effective. In a simple study, researchers taught high school students techniques for self-reward and goal maintenance, such as posting reminders, choosing achievable goals, creating a point system for self-reward, and asking their parents to reward them when they accomplished a goal (Oppezzo & Schwartz, 2013). The students then adopted the goal of increasing their intake of fruits and vegetables. Three weeks later, the students had increased their intake by one to two servings per day. In contrast, a second group of high school students who learned self-talk strategies (e.g., self-directed pep talks, blocking their own excuses) did not improve their fruit and vegetable intake.

V. Risks of Reward

People love reward. If you were as rich and powerful as Midas, you might think you could use your gold to make people behave the way you want. But nothing is ever so simple—there are specific situations where there is a hidden cost of reward.

Reward may backfire when people already find something intrinsically motivating. The promise of external rewards can commandeer those activities, so they become less satisfying in their own right. A classic study beautifully illustrates this risk (Lepper, Greene, & Nisbett, 1973). The study examined nursery school children's intrinsic motivation to draw with colored felt-tip markers, which were novel at the nursery school. To create the experimental conditions, each child met with a researcher in one of three conditions. In the Contracted for Reward condition, children heard they would receive a good

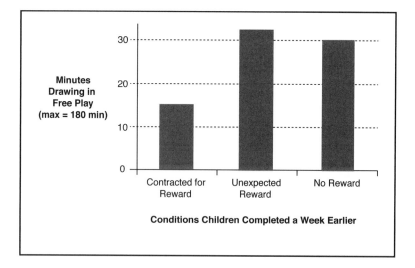

Figure R.3. The hidden cost of reward. Nursery school children who had an initial interest in drawing with felt-tip markers lost that interest if they had earlier agreed to draw for a reward. Children who received an unexpected reward or no reward maintained their interest in drawing with the markers (based on data from Lepper, Greene, & Nisbett, 1973).

player certificate and gold ribbon for making drawings with the markers. They then drew for six minutes and received the good player award. In the Unexpected Reward condition, children did not know they would receive the good player reward for drawing, but they received one after six minutes of drawing. Finally, in the No Reward condition, the children did not receive any award for their drawing and never knew other children had. A week later, the researchers set out the felt-tip markers at one of many activity tables during free play and measured how long the children chose to draw.

Figure R.3 shows that the children in the Contracted for Reward condition spent about half as much time drawing with the markers as the children in the No Reward condition. The reward caused them to lose interest in drawing with the novel markers when it was no longer for a reward! Interestingly, the children who received an unexpected reward maintained their motivation to draw. In fact, children who had lower initial intrinsic motivation for drawing increased their interest in drawing after receiving the unexpected reward. Providing a reward for a job well done increases people's motivation for tasks they did not initially find interesting. On the other hand, telling people that they will receive a reward for engaging a task they already enjoy can undermine their original motivations.

The risk of reward is greatest for people just beginning a new activity. People with more relevant experience have a deeper wellspring of resilient intrinsic motivations to draw upon. Professional artists contract for work and yet still find artwork intrinsically motivating.

A second cost of reward is a narrow cognitive focus, which undermines creativity and exploration. When people learn there is a reward for doing an activity, the activity becomes a means to an end. People want to finish the task rather than understand it more deeply by exploring alternatives (a key step in creativity). For instance, the children in the Contracted for Reward condition described above created lower-quality drawings during their six minutes with the experimenter than the other children did. The negative effect of a promised reward on creativity has been replicated many times with young and old (e.g., Amabile, Hennessy, & Grossman, 1986). Using prospective financial incentives to increase employee innovation is a bad idea. (For an engaging presentation of this concept, see the TED talk by Pink 2009.) However, reinforcing specific strategies that increase the chances of creativity (e.g., walking) may be an effective approach, because people will engage in a behavior that has the side effect of producing creative ideas (Oppezzo & Schwartz, 2014).

A more familiar risk is that people can be in thrall to reward, as found with overeating, gambling, and playing video games. Numerous behavior change techniques can help. If your child plays video games way too much for your taste, try to develop rewarding (or rewarded) alternatives. However, if you feel a person's compulsion is interfering with their abilities to function in everyday life, it is important to seek professional help.

VI. Examples of Good and Bad Use

A good example involves physical activity sensors, such as pedometers, that automatically record body movement. People can log onto a website (or smartphone) to track their activity. The websites provide bountiful rewards early for simple accomplishments (e.g., a badge for achieving 5,000 steps in a day). The setup makes it very clear what behaviors cause the reward. To shape more exercise, the website slowly requires more activity to achieve the next reward (e.g., a badge for achieving 10,000 steps in a day). In addition to shaping behavior, the scheme employs variable reinforcement, because people do not always achieve rewarded levels of activity. Variable reinforcement drives more vigorous behavior.

An entertaining but bad use of reward occurs when the learner turns the table and shapes the behavior of the reward provider. An apocryphal story describes a teacher in a downward spiral of classroom management. She ended up climbing on a desk, shouting at the students to be quiet. This would seem to be a case of the children shaping their teacher's behavior, not vice versa. When you give your dog a treat for sitting, pay close attention to whether the dog sat on your command, or whether it sat to make you give it a treat.

VII. References

Amabile, T. M., Hennessey, B. A., & Grossman, B. S. (1986). Social influences on creativity: The effects of contracted-for reward. *Journal of Personality and Social Psychology, 50*(1), 14–23.

Csikszentmihalyi, M. (1990). *Flow: The psychology of optimal experience.* New York: Harper and Row.

Lepper, M. R., Greene, D., & Nisbett, R. E. (1973). Undermining children's intrinsic interest with extrinsic reward: A test of the "overjustification" hypothesis. *Journal of Personality and Social Psychology, 28*(1), 129–137.

Malone, T. W. (1981). Toward a theory of intrinsically motivating instruction. *Cognitive Science, 4*, 333–369.

Oppezzo, M. A., & Schwartz, D. L. (2013). A behavior change perspective on self-regulated learning with teachable agents. In R. Azevedo & V. Alevan (Eds.), *International handbook of metacognition and learning* (pp. 485–500). New York: Springer.

Oppezzo, M., & Schwartz, D. L. (2014) Give your ideas some legs: the positive effect of walking on creative thinking. *Journal of Experimental Psychology: Learning, Memory and Cognition, 40*(4) 1142-1152.

Pink, D. (2009). The puzzle of motivation. TED Conferences. Retrieved, November 24, 2015 from http://www.ted.com/talks/dan_pink_on_motivation

Reeves, B., & Read, J. L. (2009). *Total engagement: Using games and virtual worlds to change the way people work and businesses compete.* Harvard, MA: Harvard Business Press.

Ryan, R. M., & Deci, E. L. (2000). Self-determination theory and the facilitation of intrinsic motivation, social development, and well-being. *American Psychologist, 55*, 68–78.

Skinner, B. F. (1986). Programmed instruction revisited. *Phi Delta Kappan, 68*, 103–110.

Wielkiewicz, R. M. (1995). *Behavior management in the schools: Principles and procedures* (2nd ed.). Boston: Allyn and Bacon.

R IS FOR REWARD

What is the core learning mechanic?

Rewarding a behavior leads people (and animals) to repeat that behavior. People can learn new behaviors by rewarding successive approximations until they achieve the desired the behavior.

What is an example, and what is it good for?

Reward can lead people to behaviors they might not otherwise engage in. A teacher wants a child to complete his homework, but the child never does it, so the teacher cannot deliver a motivating reward. To shape the child's behavior, the teacher gives a red star if he turns in a paper with just his name. After a few times, the teacher gives a green star if he turns in a paper with his name and one completed problem. The teacher then provides a gold star for turning in five problems, and so forth.

Why does it work?

Rewards, whether delivered as a prize or generated through internal satisfaction, motivate people to repeat rewarded behaviors in similar situations.

What problems does the core mechanic solve?
- People cannot motivate themselves to complete a behavior.
  - Young children may not understand why they should do something.
  - Adults may know that a behavior is desirable but still cannot make themselves do it.
- Students exhibit low interest in completing a sequence of instruction.
  - Students do not finish their math assignments.
- People need to change their behavior.
  - Classroom management is not working.

Examples of how to use it
- A teacher creates a token economy, where students receive points for bringing in homework. When students have accrued enough points, they can exchange them for extra playtime.
- A computer program provides students with x1 arithmetic problems, such as 1 x 1, 1 x 2, 1 x 3. A student's computer character grows taller for each three correct answers in a row. Once the students master these problems, the program introduces x2 problems, such as 1 x 2, 2 x 2, 3 x 2. For each five correct answers in a row, the program unlocks new pieces of clothing that the student can use to customize the computer character.

Risks

- A reward makes a behavior a means to an end—the reward.
  - Learners may engage in the behavior without any attempts at understanding, because they just want to complete the task and earn the reward.
  - When learners find a new task motivating in its own right, offering a reward for engaging in that task can supplant their natural interest, causing them to lose motivation when rewards are no longer offered.
  - The prospect of a reward can cause people to become less creative, because a single-minded drive toward the reward prevents them from exploring alternatives.
- The learning may not transfer to new situations.
  - A student learns to persevere for a reward in sports, but does not persevere in history class.
  - A person trying to quit smoking learns to break the habit of smoking after coffee, but still feels an unescable urge after lunch.

S is for Self-Explanation

Going beyond the information given

SELF-EXPLANATION IS A method of self-instruction that involves "talking it through." It supports learning from texts, diagrams, and other expository materials. Self-explanation is not about learning to read letters and words. It is about building an understanding of what an author is trying to communicate.

Words cannot dictate their own meaning. The meaning of words depends on how we interpret them. Puns are a great example. See if you can find an unintended (and dark) interpretation for each of the following actual newspaper headlines we collected over the years:

- Drunk Gets Nine Months in Violin Case
- Survivor of Siamese Twins Joins Parents
- Iraqi Head Seeks Arms
- New Study of Obesity Looks for Larger Test Group
- Kids Make Nutritious Snacks
- Miners Refuse to Work after Death (Schwartz, 1999)

Holy double entendre!

The significance of interpretation is not confined to hidden meanings; it extends to all forms of symbolic communication. Mathematics, well-written expository texts, and even diagrams depend on interpretation.

Here are two sentences from a top-selling textbook that describe the human heart:

> The septum divides the heart lengthwise into two sides. The right side pumps blood to the lungs, and the left side pumps blood to the other parts of the body.

Sometimes people do not invest the effort to develop solid interpretations. For instance, less effective readers do not slow down to connect these two sentences; they treat them as discrete facts. A good way to spot ineffective readers is that they maintain the same reading speed regardless of the content. In contrast, here is the transcript of an effective reader who takes the time to self-explain the text:

> So the septum is a divider so that the blood doesn't get mixed up. So the right side is to the lungs, and the left side is to the body. So the septum is like a wall that divides the heart into two parts . . . it kind of like separates it so that the blood doesn't get mixed up. (Chi, De Leeuw, Chiu, & LaVancher, 1994, p. 454)

This reader introduces an idea to connect the two sentences. The sentences do not say that the septum prevents the mixing of the blood; the reader did this. *If texts and diagrams stated every possible connection between ideas, they would become overwhelming.* It is up to the readers to make those connections.

Self-explanation is a constructive process. People build knowledge that goes beyond the information given. For example, self-explainers generate inferences to fill in missing information. They also make connections to their own knowledge (e.g., the lungs oxygenate blood). Ineffective readers do not take these extra efforts to construct an interpretation of a text. If anything, they merely paraphrase or reread sentences. Ineffective readers are learning a text, whereas effective readers are learning *from* a text.

Good self-explainers also monitor their comprehension. They continually test whether they can explain how a sentence or diagrammatic component fits into the whole. In the original study of self-explanation, Chi, Bassok, Lewis, Reimann, and Glaser (1989) noted that self-explainers detected nine times as many comprehension failures as ineffective readers. The self-explainers did not have more comprehension failures than the others did; they just recognized these failures because they were actively asking themselves,

"How does this sentence fit what I know and have read so far?" Given the recognition of comprehension failure, they can take steps to repair their lack of understanding.

Self-explanation requires metacognition. *Metacognition* involves explicitly monitoring and regulating how one thinks and learns—it is thinking about one's thinking. When reading, people ideally monitor their understanding by self-explaining. If they find they cannot put the text together, they regulate their reading by slowing down and looking back to earlier sentences to see if they can figure out how their earlier interpretations were incorrect.

Self-explanation brings a host of benefits associated with good understanding, including improved abilities to answer relevant questions that go beyond the exact words found in the text. For example, the self-explainer of the heart passage would easily answer the question, "Why is the distribution of oxygen to the body less efficient when there is a hole in the septum?"

I. How Self-Explanation Works

To understand how self-explanation works, we need to take a brief detour to the topic of mental models. A *mental model* is an internal representation of the world that people consult to solve problems. For instance, when moving to a new city, people typically start with an impoverished model of the street system. They may rely on a written list of turns to get from one place to another. Over time, however, people naturally build up a rich model of the streets. They can estimate the distance between two locations even if they have never traveled between them specifically. For navigation, people build a mental model that is something like a map that they can consult from a bird's eye view.

When reading a text, people also construct mental models. Consider the following two sentences:

A frog sat on a log. A fish swam under the log.

Imagine you have read many sentence pairs like these. Sometime afterward, you answer questions about what you have read. One question might ask, "Did you read the sentence, 'A fish swam under the frog?'" (Do not look back.) If you are like many people, you would answer yes. (You can look back now.) People make this mistake because they rely on the mental model they constructed from the sentences, not on the sentences themselves (Bransford, Barclay, & Franks, 1972). This type of memory error is a very typical result of a good understanding. When people understand what they have read, they tend to show memory for the gist rather than the verbatim words. They are remembering their mental model and not the precise words that led them to build the model. Testing students for an author's specific choice of words in an expository text is an ineffective way to assess whether the students have understood what they read.

In the preceding examples, people naturally create mental models. However, many expository materials require explicit efforts to build a coherent mental model. Self-explanation is a technique that fosters this explicit effort. While reading a text or interpreting a diagram, readers try to integrate each new piece of information into their growing mental model. Read the following sentences to appreciate how this works:

1. People with a fever have a higher body temperature.
2. The heat makes it difficult for bacteria to survive.
3. The body heats up by constricting the veins close to the skin.
4. Constricted veins carry less blood.
5. Blood cools when it is near the surface of the skin.
6. Without blood near the skin, people feel cold and shiver.

Effective self-explainers will evaluate each sentence against their growing mental model. Figure S.1 provides a possible schematic for sentences 3–5. For sentence 3, the student uses her prior knowledge that friction causes heat. The student quickly discards this option when reading sentence 4 and applying a chain of reasoning. Sentence 5, which explains that blood cools near the skin, is the key to making the model. Constricted veins reduce

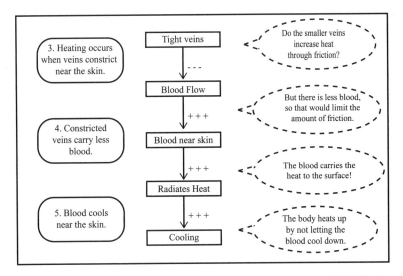

Figure S.1. An example of how people go from text to a mental model with the help of self-explanation.

blood flow to the surface, and therefore, there is less blood at the surface to cool down. By thinking through the model, the student realizes that the body does not produce more heat to make a fever. Instead, it shuts off cooling mechanisms, which yields the same effect.

Sentence 6 is interesting, because it could present a paradox. The body heats up, but people feel cold. An ineffective reader is likely to miss the potential conflict between sentences 1 and 6. A good reader notices the paradox and appreciates that it is probably the result of a comprehension failure. We leave it to the reader to self-explain the resolution to the paradox.

It is amazing just how much people must bring to bear to understand a text. There are four main moves:

- Appreciating that the goal of reading is to construct a mental model.
- Connecting the expository information with one's prior knowledge.
- Finding ways to connect separate sentences into a coherent mental model.
- Monitoring whether there are gaps or inconsistencies in one's model.

II. How to Use Self-Explanation to Enhance Learning

Self-explanation is a good complement to instruction that depends on expository materials. It has proven effective for topics that describe systems in the world (e.g., biology, physics) and topics that involve the execution of procedures (e.g., computer programming, geometry proofs).

Most instruction takes a direct approach to fostering self-explanation. A teacher explains the principles of self-explanation, complemented with examples, and then provides students with question frames to use while studying. For instance, King (1994) advocates presenting students with three principles: (1) use one's own words, (2) emphasize how and why over what, when, and where, and (3) connect incoming ideas to prior knowledge. For prompts during reading, King suggests sentence frames, for example, (a) How are X and Y similar? (b) What would happen if . . . ? (c) How does X tie in with Y, which I learned before?

Another example of a direct approach comes from a study that taught bank apprentices how to calculate interest via worked examples (Renkl, Stark, Gruber, & Mandl, 1998). A worked example shows the steps someone took to solve a problem (see Chapter W). The researchers asked students to stop after each step to write down the goal achieved by the step (e.g., "Multiplying by the percent indicates how much money was earned"). Instead of simply memorizing the steps to calculate interest, the apprentices constructed a ratio-nale for each step. Compared with control students who received the same worked examples without prompts to explain, the self-explainers were better able to apply their learning to new types of problems. A computerized sys-tem to teach geometry produced similar results when students simply selected self-explanations from a drop-down menu (Aleven & Koedinger, 2002).

There are also less direct (and less time-intensive) approaches that create a need to know and that orient students toward sense making while read-ing. They often involve presenting a driving question before engaging in the materials (see Chapter Q). For instance, in one study (Mayer, Dow, & Mayer, 2003), students learned about a battery-operated motor from an inter-active video. Some students received a question beforehand and heard that they should gather information so they could answer their guiding question. Examples of questions included, "What would you do to increase the speed of the motor?" and "What would you do to increase the reliability of an electric motor?" Compared with students who did not receive questions beforehand, these students later performed much better on novel problems. To design a good question, it is important that the answer depend on an integrated men-tal model rather than the mere retention of specific facts. For instance, for the fever sentences above, one might use the question, "How can people have a fever but still feel cold?" because the answer requires integrating across mul-tiple sentences. In contrast, "Do constricted veins carry more or less blood?" is ineffective because it simply asks students to remember what was stated by a single sentence.

III. The Outcomes of Self-Explanation

The signature learning outcomes have to do with the mental models that result from self-explanation. One outcome is that people can draw inferences about new, relevant problems. For instance, people can better answer what-if questions that describe hypothetical system changes. Given a passage about the food chain, students should be able to infer that when the grass supply on a savannah decreases, the lion population suffers, even though the passage never directly talks about the relationship between lions and grass.

A second outcome of a good mental model is that people can learn sub-sequent, related information more effectively. A fun example comes from a study that had people learn to operate a control panel shown in Figure S.2 (Kieras & Bovair, 1984). In the mental model condition, students learned that the panel controlled a phaser bank. The research was back in the day when *Star Trek* was a very popular television show, and there was invariably a

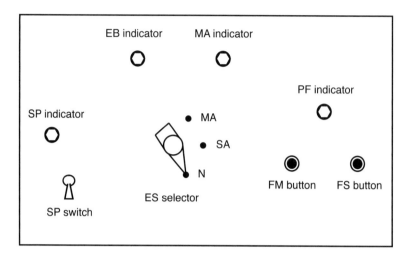

Figure S.2. A control panel for a phaser bank. People had to learn how to use the indicator lights and knobs to achieve ten different outcomes. People who had a mental model of the device that the panel controls learned the procedures more effectively. (From Kieras and Bovair, 1984.)

scene where the crew of the Starship *Enterprise* had to fire phasers at enemy ships. The students in the mental model condition received a passage explaining the device that connected to the switches and indicator lights. For example, they might read, "When the ship's power switch (SP) is turned on, power is drawn from the ship into one of the energy accumulators (EB or MA) . . ." The control condition did not receive any help in developing a model of the device controlled by the panel—they just saw the panel.

Afterward both groups received identical procedural instructions. For instance, "When the SP indicator comes on, flip the SP switch. Then, if the MA light comes on, set the ES selector to MA . . ." Participants would then try to execute a set of instructions. If they made a mistake, they would repeat until they got it right. They would then move to the next of ten total procedures.

The results were definitive. People in the model condition took about 3.2 minutes to learn the procedures, compared with 4.5 minutes for the control condition (28 percent faster). When tested a week later, the model participants were also 10 percent more accurate and 17 percent faster at executing the procedures. Thus, a good model helps people learn new material better.

The participants in the model condition were also 400 percent better at choosing the most efficient procedure when more than one was applicable. This is a useful finding. Trainers often lament the brittleness and lack of flexibility of their trainees' knowledge. Ironically, the trainers may be at fault: they may focus so tightly on ensuring that employees learn the procedures that they neglect helping them build up a strong mental model. This is a natural tendency. If people need to learn safety procedures, it is paramount that they learn them. But, there is a difference between memorizing a procedure and understanding it—self-explanation fosters the latter, which is important if there is any expectation that trainees will need to use their learning flexibly. Of course, model building and self-explanation take time, which is an important counter consideration. The mental model students may have learned more, but they also spent 20 extra minutes to build a mental model from the initial passage on the phaser device, before they received the procedural instruction.

IV. Can People Learn to Teach Themselves with Self-Explanation?

Self-explanation is primarily a tool for learning on one's own, so yes, people can learn to use it. It addresses a number of ubiquitous learning problems, including reading without comprehension (e.g., you reach the end of a page and realize you do not know what it said), reading to memorize rather than learn (e.g., searching for the bolded textbook words), and dealing with poorly written texts (e.g., some instruction manuals).

A critical first step is letting people know the goal is to build a mental model. A wonderful example comes from research with six- and seven-year-olds (Glenberg, Gutierrez, Levin, Japuntich, & Kaschak, 2004). The children read a series of simple sentences and moved figurines to match each sentence. For instance, when the children read, "The father went to bed," they would physically put the father figurine into a little bed. They did this for several passages. Afterward, the children in an Imagine condition learned that they should try to imagine doing the same thing in their head when reading. Creating the physical models of the texts helped them understand the kind of model they were supposed to make in their heads. The control children did not receive this key tip. The children in both conditions then received a new passage to read some time later. The Imagine children remembered more of the new passage and could better answer questions about the relative locations of the protagonists. Simply knowing that you are supposed to make a mental model can go a long way for learning from a text, but it is not something that children of this age (and older) spontaneously do.

The second step is to help readers learn self-explanation strategies. These strategies come from analyses of effective readers. To teach the strategies, it is useful to provide a social model of what self-explanation looks like in action. For instance, one training program with college students augmented self-explanation instruction with an opportunity to watch a video of expert self-explainers (McNamara, 2004). The students' task was to identify which of six strategies the model self-explainer was using for any given sentence: checking comprehension, paraphrasing, elaborating, using logic, predicting what the text will say next, and bridging between sentences. Lower-achieving students who received this training learned more from a future passage than students who received no training at all. (Presumably, the high-achieving college students did not show an effect of the training, because they already knew how to self-explain.)

Similarly, researchers asked college students to watch videos of effective self-explainers in the context of learning computer programming (Bielaczyc, Pirolli, & Brown, 1995). During the practice period, the researchers applied a graduated prompting scheme. If students did not self-explain, a researcher reminded them to self-explain. If they self-explained ineffectively, the researcher told the relevant strategy. If this did not work, the researcher modeled the strategy. Compared with a no-training group, students who received the training learned more from a future written lesson on programming. They also exhibited the relevant self-explanation strategies at nearly the double the rate of the control group.

V. Risks of Self-Explanation

There are three primary risks to teaching self-explanation. The first is that self-explanation is effortful and time-consuming—knowing what to do does not mean one will do it. Sometimes a text itself can trigger spontaneous sense making—a whodunit story can cause people to put together the clues of the sentences. Other times the text offers no trigger. Without strong cues, deciding when to use self-explanation is further complicated by the fact that sometimes it is just better to copy what one is told rather than sink the time into understanding. For example, when reading that the Starship *Enterprise* is traveling ten times the speed of light, is it really worth trying to figure out how that's possible? Cracking the problem of how to get people to develop an effortful habit, and wisely choose when to apply it, would constitute an advance in learning theory.

The second risk is that people may not have sufficient prior knowledge to self-explain a passage. In nearly all studies that encourage self-explanation, people's prior knowledge of the topic predicts their learning better than whether they received training in self-explanation. Without prior knowledge, it is hard to build a mental model. Consider the following passage:

> The procedure is actually quite simple. First you arrange things into different groups. Of course, one pile may be sufficient depending on how

much there is to do. If you have to go somewhere else due to lack of facilities that is the next step, otherwise you are pretty well set. It is important not to overdo things. That is, it is better to do too few things at once than too many. In the short run this may not seem important but complications can easily arise. A mistake can be expensive as well. At first the whole procedure will seem complicated. Soon, however, it will become just another facet of life. It is difficult to foresee any end to the necessity for this task in the immediate future, but then one never can tell. After the procedure is completed one arranges the materials into different groups again. Then they can be put into their appropriate places. (Bransford & Johnson, 1972)

You can probably interpret individual sentences, but you cannot self-explain your way to a model of what is going on. This is because we did not tell you that the passage title is "Washing Clothes." If you reread the passage knowing that, you will experience the power of what prior knowledge can do for making sense of a text. Of course, most of the time, the fix for prior knowledge is more complex than simply giving a title. Even the smartest new college student will likely fail to self-explain a neuroscience research paper without first learning vocabulary, scientific methods, and writing conventions.

Without prior knowledge, self-explanation cannot get very far, and instruction in self-explanation strategies will only frustrate students. Teaching self-explanation strategies using a completely novel topic would be a very unproductive way to encourage people to use those strategies.

The third risk is a familiar one, but worth reiterating: *mindlessly following procedures is a poor way to develop understanding.* Students may be inclined to parrot self-explanation prompts without using them to help build a mental model. To be effective, self-explanation needs to be a process of continual sense making.

VI. Examples of Good and Bad Use

One challenge of learning and teaching self-explanation is figuring out what counts as a good explanation. To clarify, we present bad and good explanations of the following short passage.

During a fever, the body's temperature increases by four different mechanisms. One is to shrink the veins (blood vessels) to decrease blood flow to the skin. When less blood gets near the skin, the blood cannot release as much heat through the skin.

BAD

"When less blood gets near the skin, the blood cannot release as much heat through the skin."

Repeating the text verbatim is a surefire way to learn almost nothing or, at best, to memorize the words in the text with no flexibility.

"Veins, blood, and skin are important here."

What/when/where/who statements help rote memory, but they often fail to connect the pieces into a coherent whole.

BETTER

"When veins get skinnier and/or shorter, not as much blood can get through them to the skin."

Restating ideas in one's own words helps readers integrate new material into their mental models and catch misunderstandings/contradictions.

"Wait, body temperature increases? I thought it decreases since you feel cold."

Monitoring and repairing faulty knowledge keeps one's mental models coherent and accurate.

"It says your body temperature increases by keeping blood heat in the body. So the temperature must decrease by letting blood heat out."

Generating inferences to fill in missing information is an example of learning more than is directly stated.

"Four ways. Three other ways besides keeping heat away from the edges of the body."

Explanations that integrate information within the study materials help to strengthen the connections between the ideas in one's mind.

"When the heat comes out through your skin, it probably warms up the skin a little. Maybe my heat and cold sensors are on my skin, and maybe I feel cold during fever because there's no blood heating up the skin."

Explanations that integrate information with prior knowledge help build new information into mental models. These statements tend coincidentally to include restatement and who/what/when/where details, so they essentially integrate three types of explanation into one.

VII. References

Aleven, V. A., & Koedinger, K. R. (2002). An effective metacognitive strategy: Learning by doing and explaining with a computer-based cognitive tutor. *Cognitive Science, 26*(2), 147–179.

Bielaczyc, K., Pirolli, P. L., & Brown, A. L. (1995). Training in self-explanation and self-regulation strategies: Investigating the effects of knowledge acquisition activities on problem solving. *Cognition and Instruction, 13*(2), 221–252.

Bransford, J. D., Barclay, J. R., & Franks, J. J. (1972). Sentence memory: A constructive versus interpretive approach. *Cognitive Psychology, 3*(2), 193–209.

Bransford, J. D., & Johnson, M. K. (1972). Contextual prerequisites for understanding: Some investigations of comprehension and recall. *Journal of Verbal Learning and Verbal Behavior, 11*, 717–726.

Chi, M. T., Bassok, M., Lewis, M. W., Reimann, P., & Glaser, R. (1989). Self-explanations: How students study and use examples in learning to solve problems. *Cognitive Science, 13*(2), 145–182.

Chi, M. T., De Leeuw, N., Chiu, M. H., & LaVancher, C. (1994). Eliciting self-explanations improves understanding. *Cognitive Science, 18*(3), 439–477.

Glenberg, A. M., Gutierrez, T., Levin, J. R., Japuntich, S., & Kaschak, M. P. (2004). Activity and imagined activity can enhance young children's reading comprehension. *Journal of Educational Psychology, 96*(3), 424-436.

Kieras, D. E., & Bovair, S. (1984). The role of a mental model in learning to operate a device. *Cognitive Science, 8*(3), 255–273.

King, A. (1994). Guiding knowledge construction in the classroom: Effects of teaching children how to question and how to explain. *American Educational Research Journal, 31*(2), 338–368.

Mayer, R. E., Dow, G. T., & Mayer, S. (2003). Multimedia learning in an interactive self-explaining environment: What works in the design of agent-based microworlds? *Journal of Educational Psychology, 95*(4), 806-812.

McNamara, D. S. (2004). SERT: Self-Explanation Reading Training. *Discourse Processes, 38*(1), 1–30.

Renkl, A., Stark, R., Gruber, H., & Mandl, H. (1998). Learning from worked-out examples: The effects of example variability and elicited self-explanations. *Contemporary Educational Psychology, 23*(1), 90–108.

Schwartz, D. L. (1999). The productive agency that drives collaborative learning. In P. Dillenbourg (Ed.), *Collaborative learning: Cognitive and computational approaches* (pp. 197-218). NY: Elsevier Science.

S IS FOR SELF-EXPLANATION

What is the core learning mechanic?
Silently talking through expository materials to improve comprehension.

What is an example, and what is it good for?
"Dark matter is a type of matter hypothesized in cosmology to account for a large part of the mass that appears to be missing from the universe." Effective readers work to make sense of this sentence, for example, by asking how matter can be missing from the universe yet still be there. They try to construct a mental model of the text by explicitly looking for connections across sentences and connections to their own knowledge. This includes looking for gaps in understanding. The resulting mental model improves memory for meaning and makes it easier to draw inferences and have insights.

Why does it work?
People often think learning means memorizing, and their study habits reflect it—repeatedly reading a text and reciting facts verbatim. However, a text cannot state all the relevant connections among ideas, so students need to construct an understanding that goes beyond memorizing sentences. Self-explanation works because people fill in missing information to make a coherent explanation.

What problems does the core mechanic solve?
- Students fail to recognize misunderstanding.
  - A student contradicts herself.
  - A student is surprised to find he has done poorly on a test.
- Students fail to comprehend what they read.
  - A student speeds through a textbook chapter but doesn't remember a thing.
- Students miss the point of a text.
  - When taking a test a student protests, "But we didn't learn this!" whenever questions cannot be answered by quoting the textbook.

Examples of how to use it
- To learn from explanatory texts.
  - Provide prompts that ask students to explain how what they are reading is related to what they already know.
- To learn from procedural examples.
  - After each step in a math procedure, ask students to explain its purpose.

Risks

- Students may not know enough about a topic to self-explain.
- Students may find the process too effortful and time-consuming.
- Students may parrot self-explanation prompts rather than use them to help build a mental model.

T is for Teaching

Taking responsibility for others' understanding

LEARNING BY TEACHING occurs when people accept the responsibility of teaching others and develop their own understanding so they can teach well. Teaching is not just for pupils; the teacher learns too. Teaching creates a confluence of felicitous conditions for learning. These include a motivating sense of responsibility, a need to organize and explain information, and feedback based on one's pupils' performances. When learning by teaching, people develop chains of connected ideas.

Professors often say they never really understood a topic until they had to teach it. Students can also benefit when they have a chance to teach. In peer tutoring, students teach other students face-to-face. In a review of thirty-eight peer-tutoring studies, Cohen, Kulik, and Kulik (1982) found that 87 percent of the studies exhibited a learning benefit for the tutors that was nearly as large as the benefit for the tutees! Engaging in teaching can be a powerful way for students to learn.

I. How Learning by Teaching Works

Learning by teaching is a complex recipe with many ingredients. The flame that cooks the ingredients together is a strong social motivation. Chase, Chin,

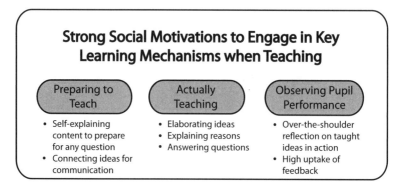

Figure T.1. Three phases of teaching. Each phase depends on several important learning mechanisms. A strong sense of responsibility leads teachers to engage these mechanisms so they can teach well.

Oppezzo, and Schwartz (2009) demonstrated a protégé effect: students make greater efforts to learn on behalf of others than they do for themselves. For instance, they found that adolescents spent nearly twice as long reading science material in preparation for teaching someone else compared with studying for themselves. Most teachers feel a responsibility to their pupils and want them to do well. There are also social motivations to appear capable—few things are more humiliating than teaching a class unprepared.

Teaching can take many different forms and at different time scales: full-blown semesters of classroom instruction, a one-hour videotaped lecture, thirty minutes of face-to-face tutoring, a ten-minute class presentation and discussion. Figure T.1 provides an analytic distinction among three phases that occur more or less for all types of teaching: preparing, teaching, and observing.

PREPARING TO TEACH

People learn better when they prepare to teach a pupil who will take a test than when they prepare to take the test themselves. On posttests of learning, the benefits especially appear on high-level questions that require connected ideas (Benware & Deci, 1984). This is because teachers need to consider what and how to communicate their knowledge. This requires producing a framework that puts all the relevant information together so teachers can move from one idea to the next (see Chapter S). Moreover, teachers need to prepare themselves for any question that students might ask. In contrast, when students prepare for a test, they only need to guess the types of questions that will be on the test and memorize the answers to those questions.

THE ACT OF TEACHING

The very act of teaching also helps learning. Fiorella and Mayer (2013) found that college students who prepared to teach and then delivered a videotaped lecture learned more than students who only prepared to teach. In practice, teaching has moments of improvisation, where teachers need to explain and elaborate ideas on the fly. The process of meaningfully connecting ideas improves memory and understanding (see Chapter E). For example, students who provide explanations in cooperative groups learn more than those who receive them (Webb, 1989). Answering questions from pupils is an excellent catalyst to elaboration and explanation.

Questions asked by pupils can also lead teachers to recognize and repair gaps in their own understanding. Borko and colleagues (1992) provide a canonical example. A preservice teacher was asked by a student why people invert fractions for multiplication, and she realized that she did not know the conceptual reason. Roscoe and Chi concluded, "[Questions from] tutees were responsible for about two-thirds of tutors' reflective knowledge-building activity" (2007, p. 23). Finally, teachers are "on" when teaching, which yields a high degree of attention and arousal (see Chapter X).

OBSERVING STUDENT PERFORMANCE

Often, when we ask learners to teach, we leave out the part where they get to see their pupils use what they have learned. For example, when students give a class presentation on an original project, this is a form of teaching. Even so, the presenting student rarely has an opportunity to find out what the audience actually learned from the presentation. This is a mistake. Seeing your pupils use what they learn is a uniquely powerful form of informative feedback (see Chapter F). Even fourteen-month-old infants show enhanced neural activity when they see other people imitate their own behaviors (Marshall & Meltzoff, 2014).

Okita and Schwartz (2013) demonstrated that students learn more when they see their pupils answer questions than when they answer the same questions themselves. In their study, college adults read a one-page passage on a biology topic. They briefly prepared to teach and then actually did teach another student on the topic. The experimental manipulation occurred in the next phase of the study. In the Self condition, the adults answered a set of relevant biology questions. In the Observe condition, the adults did not answer the questions but instead observed their pupil answer the questions. There was no feedback about the quality of the answers for either condition. Nevertheless, on a posttest of learning, the students who saw their pupils answer questions did better even on brand-new questions.

Two mechanisms likely contribute to the special benefit of observing one's pupil. First, teachers pay close attention to where their pupils succeed and fall short. A coach, for example, may discount negative feedback about herself, but when she sees her players doing poorly in a game, she is actively looking for a way to improve her teaching and her understanding of the situation. Second, seeing a pupil's performance is a special kind of "over-the-shoulder" observation. When performing a task yourself, you are concentrating on executing the task, and you may not have any remaining cognitive resources for reflecting on your performance. In contrast, when watching your pupils, you can be fully reflective because you do not need to do the task simultaneously. Moreover, you know what the pupil has in mind because you put it there. This permits you to monitor and repair gaps in the knowledge that you originally relied upon for teaching.

II. How to Use Teaching to Enhance Learning

There are many possible arrangements for learning by teaching. In peer tutoring, one student has the responsibility of tutoring another student. Students who are excelling in a class can learn more deeply by teaching other students who need some help. This arrangement has the added benefit that the students who need help receive individual attention.

Figure T.2 shows a useful collaborative learning arrangement called Jigsaw. In Jigsaw, all the students have an opportunity to teach. This arrangement is nice because there is interdependence within the group—no student can complete the task alone, and success depends on the teaching of the other students.

It is important to create a reason for teachers to care about their pupils. It makes the teaching real rather than a thin cover story. In a classroom, one approach is to assign the grade of the pupil to the teacher. If you taught Johnny, and he got a C– on his test, you would receive his C– averaged into your grade on the test. We are not fans of this approach because students do not like it, and it invites blaming. Instead, it is better to create situations where teachers have an opportunity to observe their pupil's subsequent performance. This taps into most people's sense of social responsibility. *Observing one's pupil is not just good feedback for teacher learning; it is also a good motivation for teaching well.*

People also need resources so they can learn what they are supposed to teach. These resources can be whatever you usually provide students for learning. Students just need a chance to organize and think about the material before teaching. Thus, a good teaching arrangement gives teachers a way to prepare, an opportunity to teach, and a chance to observe their students' independent performance after being taught.

Jigsaw in Cooperative Learning

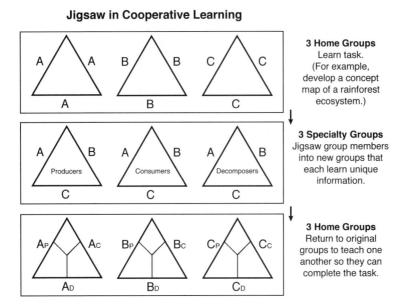

3 Home Groups
Learn task.
(For example,
develop a concept
map of a rainforest
ecosystem.)

3 Specialty Groups
Jigsaw group members
into new groups that
each learn unique
information.

3 Home Groups
Return to original
groups to teach one
another so they can
complete the task.

Figure T.2. Jigsaw in cooperative learning. Each capital letter stands for a student. Students start with their home groups and a larger task. Students then switch to their specialty groups. Each specialty group learns a different body of information relevant to completing the larger task. The students return to their home group, and they teach one another what they learned, so they can combine their knowledge to complete the task together.

III. The Outcomes of Teaching

Teaching requires connecting ideas to make a coherent narrative. Furthermore, answering pupil questions often involves such statements as "because fire depends on oxygen," "because water puts out fire," and "if you did not have water the oxygen could reach the fire." The result of all this, not surprisingly, is that the teacher develops chains of ideas. For instance, instead of learning the brute fact that water puts out a fire, a student might learn that water puts out fire because it blocks oxygen from reaching the flame.

A technology called a Teachable Agent (TA) fosters chains of ideas in the extreme (Blair, Schwartz, Biswas, & Leelawong, 2007). With TA, students teach a computer character. Figure T.3 shows some components of the teaching interface. To teach a TA, students build their agent's brain by adding nodes and connecting them. In Figure T.3, a student has taught the TA about global warming. For example, the student added two nodes: landfill and

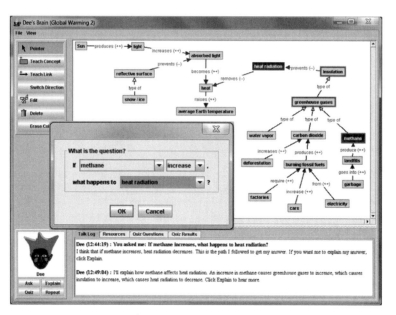

Figure T.3. A Teachable Agent. Students teach a computer character by creating a concept map that shows the causal relations among nodes in the map. Once they have taught their agent, they can ask it questions, as shown in the foreground panel. The agent visually reasons through the concept map to determine the answer.

methane. The student also connected the two concepts with a causal relation, indicating that an increase in landfill produces an increase in methane. Once taught, the TA can answer questions. The panel in the foreground of Figure T.3 shows the student asked the TA, "If methane increases, what happens to heat radiation?" The TA reasons through the concept map, graphically highlighting how it traverses the nodes and links. In the example, the TA reasons that an increase in methane decreases heat radiation by following the path: methane is a type of greenhouse gas; greenhouse gas is a type of insulation; an increase in insulation decreases heat radiation. The TA can also take quizzes or compete with other students' TAs in a game show format. Students teach their agent using the familiar schema of teach-test-remediate. If TAs give an incorrect answer, the students need to track down the mistake in the concept map and remediate their agent's knowledge (and their own in the process).

Compared with simply making a concept map, when students teach the TA they learn to make longer chains of inference (e.g., why an increase in cars can be bad for polar bears that are far away). Moreover, even after the technology is no longer in use, the students spontaneously learn to use causal relations to understand new topics (Chin et al., 2010). So, with TAs, children not only connect ideas but, further, learn how to connect ideas with causal relations to learn new material. The TA is a specific technology designed to support learning by teaching. The benefits can be generalized, however, to people teaching people. The key addition is that it is worthwhile to include some sort of visual representation that makes thinking visible. For example, if students are teaching about rhyming in poetry, it can be useful to have students build a visual representation that stands for the rhyming patterns. People's thoughts can be hard to decipher when only relying on words. A visual representation can make it easier to know what another is thinking (see Chapter V).

IV. Can People Learn to Teach Themselves by Teaching?

Teaching is uniquely native to the human species. Humans and some animals teach their young, but unlike animals, human parents look to see if their children have learned. Moreover, people like to share what they know, and they find excuses to teach. You probably have a friend who has expertise in wine, macrame, cars, or whatever. This friend is happy to teach you all manner of subtle distinctions that you would have never guessed matter to anybody.

Even so, people may not know that teaching is a good way to learn. Before college students write an essay, ask them to teach another student about their topic. Tell them this is a good way to learn and organize their knowledge. With enough practice, they will begin to find the value in it.

V. Risks of Teaching to Learn

Teaching is a robust way to learn and stands up to all sorts of variation. However, there are three risks worth monitoring, and they all occur during the act of teaching. The first is that students may adopt a poor teaching style. For example, tutors can slip into a didactic style, which can eliminate opportunities for pupils to ask questions that would otherwise support the tutors' own learning (Chi, Roy, & Hausmann, 2008). Try to arrange situations that enhance interactive teaching, so that the teacher can see or hear how the pupil is thinking about the content. Second, the strong motivational aspects of teaching need judicious management, because they can elevate into performance anxiety. Third, when students teach other students, such as in peer tutoring, the tutors may have incomplete knowledge of their own misconceptions, which can lead to confusion for the students being tutored. Having an expert teacher monitor and facilitate a peer teaching interaction can alleviate this concern.

VI. Examples of Good and Bad Use

Bad: A teacher tells a pair of students to study the same fairly simple math formula and then teach each other what they have learned. This is not a bad idea for getting students to practice articulating what they know, but it is not really teaching. Students do not believe they are really teaching or that their counterpart is really learning. The sense of social responsibility is not in place. Moreover, pretend pupils do not ask good questions.

Good: A teacher asks a student, Jill, to develop knowledge unknown to her peers (e.g., by doing a project or reading a book). Jill receives time to prepare to teach the class. Jill teaches the class about what she has learned, and then gets to see how the other students respond to questions posed by the teacher. Jill has an opportunity to reflect and address the class again the next day, improving her teaching based on the students' responses.

VII. References

Benware, C. A., & Deci, E. L. (1984). Quality of learning with an active versus passive motivational set. *American Educational Research Journal, 21,* 755–765.

Blair, K., Schwartz, D. L., Biswas, G., & Leelawong, K. (2007). Pedagogical agents for learning by teaching: Teachable agents. *Educational Technology, 47*(1), 56–61.

Borko, H., Eisenhart, M., Brown, C. A., Underhill, R. G., Jones, D., & Agard, P. C. (1992). Learning to teach hard mathematics: Do novice teachers and their instructors give up too easily? *Journal for Research in Mathematics Education, 23,* 194–222.

Chase, C., Chin, D. B., Oppezzo, M., & Schwartz, D. L. (2009). Teachable agents and the protégé effect: Increasing the effort towards learning. *Journal of Science Education and Technology, 18,* 334–352.

Chi, M. T. H., Roy, M., & Hausmann, R. G. M. (2008). Observing tutorial dialogues collaboratively: Insights about human tutoring effectiveness from vicarious learning. *Cognitive Science, 32*(2), 301–341.

Chin, D. B., Dohamen, I., Oppezzo, M., Cheng, B., Chase, C., & Schwartz, D. L. (2010). Preparation for future learning with teachable agents. *Educational Technology Research and Design, 58,* 649–669.

Cohen, P. A., Kulik, J. A., & Kulik, C.-L. C. (1982). Educational outcomes of peer tutoring: A meta-analysis of findings. *American Educational Research Journal, 19,* 237–248.

Fiorella, L., & Mayer, R. E. (2013). The relative benefits of learning by teaching and teaching expectancy. *Contemporary Educational Psychology, 38*(4), 281–288.

Marshall, P. J., & Meltzoff, A. N. (2014). Neural mirroring mechanisms and imitation in human infants. *Philosophical Transactions of the Royal Society of London, Series B, Biological Sciences, 369,* 20130620.

Okita, S. Y., Schwartz, D. L. (2013). Learning by teaching human pupils and teachable agents: The importance of recursive feedback. *Journal of the Learning Sciences, 22*(3), 375-412.

Roscoe, R. D., & Chi, M. T. H. (2007). Understanding tutor learning: Reflective knowledge-building and knowledge-telling in peer tutors' explanations and questions. *Review of Educational Research, 77,* 534–574.

Webb, N.M. (1989). Peer interaction and learning in small groups. *International Journal of Education Research, 13,* 21-39.

T IS FOR TEACHING

What is the core learning mechanic?
Teaching improves the teacher's own knowledge.

What is an example, and what is it good for?
Teaching is not just good for pupils; it is good for the teacher, too. Professors often say they never really understood a topic until they had to teach it. Asking older students to tutor younger students is an excellent example of learning by teaching. Tutors improve their understanding nearly as much as the tutees. The outcome of teaching is well-connected ideas.

Why does it work?
Teaching brings strong social motivations that cause teachers to engage content carefully. Teachers need to organize the information and be prepared to answer any question that might arise. Pupil questions lead teachers to elaborate and explain how ideas fit together. Teachers observe their pupils use what they have been taught, which provides useful feedback on how well the teachers connected their own ideas.

What problems does the core mechanic solve?
- People do not connect intermediate ideas together.
  - After a science lesson, a student knows that a battery turns on a light bulb, but not that the wires need to make a loop from the battery to the bulb and back.
- People do not pay attention to feedback.
  - A student only skims the feedback on an essay looking for positive marks such as "good," "nice," and smiley faces.
- People are unmotivated to learn.
  - A student does not read an assigned chapter carefully.

Examples of how to use it
- Use cross-age peer tutoring.
  - A student who has already completed algebra tutors a younger student taking algebra.
- Have students complete collaborative activities using Jigsaw.
  - One group of students learns about rainforest consumers, another about producers, and a third about decomposers. Create new groups that include one student from each of the specialization groups.

Students teach one another what they learned, so they can jointly solve a problem about the rainforest ecosystem.

Risks

- Students may not believe they really have responsibility for their pupil's learning.
- The strong social motivations that drive teaching may also produce performance anxiety.

U is for Undoing

Overcoming misconceptions and misplaced reasoning

UNDOING HELPS TO weaken mistaken ideas that are often resistant to change. People regularly develop beliefs and ways of reasoning that work much of the time but are still formally incorrect and can occasionally cause problems. This includes bad habits, misconceptions, and faulty ways of reasoning. It is important to undo this prior learning lest it interfere with future learning. Undoing requires identifying and replacing the source of the incorrect thinking, rather than just correcting each mistaken answer.

Not all mistakes are created equal. Some mistakes are simple errors and guesses. Other mistakes grow from years of experience. They have extensive root systems that can be difficult to extricate and replace. *Simply correcting a mistake may only relieve the symptom but not cure the cause.*

Many systematic errors result from borrowing ways of thinking that usefully simplify the world but also introduce distortions. Try the following question, the first of many "fun" tests of your own mental representations in this chapter: "Is San Diego to the east or west of Reno?" Most people answer incorrectly, because they have a rectified spatial representation. *Rectified* means they make things more orderly than they really are. They make the states line up more neatly in their minds so political and geographical boundaries work

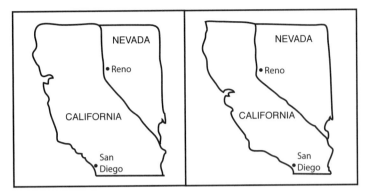

Figure U.1. Is San Diego to the east or west of Reno? An example of how people simplify the world to make it easier to think about.

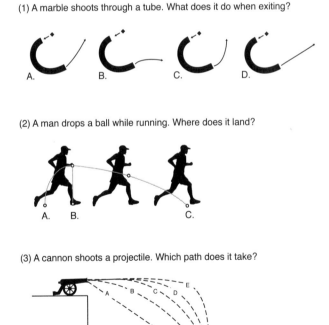

Figure U.2. Three examples of physics problems that often reveal naïve physics misconceptions.

together. Figure U.1 provides an example of what people's thoughts might be like. The right panel is correct.

We consider three sources of mistakes: misconceptions, reasoning biases, and simple errors.

MISCONCEPTIONS

Through everyday experience, people develop beliefs that work well in most circumstances but are nevertheless incorrect. Over time these experiences can evolve into loosely knit misconceptions. Sometimes people's errors appear systematic, as though the misconception is an intuitive theory (McCloskey, 1983). Other times, the misconceptions lack the integrated coherence and consistent application of a theory; people's beliefs appear to be "knowledge in pieces" (DiSessa, 1988). People's naïve physics conceptions reveal both properties at the same time—intuitive theory and inconsistent application. To see how, generate your answers for the three problems in Figure U.2.

The correct answers are 1D, 2C, 3B. If you gave the combined answers of 1A or 1C, 2B, and 3C, 3D, or 3E, you may have an impetus theory of motion (McCloskey, 1983). Roughly stated, the theory might be something like, "A moving object carries an internal force (impetus), which eventually gets used up." For answer 1A/C, the object holds a curvilinear force so it continues going in a circle for a while. For answer 2B, the object falls straight down because it is dropped rather than gathering an internal force from a push. For answer 3C/D/E, the object continues straight until its impetus drains and then it starts falling. Although wrong in each case, the mistakes appear to be consistently derived from the same naïve theory.

At the same time, misconceptions are often applied inconsistently and appear less general than a theory. For problem 1, imagine that, rather than a marble, it is water shooting out of the tube (as if through a coiled hose). Even people with an apparent impetus theory predict the water comes out straight. One implication of the unevenness of misconceptions is that fixing people's beliefs about one problem (e.g., thinking of water instead of a marble) may have little influence on displacing their naïve theory for other problems.

REASONING BIASES

In the 1930s, the American Child Health Association (1934, pp. 80-96) was concerned by the tonsillectomy rate because of the surgery costs and associated risks of anesthesia death. (They used chloroform back in the day.) The association sampled one thousand eleven-year-olds in New York City and found that 61.1 percent had had their tonsils removed. (Nowadays, the rate of tonsillectomy hovers around 1 percent.) The study gets interesting in the next step. They managed to have the remaining 389 children meet with a new group of physicians. These physicians recommended that 45 percent of these previously undiagnosed children receive a tonsillectomy. If that were not enough, the researchers repeated the procedure, so that the children who had passed through two diagnostic filters went to yet another group of physicians. These physicians recommended that 46 percent of these remaining children receive a tonsillectomy. Finally, the remaining undiagnosed children went to another group of doctors, who sure enough, recommended that 44 percent get a tonsillectomy. By the end, only 65 of 1,000 children remained without a diagnosis for tonsillectomy. How is this absurdity possible? One likely explanation is that the doctors had learned that around 45 percent of children need tonsillectomies in general. They matched that percentage in their diagnoses.

As patients, we hope that symptoms uniquely identify a cause and treatment. Unfortunately, evidence is rarely definitive, which is one reason it is wise to get a second opinion. Doctors often need to make a judgment under uncertainty. When there is uncertainty, reasoning biases can slip in, such as the belief that 45 percent of children in any given sample should receive a tonsillectomy.

Here is another problem from Tversky and Kahneman (1983) that requires a judgment under uncertainty:

Linda is thirty-one years old, single, outspoken, and very bright. She majored in philosophy. As a student, she was deeply concerned with issues of discrimination and social justice, and she also participated in antinuclear demonstrations. Which is more probable?

1. Linda is a bank teller.
2. Linda is a bank teller and is active in the feminist movement.

The description of Linda reads as though she could very well be a feminist, and 85 percent of people incorrectly choose 2 as their answer. How can choice 2 be wrong? Linda sure sounds like a feminist! Choice 2 is wrong because the odds of being a feminist and a bank teller have to be lower than the odds of just being a bank teller. There is no situation where the odds of two things happening together are greater than either one of them happening alone. (Imagine the Venn diagram.)

For judgments under uncertainty, people should use probabilistic reasoning. Instead, people typically draw upon comfortable heuristics. A *heuristic* is a rule of thumb or judgmental shortcut that works most of the time. (In contrast, an algorithm yields a correct answer every time.) For the Linda problem, people use a heuristic termed *representativeness*: choice 2 is more similar to, or representative of, the description of Linda than choice 1. Using representativeness leads people to ignore issues of probability. Reasoning about the similarity of things is very natural, but in this case it is the wrong type of reasoning.

People often draw on heuristics, because they do not know how to reason about probabilistic outcomes. Konold (1989) interviewed people about the following problem:

A six-sided die has five sides painted black and one side painted white. You roll it six times. Which outcome is more likely?

1. Five blacks and one white
2. Six blacks

Many people chose option 2. They reason that for a single roll, the odds favor a black side coming up. Therefore, if they rolled it six times, each time the odds would favor a black side, hence six blacks. It is a compelling piece of intuitive reasoning, but again, it is wrong. The chance of six blacks is .335, whereas the chance of five blacks is .402. The source of the mistake is that people tend to think in terms of single trials, but with probability one needs to think about the aggregate outcome of all the trials.

Just because these examples are so fun, here is yet another from Daniel Kahneman (2002), when he received the Nobel Prize for his pioneering work on judgment under uncertainty:

At the air force academy, an instructor has followed the policy of rewarding the best pilot of the day and punishing the worst pilot. He noticed that on the next day the best pilot usually did worse while the worst pilot usually did better. He concluded that he should change his instructional model so he should no longer give rewards but instead only punish. What would you tell the flight instructor?

It is tempting to argue with the flight instructor by saying that reward is a good motivator. This argument reveals how naturally we spill into causal reasoning. Probabilistic reasoning is more appropriate here. Just by chance, some people have a good day (or bad day) that yields an exceptional performance. Odds are that the next time, they will slip back toward the average, which is termed *regression to the mean*. A pilot who has an exceptionally bad day will do better on the next day, punishment or not. A pilot who has an exceptionally good day is likely not to do as well on the next day, reward or not. A more familiar version of this is the rookie jinx: In baseball, a rookie has an exceptional year, wins an award, and appears on the cover of a sports magazine. The next year the rookie does less well. Sometimes people argue that being on the cover of the magazine is a jinx or that the success distracts the rookie from his craft. Again, probability is likely more appropriate here. To be the very best of all the rookies in a given year requires some good luck for the rookie and some bad luck for all the others. In the following year, the rookie will regress toward the average of all rookies, because it is unlikely that all the lucky events will occur again.

Reasoning biases are not confined to judgments under uncertainty. Hammer (1994) also points to people's discipline-specific beliefs about learning and knowledge—their epistemic beliefs. These beliefs can become an impediment to learning. For instance, students may believe that physics is a set of unconnected facts, or they may believe that physics understanding comes from authority rather than something one develops for oneself. Here is one of our favorite interview excerpts:

> I feel that proving the formula is not really necessary for me, it doesn't matter if I can prove it or not, as long as I know that someone has proven it before . . . there's a concept, and . . . here I am paying 15,000 dollars a year. . . . I'm not going to derive this thing for them; they're going to derive it for me and explain to me how it works. (Hammer, 1994, p. 159)

It is not obvious whether the student is lazy or really believes the point of physics learning is to receive the authoritative answer. Regardless, unchecked, it is an unproductive attitude. Epistemologies like this are probably the result of instruction, unlike intuitive beliefs and natural heuristics. It is a reasonable prediction that this type of student epistemology arises after instruction that emphasizes pushing equations dictated by a professor.

SIMPLE ERRORS

Errors that come from isolated mistakes are relatively easy to undo. Many home cooks believe that simmering a sauce boils off the alcohol from added wine. This belief is in error. After an hour of simmering, 25 percent of the alcohol remains (Augustin, Augustin, Cutrufelli, Hagen, & Teitzel, 1992). This is an easy mistake to fix. In fact, your misunderstanding probably disappeared just by reading this paragraph. It is an isolated fact that shows up in only one place in your life: when cooking with alcohol. Undoing simply requires noticing the wrong fact and replacing it.

A common source of simple errors is that people make up answers on the fly. Many people have never really thought about the causes of the seasons. When asked, they reach for an easy analogy: the closer something is to a heat source, the hotter it gets. They conclude that the earth must be closer to the sun in the summer. It is probably sufficient to debug this misconception by pointing out that the analogy does not work very well, because it implies that the northern and southern hemispheres experience summer at the same time. From there, one can simply teach how the earth's tilt causes the seasons. Of course, this is a nontrivial teaching task, but at least there won't be interference from a deep misconception. Errors with shallow roots do not create bedeviling problems for undoing, as long as one discovers them.

I. How Undoing Works

Jean Piaget, the famous developmental psychologist who proposed stages of cognitive development, theorized that children improve their reasoning about the world through processes of assimilation and accommodation. *Assimilation* occurs when people make new information fit their current ideas. *Accommodation* occurs when people change their ideas to fit new information. Undoing depends on accommodation, which can be difficult—changing beliefs is harder than confirming them.

There are two reasons that accommodation is hard. First, people's intuitive beliefs and ways of reasoning do not have the rigid texture of formal theories. A single piece of evidence can falsify a formal theory but not a hazy misconception. Second, people are unlikely to give up their ideas when there are no alternatives.

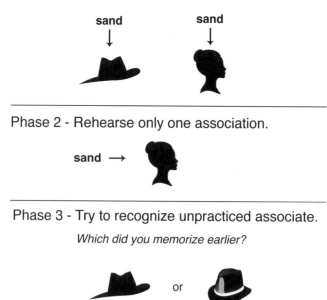

Phase 1 - Memorize two associations to one word.

sand

sand

Phase 2 - Rehearse only one association.

sand →

Phase 3 - Try to recognize unpracticed associate.

Which did you memorize earlier?

or

Figure U.3. A study to test whether memories fade when intentionally suppressed.

Accommodation occurs when alternative ideas develop enough strength that they can compete with original ideas. Chen and Siegler (2000) describe how children can continue to give a wrong prediction and explanation (e.g., that three cookies spread apart are more than three cookies close together), but in the background an alternate representation is slowly being strengthened. With enough experience, the slowly strengthening representation can assert itself into consciousness, so that children eventually give the right answer, and now that they know the correct answer, they can construct an explanation for why.

An enduring question is whether old misconceptions go away or, rather, sit quietly in the brain, waiting for their chance to cause mischief. For simple associative memory, there is some evidence of retrieval-induced forgetting, though it is unknown if it also applies to misconceptions. In one study, people learned to associate unrelated words with two separate images (Wimber, Alink, Charest, Kriegeskorte, & Anderson, 2015). Figure U.3 shows the study timeline. Participants memorized two possible associations to a word. (They did this for lots of words, not just the one shown in the figure.) Afterward, when people read the word, the researchers could detect brain activation for both of the image associates. In the next part of the study, people had to practice retrieving only one of the images. Upon reading the word in Figure U.2, they were told to recall only the image on the right (woman). They completed this activity over five different sessions, and by the end, they recalled the image on the right (woman) about 80 percent of the time. The question is what happened to the memory for the other image (hat). People saw pictures of hat images and had to decide which one they had seen earlier. People became worse at recognizing the hat image they had seen, and they showed less organized brain activation for that image in memory. One interpretation is that the old memory was slowly dissolving, because the effort to remember the woman required actively suppressing the memory of the hat.

When this observation is applied to misconceptions, one potential implication is that it is helpful to have people make their misconceived ideas explicit and precise, so it is possible to suppress them when entertaining the alternate conception.

Sometimes people apply good concepts to the wrong situations, as in the case of using proximity to the sun to explain the seasons. Being closer to a heat source does heat things up, but it is misapplied to explain the seasons. Here, undoing does not require eliminating prior concepts. It requires realigning the associations between concepts and the situations that call for them. As before, people need multiple experiences so that the new association (i.e., it is the tilt of the earth) can outweigh the old one (i.e., it is the proximity to the sun). The implication is that telling people they have misapplied a concept one time will not work very well, because this is insufficient to build up a competing association that can take its place.

II. How to Use Undoing to Enhance Learning

The first step for undoing is to become aware that a student's misconception or reasoning bias may exist. Sadler, Sonnert, Coyle, Cook-Smith, and Miller (2013) showed that teacher knowledge of potential student misconceptions correlated with improved student learning. About two hundred middle school physical science teachers, and their ten thousand students, completed a multiple-choice test at the start of the year. The teachers additionally had to predict the most common answers among students. Here is an example of a question and the percentage of students who chose each answer (Sadler et al., 2013, p. 1030):

> Eric is watching a burning candle very carefully. After all of the candle has burned, he wonders what happened to the wax. He has a number of ideas; which one do you agree with most?
>
> a. The candle wax has turned into invisible gases. (17 percent)
> b. The candle wax is invisible and still in the air. (6 percent)
> c. The candle was has been completely destroyed after burning. (8 percent)
> d. All the wax has melted and dripped to the bottom of the candle holder. (59 percent)
> e. The candle wax has turned into energy. (10 percent)

The finding that 59 percent of students chose option d indicates that there is a relatively common misconception among the students. (The correct answer, by the way, is a.)

The researchers then measured how much students learned over the year. The results showed that if teachers did badly on the test themselves, their classes did not exhibit strong gains, as one should expect. More relevant here, the students of those teachers who correctly predicted likely student misconceptions gained the most. To be an effective teacher, one needs content knowledge *and* knowledge of how students think about that content (Shulman, 1986). Pedagogical content knowledge—PCK, as it is fondly called—includes the likely points of student confusion and how to address them (e.g., Ball, Thames, & Phelps, 2008).

There are useful premade assessments, for example, in physics, to help reveal student misconceptions (e.g., Hestenes, Wells, & Swackhamer, 1992) and reasoning biases (e.g., Adams et al., 2006). Without the benefit of a preexisting test, one way to learn about student misconceptions is to use the predict–observe–explain (POE) cycle (White & Gunstone, 1992). Students predict the outcome of an experiment, observe the results (typically discrepant), and then explain why their hypothesis was wrong and how to fix it. The latter part brings student reasoning and beliefs to the surface, which makes POE a useful formative assessment for making instructional decisions.

Sometimes instructors also use POE as a method of instruction, on the assumption that cognitive conflict will induce students to correct their misunderstandings. Evidence suggests this is not an effective strategy in and of itself (Limón, 2001). The cognitive disequilibrium caused by a result that conflicts with a prediction is typically inadequate, because people can find many ways to patch their faulty predictions without learning the correct general principle (e.g., Shemwell, Chase, & Schwartz, 2015).

The next step is doing something about the misconception. There is no magic bullet, but three instructional features seem especially important. First, increase students' precision of thought, so they can recognize differences between their intuitive beliefs and correct explanations. The precision helps students avoid the natural tendency to assimilate new ideas and findings into their naïve framework, because they can recognize the old and new ideas do not fit together. Vosniadou, Ioannides, Dimitrakopoulou, and Papademetriou (2001), who teach science through student inquiry, begin by having students clarify their own beliefs, perhaps by working in groups to make specific predictions and explanations of those predictions. Students also learn to take precise measurements, and there is a concerted effort to help students differentiate frequently conflated terms (e.g., force and energy).

Second, students need an alternative conception that can replace the original misconception. Here, Vosniadou and colleagues provide students with external representations, such as force vectors and energy meters that provide students a new way to think about and explain the phenomenon. Alternatively, one might help students reframe a problem so it relies on a different concept. For example, instead of thinking of electrical current as water flowing through a pipe, one might think of it as a teeming crowd trying to squeeze through a tunnel. (The latter is better for thinking about resistance.)

Third, people need time for the new explanations to build up the strength to compete with the original misconception. Students also need to learn the range of situations to which the new explanation applies. Vosniadou and colleagues are willing to sacrifice breadth of science coverage to ensure students learn fundamental concepts more deeply. Undoing misconceptions does not happen in a day.

III. The Outcomes of Undoing Learning

Undoing misconceptions and reasoning biases helps people reach correct conclusions. In the practical world, this has far-reaching consequences. For instance, you can correctly conclude that one good year for a financial broker does not assure that the broker is any better than other brokers. Somebody can have a good year by chance, and maybe your broker just got lucky. The second outcome is greater ease in learning new related content. We provide a simple example at the end of the chapter.

IV. Can People Learn to Teach Themselves Undoing?

There is little compelling evidence that people can readily learn to undo their own mistaken concepts and reasoning habits in general. The reason is simple: people do not know which concepts and ways of reasoning are wrong, let alone how to replace them. For example, Europeans believed the earth was flat for a very long time.

The primary hope for learning to self-correct is to pay attention to discrepant information and adjust accordingly. The problem is that people have yet another reasoning bias called *confirmation bias*: people use reasoning to prove ideas correct, not to disprove them. A simple example is wishful thinking. People spend billions of dollars on unproven and unlikely health solutions (e.g., antiaging pills). Sometimes people just want to believe, and they interpret every new fact as support for their desired beliefs.

Confirmation bias runs deep and does not solely depend on wishful thinking. Figure U.4 shows the selection task made famous by Wason (1966). People who believe they should turn over A and 4 exhibit a confirmation

If a card has a vowel on one side, it has an even number on the other side.

Which card or cards should you turn over to see if these four cards follow the rule?

Figure U.4. The selection task (based on Wason, 1966).

If a person is drinking alcohol, the person needs to be 21 or over.

Which of the four people do you check to see if they are following the rule?

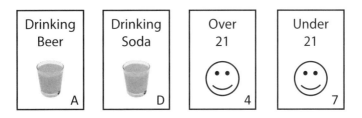

Figure U.5. The selection task becomes trivially easy in the context of familiar social rules.

bias. A is a correct choice, but 4 is irrelevant to the rule. If the other side of 4 is a vowel it confirms the rule. If it is a consonant, it does not falsify the rule. (The rule does *not* say, "If there is an even number, then the other side has to be a vowel.") Choosing 4 is trying to find an instance that confirms the rule. To test the rule, one needs to turn over the 7. If there is a vowel on the other side, then the card violates the rule. If that explanation does not work for you, let us change the context. Look at Figure U.5. The correct answer should be obvious. People are much better at handling this logic problem when framed as a social problem of permission. In this case, borrowing an intuitive reasoning scheme (catching cheaters) actually helps!

Even when people do recognize that an outcome falsifies their theory, they may apply ad hoc reasoning. They find ways to maintain their beliefs by making special-case adjustments. A wonderful example comes from children who conducted experiments to test their theory that sweaters produce heat. Their teacher put a thermometer in a sweater and set it aside. The children predicted that the next day the thermometer would show triple-digit temperatures. When the thermometers showed no increase the next morning, the children argued that the thermometer was not in there long enough and that cold air got in there somehow (Watson & Konicek, 1990).

All is not lost. People can learn to avoid a confirmation bias, especially in their domain of expertise. Dunbar (2000) videotaped top-flight biology laboratory meetings for months. He found that when an experiment came up with a result that falsified the leading hypothesis, scientists did not simply try to explain it away. They began the process of considering alternative explanations of the result, including new types of theories that could explain them and what tests would falsify those new theories. Thus, there is some hope that people can learn to undo their own beliefs based on reasoning and evidence, but remember, these scientists had received decades of training to do just that in their domain of expertise. At home, when reasoning about where to find the source of a leak in the roof, they may exhibit the same confirmation bias as the rest of us and keep searching in the same (wrong) spot.

V. Risks of Undoing

Undoing has three major risks. The first is that a helpful explanation may cause another misconception. For instance, if you explain to a child that the world is not flat, but round like a ball, they may develop the misconception that if they walk far enough they will fall off the earth. The second risk is that teachers can fool themselves that students understand because the students can apply quantitative procedures to compute the correct answers. Herein resides a deep truth about human learning: *The greatest strength of procedures is that people can use them to get the right answers without understanding; it is also their greatest weakness.* This truth came to light in college physics classes with the development of the Force Concept Inventory (Hestenes et al., 1992). The inventory is a test composed of items similar to those in Figure U.2. With this test, professors discovered that their students had deep misconceptions about Newtonian physics, despite the students doing relatively well on tests that emphasized procedural applications of equations. One might even propose that the professors previously had a confirmation bias because they wanted to believe their students had learned well, so they did not probe for evidence to the contrary. The third risk is that instructors may spend so much time highlighting misconceptions that students are left feeling incompetent.

VI. Examples of Good and Bad Use

Imagine a child gives the following answers:

19	13	11
−6	−7	−9
-----	----	----
13	14	18

Bad: You tell the child that the correct answers are 13, 6, and 2.

Better: You recognize that the child has learned the following rule: One cannot subtract a bigger number from a smaller number (e.g., 3 − 7). The child probably figured that she should subtract the smaller from the bigger (e.g., 7

– 3, which explains the 4 in the answer 14). To solve this misconception, you explain that the rule she learned is not true. In fact, one can subtract bigger numbers from smaller numbers, which is why we have negative numbers.

Best: You further realize that the child has a second misconception that is the deeper source of the problem. The child is treating each column as a separate subtraction, and the child does not appreciate that one should be subtracting 7 from 13, not 7 from 3. To solve this misconception, you back up to undo the root misconception. Then you reteach carrying from the beginning, now that the child has the right conception of place value to build upon.

VII. References

Adams, W. K., Perkins, K. K., Podolefsky, N. S., Dubson, M., Finkelstein, N. D., & Wieman, C. E. (2006). New instrument for measuring student beliefs about physics and learning physics: The Colorado Learning Attitudes about Science Survey. *Physical Review Special Topics—Physics Education Research, 2*(1), 010101-1–010101-14.

American Child Health Association. (1934). *Physical defects: The pathway to correction. A study of physical defects among school children in New York City.*. New York: American Child Health Association.

Augustin, J., Augustin, E., Cutrufelli, R. L., Hagen, S. R., & Teitzel, C. (1992). Alcohol retention in food preparation. *Journal of the American Dietetic Association, 92*(4), 486-488.

Ball, D. L., Thames, M. H., & Phelps, G. (2008). Content knowledge for teaching: What makes it special? *Journal of Teacher Education, 59*(5), 389–407.

Chen, Z., & Siegler, R. S. (2000). II. Overlapping waves theory. *Monographs of the Society for Research in Child Development, 65*(2), 7–11.

DiSessa, A. A. (1988). Knowledge in pieces. In G. Forman & P. Pufall (Eds.), *Constructivism in the computer age* (pp. 49–70). Hillsdale, NJ: Erlbaum.

Dunbar, K. (2000). How scientists think in the real world: Implications for science education. *Journal of Applied Developmental Psychology, 21*(1), 49–58.

Hammer, D. (1994). Epistemological beliefs in introductory physics. *Cognition and Instruction, 12*(2), 151–183.

Hestenes, D., Wells, M., & Swackhamer, G. (1992). Force concept inventory. *Physics Teacher, 30*(3), 141–158.

Kahneman, D. (2002). Maps of bounded rationality: A perspective on intuitive judgment and choice. In T. Frangsmyr (ed.). *Les Prix Nobel: The Nobel Prizes 2002* (pp. 449-489). Stockholm, Nobel Prize.

Konold, C. (1989). Informal conceptions of probability. *Cognition and Instruction, 6*(1), 59–98.

Limón, M. (2001). On the cognitive conflict as an instructional strategy for conceptual change: A critical appraisal. *Learning and Instruction, 11*(4), 357–380.

McCloskey, M. (1983). Intuitive physics. *Scientific American, 248*(8), 122–130.

Sadler, P. M., Sonnert, G., Coyle, H. P., Cook-Smith, N., & Miller, J. L. (2013). The influence of teachers' knowledge on student learning in middle school physical science classrooms. *American Educational Research Journal, 50*(5), 1020–1049.

Shemwell, J. T., Chase, C. C., & Schwartz, D. L. (2015). Seeking the general explanation: A test of inductive activities for learning and transfer. *Journal of Research in Science Teaching, 52*(1), 58–83.

Shulman, L. S. (1986). Those who understand: Knowledge growth in teaching. *Educational Researcher, 15*(2), 4–14.

Tversky, A., & Kahneman, D. (1983). Extension versus intuitive reasoning: The conjunction fallacy in probability judgment. *Psychological Review, 90*(4), 293–315.

Vosniadou, S., Ioannides, C., Dimitrakopoulou, A., & Papademetriou, E. (2001). Designing learning environments to promote conceptual change in science. *Learning and Instruction, 11*(4), 381–419.

Wason, P. C. (1966). Reasoning. In B. M. Foss (Ed.), *New horizons in psychology* (pp. 135–151). Harmondsworth, UK: Penguin.

Watson, B., & Konicek, R. (1990). Teaching for conceptual change: Confronting children's experience. *Phi Delta Kappan, 71*(9), 680-685.

White, R. T., & Gunstone, R. F. (1992). *Probing understanding.* London: Falmer.

Wimber, M., Alink, A., Charest, I., Kriegeskorte, N., & Anderson, M. C. (2015). Retrieval induces adaptive forgetting of competing memories via cortical pattern suppression. *Nature Neuroscience, 18*(4), 582–589.

U is for Undoing

What is the core learning mechanic?
Undoing is the process of identifying and replacing misconceptions and faulty methods of reasoning.

What is an example, and what is it good for?
A child answers that $13 - 7 = 14$. Is this a random mistake, or is there a deeper cause? The child may believe that one cannot subtract 7 from 3, so she subtracts 3 from 7 instead. To undo this misunderstanding, we cannot simply tell the child, "You cannot just switch the numbers." This will not solve the deeper misconception that subtraction refers to only one column at a time. This requires teaching place value so the student understands that 13 refers to a single quantity. This will smooth the student's abilities to learn future arithmetic concepts.

A rookie baseball player wins most valuable player of the year and appears on the cover of a sports magazine. Next year the player does not perform as well, and people blame it on the distraction of media coverage. This explanation uses causal reasoning, when probabilistic reasoning is more appropriate—the rookie would have to be very lucky to have another year just as good. People need extensive practice in probabilistic reasoning to overcome their everyday heuristics for making judgments under uncertainty.

Why does it work?
Misconceptions and faulty ways of reasoning work most of the time, and they become entrenched and hard to detect. Undoing helps identify the underlying problem and then strengthens a competing mental representation that can replace the erroneous way of thinking.

What problems does the core mechanic solve?
- Teachers do not realize there is a confusion that interferes with future learning.
  - Physical science instructors are unaware that students have a problematic intuitive theory, and they correct only the symptoms rather than the cause.
- People assimilate new information to fit within their existing beliefs.
  - People pay attention only to information that supports their fad diet.

Examples of how to use it
- Use tests or tasks explicitly designed to reveal student misconceptions.

- ◦ Ask students to predict the trajectory of a marble shot out of a coiled tube.
- Build up an alternative framework that can replace faulty beliefs.
  - ◦ Teach probability as an alternative to causal analysis.

Risks

- Educators may think students understand because they can solve procedural tasks.
- The solution to one misconception may introduce another.
- Relentlessly highlighting misconceptions can make people feel incompetent.

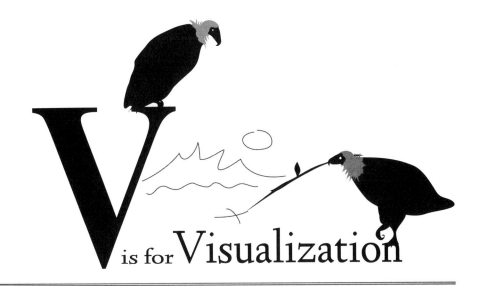

V is for Visualization

Inventing structure for complex information

Visualization is the process of making an external spatial representation of information. Visualizing is a useful strategy for discovering structure and organizing information efficiently.

People often want to know the best way to communicate effectively with visualizations (McElhaney, Chang, Chiu, & Linn, 2014). In this chapter, we discuss a different matter: getting learners to create their own visualizations. It has many benefits and is rarely included in instruction, so we emphasize it here.

Maps, diagrams, sketches, and Venn diagrams are all external visualizations. One can find them in nearly every business report, textbook, and newspaper. There is a reason for this: spatial representations help people see structure and search for relations across different pieces of information. Visualizing for oneself can have the same benefits. As a simple example, try to solve the following problem:

3rd Street is to the north of 4th Street. Peach Avenue runs perpendicular to 3rd and 4th streets. On the southeast corner of 4th and Peach is a coffee shop. On the northwest corner of 3rd and Peach is a tea store.

How many streets does a person need to cross when walking from the coffee shop to the tea store?

The question would be much easier to answer if one had drawn the map that we conveniently provide as Figure V.1. The map makes it easier to grasp the layout of the streets and to search for different paths from the coffee shop to the tea store.

Diagrams and maps share the spatial structure of their referents. They are abstractions that result from many decisions about which spatial relations to preserve and which details to eliminate (the shape of the coffee shop). Some symbolic visualizations are even more abstract and do not look like their referents at all. Consider the following logical expressions:

All X are Y. No Z is Y.

In Figure V.2, it does not really matter what X, Y, and Z stand for. Even so, the visualization of the logical premises confers similar benefits as the map. The drawing makes a spatial structure that organizes relations and makes it easier to answer questions. One merely needs to read off the Euler diagram to answer the question, "Are any Xs also Zs?"

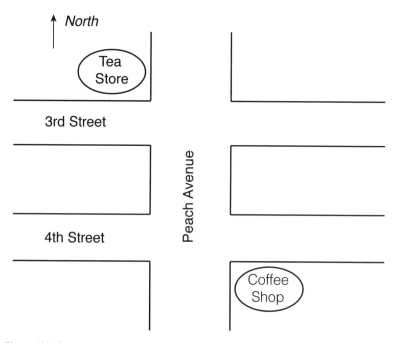

Figure V.1. A map makes it easier to reason about spatial relations.

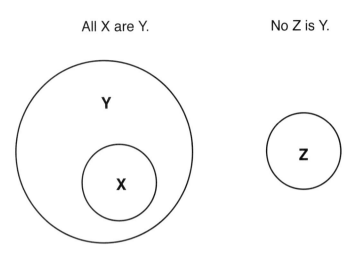

Figure V.2. A Euler diagram is a visualization that makes it easier to reason about logical relations.

Visualizations can also be text based when they take advantage of position and order. The periodic table is an impressive example of a text-based matrix where the rows, columns, and regions identify important properties and relations among atoms. It is a fun debate to decide on the greatest visualization format of all time. (We vote for the Cartesian graph.)

I. How Visualization Works

Visualization depends on making an external, spatially organized representation of ideas and information. Architects, for example, can sketch possible layouts to see what forms appear. Even though the sketches come from their minds, they hope to see new patterns in their handiwork. People can engage in a similar discovery process when writing their ideas in prose, but visualization brings very specific benefits.

DISTRIBUTING COGNITION

Visualization offloads the demands of maintaining too much information in one's mind simultaneously. It is a form of *distributed cognition*, where the world serves as a memory store. Roy Pea describes the benefits of distributed cognition as follows:

> Make external the intermediate products of thinking . . . which can then be analyzed, reflected upon, and discussed. Transient and private thought processes subject to the distortions and limitations of attention and mem-

ory are "captured" and embodied in a communicable medium that persists, providing material records that can become objects of analysis in their own right—conceptual building blocks rather than shifting sands. (1987, p. 91)

With a drawing, one can visually search for information rather than having to search one's memory (and forgetting what else one may have been thinking at the time).

RELATIONAL SPECIFICITY

A special benefit of visualization is that a drawing tends to be more relationally determinate than words. For instance, consider the sentence pair:

The cross is above the rectangle. The triangle is next to the rectangle.

The expression *next to* is indeterminate. When drawing, you have to put the triangle to the left or right of the rectangle. Moreover, you have to decide

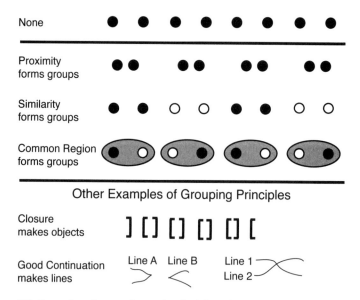

Figure V.3. Examples of several gestalt principles of grouping. The visual system automatically finds structure among discrete elements. The first examples show three different ways to make visual groups from eight dots. The remaining examples demonstrate two other gestalt principles: people see a single visual entity based on whether they can close or continue the lines and edges.

what type of rectangle (e.g., a square, a tall rectangle, or a wide rectangle). Visualization makes linguistically vague relations spatially specific and thus available for finding relational structure.

The determinacy of spatial representations makes drawing an excellent way to assess understanding (and fun for the students). Ask several friends to draw an image showing what causes an earthquake. You will see the differences in their understanding.

EMERGENT STRUCTURE

A third special benefit of visualization is that our visual system naturally imposes structure on spatial arrangements. When people depict their ideas, they can begin to see new patterns that they had not anticipated. The gestalt psychologists were interested in how people find global structure from component pieces. Max Wertheimer (1923/1938) discovered multiple principles that determine the emergence of visual structure. The rows in Figure V.3 demonstrate some of these principles. The Common Region row shows that a bounding region will cause the dots inside to appear as a group, even though they are relatively far apart and different colors. The visual system does this effortlessly.

Figure V.4. The structure of a visualization invites interpretation. Three different visualizations of proper diet from the U.S. Department of Agriculture.

INTERPRETIVE EASE

A fourth source of benefit is that people readily interpret visual structure. Familiar shapes, size differentials, and representational conventions invite interpretation. Figure V.4 shows the evolution of the U.S. Department of Agriculture (USDA) food recommendations. On the left, the 1992 food pyramid invited the inference that the grain-based foods at the bottom are foundational and we should eat more. The 2006 food pyramid in the center does not invite this foundational interpretation, but then it does not really invite any interpretation based on the triangular shape (and anyway, why is the person walking up the triangle away from the food?) The USDA abandoned the pyramid for a more literal representation that maps the size of portions to a plate.

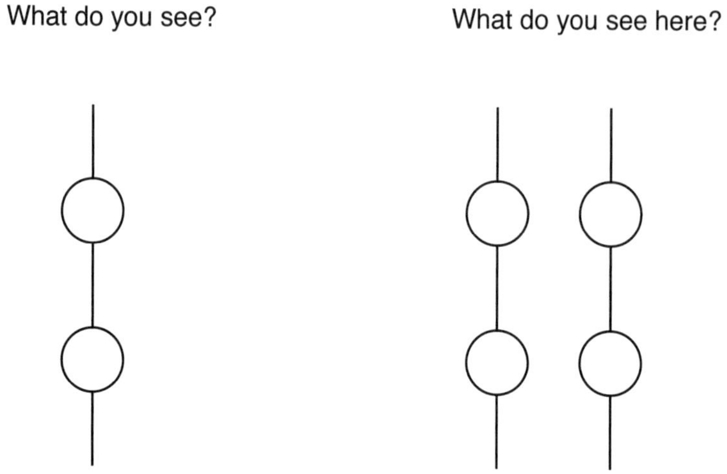

What do you see?   What do you see here?

Figure V.5. Reorganizing visual structure. Begin with the figure on the left. Decide what it represents. Then look at the figure on the right and decide what it represents.

REORGANIZATION

An explicit effort to reinterpret a spatial representation can help people reorganize what they see. Look at the left figure in Figure V.5. What might it represent? Some people think it is two olives on a toothpick. Others interpret it as a propeller plane flying sideways. Now, look at the figure on the right. What does it represent? Often, people will just say a pair of whatever they saw on the left. We will tell you in a second. When we tell you, notice how the two vertical lines restructure.

The figure on the right represents a bear cub clinging to the backside of a tree. The circles represent its paws. Did you notice how the two vertical lines became part of one shape (a tree) rather than two separate lines? The possibility of visual reorganization is one reason that it is good to avoid locking into a single interpretation—you may miss other structures that are available in the image.

II. How to Use Visualization to Enhance Learning

Symbolic visualization requires choosing some conventions. Should you use a hierarchical tree or a Gantt chart? Will a line represent a boundary, as in a Venn diagram, or a quantity, as in a Cartesian graph? Should you include arrows in your representation of river flow? Different visual representations reveal different structural possibilities that can have large effects on interpretation and problem solving (Zhang, 1997). For fun, do an image search on *molecule*. Each of the different conventions emphasizes different structural properties. The visual convention one chooses will have a major influence on the structure that one discovers, and it is often a good idea to try different approaches before committing to one.

Consider the task of writing a paper or preparing a presentation. There are many different ideas, facts, and tidbits you may wish to include. A flat list of bullet points will not go very far for the audience or your own understanding. Instead, you need to find some sort of structure that helps organize as many of the points as possible (and the rest you should just leave behind). People often dive into writing and try to make a hierarchical outline using section headings like II.A and II.B. A hierarchy is only one of many possible ways to produce structure. Another strategy is to write down everything you want to include. Then, start to make different visualizations to organize the information. The experience should be something like sketching but with familiar visual conventions. You might try a Venn diagram, a hierarchical tree, a two-dimensional graph, a metaphorical landscape. The process of visualizing helps find a structure that organizes the information. Keep moving through different visualizations. Do not be afraid to invent your own visualizations (maybe there is a way to combine a Venn diagram with a Cartesian graph). Once you have found an effective visual structure to organize the ideas, the task of writing a well-structured paper or talk is much easier.

One does not need to be an expert in visualization or graphic design to make useful visualizations. DiSessa and Sherin (2000) have referred to people's surprising visualization abilities as *meta-representational competence*.

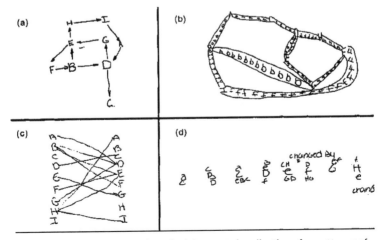

Figure V.6. Schematic examples of adolescent visualizations for patterns of disease transmission. (From Schwartz, 1993).

As an example, Schwartz (1993) asked adolescents to invent their own visualizations for organizing information about disease transmission. Students received written propositions of the form "F can pass the disease to B, E can pass the disease to F, B can pass the disease to E and D," and so forth. The students learned that their visualizations should help doctors determine the best groups to vaccinate next when a disease shows up. Figure V.6 shows some of their clever solutions. These representations distill the complex verbal information into a visual format that simplifies searching for paths of transmission. For similar demonstrations with primary school students learning statistical concepts, see Lehrer and Schauble (2000).

III. The Outcomes of Visualization

Once upon a time, the educated person took classes in drawing. Not anymore. Although schools still focus on helping students interpret visual representations, they rarely provide students with an opportunity to learn how to produce their own visualizations. Ideally, advancements in graphics tools and the ability to share products electronically will bring visualization back into the curriculum. Ainsworth, Prain, and Tytler (2011) advocate bringing drawing into the science curriculum because visualization

- enhances student engagement,
- helps students learn how to represent information,
- helps students learn to reason in science,
- is a major way to communicate scientific data and models, and
- is a learning strategy.

Here, we primarily focus on visualization as a strategy for discovering new relations and putting those relations into an orderly structure. Like all strategies for enhancing creativity and discovering something new, there can be no guarantee of success. Arranging and rearranging sticky notes does not always work, but it is still a good idea. Visualizing improves the odds.

A good spatial organization can help people search through large amounts of information. A train schedule organizes information so it is easy to find departure and arrival times for all the locations. The eyes can swiftly move from location to location, knowing what to expect at each. Imagine instead train times and locations written over several paragraphs. You would not know where to look for information, so you would have to guess or work your way down from the very beginning to make sure you did not miss what you were looking for.

IV. Can People Learn to Teach Themselves with Visualization?

Not only do people learn to use visualizations they have been taught; they also learn the very idea of inventing their own visualizations to handle novel problems. A study with adolescents shows that people transfer the use and invention of visualizations (Schwartz, 1993). Two weeks before the start of instruction on visualization, students received a packet of science problems. In the middle of the packet was a science problem that involved complex causal relations (e.g., food webs). Similarly, two weeks after instruction, students received another packet, and in the middle was another complex problem. Both questions were suitable to path diagrams that show how one entity influences another (e.g., as shown in Figure V.6a). The question was whether students would spontaneously construct visualizations to help solve the problems.

In between the pre- and posttest, students completed instruction on visualization. They received complex information and tried to create a visualization of their own. Afterward, the instructor showed the visualizations that experts use for these types of problems. This occurred for three different types of visualizations, one per day. Students completed one of two possible sequences of visualizations. The primary difference was that one group learned how to make path diagrams and the other did not.

Path Condition: matrices → path diagrams → permutation lists
No-Path Condition: matrices → Cartesian graphs → permutation lists

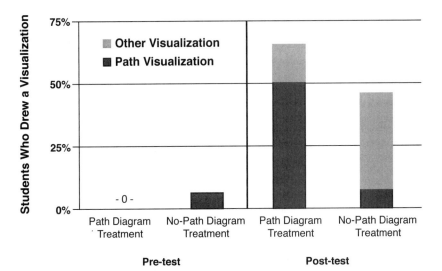

Figure V.7. Spontaneous use of visualization before and after instruction (based on data from Schwartz, 1993).

Figure V.7 shows that very few students made visualizations at pretest. At posttest, students were much more likely to create visualizations to help solve the complex problem, despite the fact that nothing in the problem told them to visualize. (They squeezed drawings into the margins of the worksheet.) Of special interest is the difference between the Path and No-Path conditions. In the Path condition, 78 percent of the students' visualizations were path diagrams. They had learned to recognize the sort of information that was appropriate for a path diagram, and they appreciated the value of path diagrams enough that they took the time to make one. This is a strong demonstration of spontaneous transfer. Even more compelling, nearly 50 percent of the students in the No-Path condition visualized. These students never learned about path diagrams, which is why only 18 percent of their visualizations were path diagrams. Instead, they transferred the very idea of making visualizations for complex information and made up their own representations for the posttest problem.

Once people learn how much visualizations can help, they are more likely to use them. Martin and Schwartz (2009) provided undergraduate and graduate students in science with a series of diagnosis problems. The students received twelve sheets of paper that each described the symptoms and disease of a prior patient. The students had to use this information to help diagnose new patients. Each graduate student created a visualization of the information on the sheets before trying to diagnose the first new patient (e.g., by making a matrix of diseases by symptoms). Once they had made their visualization, often spending up to twelve minutes, they never referred back to the original twelve sheets of paper. In contrast, 82 percent of the undergraduates jumped straight into diagnosing the new patients. They shuffled through the sheets of paper for each new patient and never made visualizations. The authors speculated that the graduate students had much more experience working with their own data and trying to figure out what was going on. They had experienced the value of organizing data visually, even though it takes more time at the outset.

V. Risks of Visualization

The visual system excels at finding patterns, but vision does not permit conflicting interpretations simultaneously, as demonstrated by Figure V.8 (Schwartz & Heiser, 2006). This creates the risk of overcommitting to one pattern at the expense of another possibility. If one locks into an interpretation, other possible interpretations can be blocked. Csikszentmihalyi and Getzels (1970) studied creativity among painters. The painters received

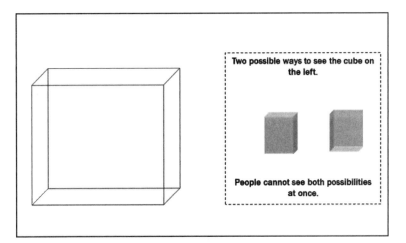

Figure V.8. The Necker cube. The visual system is deterministic and cannot see two alternatives simultaneously. (From Schwartz and Heiser, 2006.)

items to paint into a still life. Some of the painters arranged the items and began painting quickly. They had formed an early interpretation of what there was to see, and they spent their time executing that interpretation. Other painters kept rearranging the items while painting. They were trying to develop new possible interpretations. Not only were this latter group's paintings judged as more creative, but these painters were also more likely to be successful, practicing artists many years later (Csikszentmihalyi, 1990).

One way to summarize the risk of an early interpretation is that it can cause verbal overshadowing. A verbal interpretation of visual information can preempt further visual pattern finding. As a stunning example, Schooler and Engstler-Schooler (1990) showed people a videotape that included a salient individual. Some people had to describe the individual's face, and some did not. Those people who had described the person's face did worse at recognizing the person later! They relied on their less precise verbal memory instead of their visual memory.

To mitigate the risk of premature interpretive closure, one can explicitly make multiple, different visualizations. Do not be content with the clever Venn diagram you invented; also try to make a 2 ′ 2 table of the same information. This way you can see a range of possible visual structures rather than just refining whatever idea happened to come first (Dow et al., 2010). In a classroom, it is possible to capitalize on the natural variability across students. Students can work individually or in small groups to create their representations, and then work collectively to find the best elements across the visualizations. From there, they can create a final representation best suited to the task (Danish & Enyedy 2007).

A second risk is that students may slavishly follow a visualization procedure. Heckler (2010), for example, gave a physics word problem to undergraduate students. Half of the students received only the word problem. The other half were prompted to make a force diagram of the problem first, as they had learned earlier in the physics course. The students told to make the diagram did worse on the problem! They treated the visualization as a chore rather than as a tool. This finding does not imply that it is bad to suggest that students use visualizations to help solve problems—it is generally a useful strategy. Rather, the risk occurs when visualization becomes so proceduralized and prescribed that it no longer supports student discovery of structure.

VI. Examples of Good and Bad Use

Imagine that someone receives the task of visualizing four major components of visualization (and assume the person understands what they mean):

> 1. *Flexible abstraction:* deciding which elements to include
> 2. *Combination:* integrating elements
> 3. *Borrowing structure:* integrating conventional representational formats
> 4. *Reinterpretation:* seeing relations in new ways

A terrible approach begins with, "I am not a spatial thinker; I cannot do this." Spatial thinking comprises very many distinct skills (Newcombe & Shipley, 2015), and it is extremely unlikely that a person is so dismal at every single skill that visualization is useless. Moreover, in a review of 217 studies, researchers found that spatial abilities improve through practice (Uttal et al., 2013). Regardless of people's self-attributions, visualization depends on their willingness to try, not their spatial abilities.

A better approach is to sketch out some different possibilities. The top panel of Figure V.9 shows two early visualizations produced by Martin and Schwartz (2014) but never published. The Venn diagram captured the idea that people can combine the four major components during visualization. The two horizontal lines reflect the authors' attempt to dimensionalize aspects of visualization. The bottom panel combines these two ideas into an integrated matrix format. Whether or not the final visualization is ideal, the process of visualizing led to the realization of structure that goes beyond the original list of four major components.

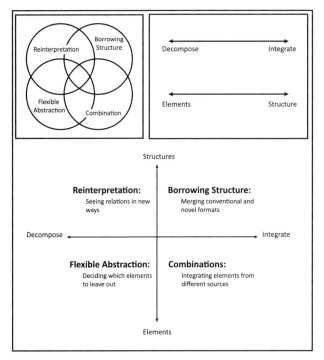

Figure V.9. Progressive visualizations that ultimately resulted in the bottom panel. (From Martin and Schwartz, 2014.)

VII. References

Ainsworth, S., Prain, V., & Tytler, R. (2011). Drawing to learn in science. *Science, 333*, 1096–1097.

Csikszentmihalyi, M. (1990). The domain of creativity. In M. A. Runco & R. S. Albert (Eds.), *Theories of creativity* (pp. 190–212). Newbury Park, CA: Sage.

Csikszentmihalyi, M., & Getzels, J. (1970). Concern for discovery: An attitudinal component of creative production 1. *Journal of Personality, 38*(1), 91–105.

Danish, J. A., & Enyedy, N. (2007). Negotiated representational mediators: How young children decide what to include in their science representations. *Science Education, 91*(1), 1–35.

DiSessa, A. A., & Sherin, B. L. (2000). Meta-representation: An introduction. *Journal of Mathematical Behavior, 19*(4), 385–398.

Dow, S. P., Glassco, A., Kass, J., Schwarz, M., Schwartz, D. L., & Klemmer, S. R. (2010). Parallel prototyping leads to better design results, more divergence, and increased self-efficacy. *ACM Transactions on Computer-Human Interaction, 17*(4), Article 18:1-24.

Heckler, A. F. (2010). Some consequences of prompting novice physics students to construct force diagrams. *International Journal of Science Education, 32*(14), 1829–1851.

Lehrer, R., & Schauble, L. (2000). Inventing data structures for representational purposes: Elementary grade students' classification models. *Mathematical Thinking and Learning, 2*(1–2), 51–74.

Martin, L., & Schwartz, D. L. (2009). Prospective adaptation in the use of external representations. *Cognition and Instruction, 27*(4), 370–400.

Martin, L., & Schwartz, D. L. (2014). A pragmatic perspective on visual representation and creative thinking. *Visual Studies, 29*, 80–93.

McElhaney, K. W., Chang, H. Y., Chiu, J. L., & Linn, M. C. (2014). Evidence for effective uses of dynamic visualisations in science curriculum materials. *Studies in Science Education, 51*(1), 49-85.

Newcombe, N. S., & Shipley, T. F. (2015). Thinking about spatial thinking: New typology, new assessments. In J. S. Gero (Ed.), *Studying visual and spatial reasoning for design creativity* (pp. 179–192). New York, NY: Springer.

Pea, R. D. (1987). Cognitive technologies for mathematics education. In A. Schoenfeld (Ed.), *Cognitive science and mathematics education* (pp. 89–122). Hillsdale, NJ: Erlbaum.

Schooler, J. W., & Engstler-Schooler, T. Y. (1990). Verbal overshadowing of visual memories: Some things are better left unsaid. *Cognitive Psychology, 22*(1), 36–71.

Schwartz, D. L. (1993). The construction and analogical transfer of symbolic visualizations. *Journal of Research in Science Teaching, 30*(10), 1309–1325.

Schwartz, D. L., & Heiser, J. (2006). Spatial representations and imagery in learning. In K. Sawyer (Ed.), *Handbook of the learning sciences* (pp. 283–298). Cambridge, UK: Cambridge University Press.

Uttal, D. H., Meadow, N. G., Tipton, E., Hand, L. L., Alden, A. R., Warren, C., & Newcombe, N. S. (2013). The malleability of spatial skills: A meta-analysis of training studies. *Psychological Bulletin, 139*(2), 352-402.

Wertheimer, M. (1938). Laws of organization in perceptual forms. In W. D. Ellis, *A source book of gestalt psychology* (pp. 71–88). London: Routledge and Kegan Paul. (Original work published 1923)

Zhang, J. (1997). The nature of external representations in problem solving. *Cognitive Science, 21*(2), 179–217.

V IS FOR VISUALIZATION

What is the core learning mechanic?
Drawing a spatial representation helps organize ideas and information. Some examples include maps, diagrams, sketches, graphs, Venn diagrams, trees, and matrices.

What is an example, and what is it good for?
In the early 1900s, Harry Beck created a visualization of the London subway that sacrificed exact geographic detail for a structure more relevant to the subway passenger. It led to the modern subway map used by nearly every subway system. Visualization is a strategy for organizing complex information. It works for inherently spatial information, as may be found in many science topics. It also works for nonspatial information, as in the case of a calendar, which uses space to represent time. Visualization can help people discover new structure that improves learning and future problem solving.

Why does it work?
Creating a spatial organization of ideas helps the visual system find patterns. Visual patterns support the discovery of structure, new interpretations, and the efficient search of information.

What problems does the core mechanic solve?
- People cannot think of a way to structure their ideas.
  - A presentation just marches through a series of ideas rather than providing a framework.
- People find themselves overwhelmed by complex information.
  - A taxi driver needs to learn the roads and the best routes.
- Student ideas are too vague.
  - A student says, "There is an earthquake because the land collides."

Examples of how to use it
- Construct a visualization to organize a presentation.
  - Present a Venn diagram. Explain each circle separately and then their overlap.
- Use a spatial representation that helps set out the alternatives.
  - Make a flow chart to show the sequence and decision points in a process.
- Diagram a complex situation so it is possible to keep track of all the factors.

○ Draw the multiple pathways of influence in social situations. It may be useful to try several ways of visualizing the information.

Risks

- People may reach premature closure and miss other possible structures.
- People treat visualization as a chore to follow rather than as a way to discover structure.
- People believe they are not spatial thinkers and that therefore they cannot visualize.

W is for Worked Examples

Acquiring skills and procedures

WORKED EXAMPLES ARE models of expert solutions. Novices can follow the expert's procedures and explanations to learn how to solve similar problems on their own.

A major challenge for instruction is how to help people get started learning (see Chapter P). Worked examples are particularly useful when novices might flounder needlessly when they have to solve problems on their own. For example, imagine you borrowed your friend's bike. It gets a flat tire. You have the tools to fix it but do not know how. What would you do?

(a) Hire someone else to fix it.
(b) Try to figure out how to fix it on your own.
(c) Observe someone else fixing a tire.
(d) Watch a video on YouTube with step-by-step instructions on how to fix a tire.

If you have the money and zero desire to dirty your hands, (a) is a good choice. Otherwise, the better choice is (d), which is the worked example. A worked example differs from (b), which is solving problems on your own. Instead of having to figure it out, the worked example just shows you. A worked example also differs from (c), which is pure observation. Worked examples break down the steps to completing a task, and at their best, they explain the reason for each step. Highlighting each separate step helps people notice each move they need to take, and the explanation helps people understand each step so they can adapt them to their specific circumstance (which may differ slightly from the video).

I. How Worked Examples Work

In their simplest form, worked examples extend observational learning (see Chapter O). Through observation, people can learn to imitate another person. Worked examples help solve two challenges inherent to pure observation. The first is that a learner can have difficulty segmenting an observed behavior into simple, imitable components. For example, juggling happens quickly with many simultaneous moves. Should a learner pay attention to the balls in the air, the movement of the hands, the position of the juggler's legs? A worked example separates the elements, so the learner can see and practice each one. The second challenge of observational learning is that people may not know what the model has in mind. This can make it hard to figure out the purpose for a specific behavior, which leads to brittle imitation. For instance, the juggler may do certain moves with extra flair. Without knowing that this is to entertain the audience, the learner might always try to imitate the flair. A good worked example explains the goal or reasons for each component behavior. This way, learners can figure out which aspects of the behavior are critical and how they can adapt them to their own purposes.

Worked examples can also work without a human model. A worked example can show a series of algebraic transformations, one per line, without showing a person actually writing out each step. Even though there is no person, the worked example shows the steps of an expert, and ideally, it reflects the expert thinking as well.

When doing algebra, and the many other symbolic tasks in school, it is easy to forget the steps reflect someone else's thoughts about the problem. Worked examples try to make the hidden expert thinking more explicit. A good worked example shows how the expert decomposed a larger problem into subgoals and the steps taken for each. It also explains what the expert had in mind to a useful degree.

Which of the following do you find most helpful?

Example A

Solve for a:
$(a + b)/c = d$

$$a + b = dc$$
$$a = dc - b$$

Example B

Solve for a:

$(a + b)/c = d$	Try to isolate a on one side of the equation.
$a + b = dc$	Multiply both sides by c to get rid of the $1/c$ term on the left.
$a = dc - b$	Then subtract b from both sides to isolate a.

If you remember your algebra, example A is probably sufficient. It simply shows the steps, and you can fill in the reasons for each step. If you are just starting, example B is probably better. It explains the purpose of each subgoal, which may help students flexibly apply the steps to new situations that do not involve exactly solving for a.

Scholars who study worked examples often compare their benefits against learning by problem solving. In a worked example, people are shown what to do and why. In problem solving, people need to figure out what to do and why. A disadvantage of problem solving for beginners is that they may never actually figure out how to solve a problem, or they may waste time on false leads before finally figuring out the solution. Worked examples help ensure learners do not spend time fuddling through mistakes, because the way to solve the problem is modeled for them.

A nonintuitive finding is that, compared with problem solving, following a worked example can lead to better encoding and memory of solution procedures. The reason is that worked examples reduce cognitive load (Sweller, 1994). *Cognitive load* refers to the amount of information people need to track simultaneously to accomplish a task: more information = more cognitive load. Working memory is the memory system that enables the conscious manipulation of information (see Chapter E). Problem solving requires managing more information in working memory and increases cognitive load. People need to remember their prior tries; they need to search for the next thing to do; they need to decide on problem-solving strategies; they need to figure out which information is relevant. The result is that fewer cognitive resources are available for learning the relevant information. When people are being interviewed for a job, they can concentrate so hard on giving good answers that later in the day they cannot remember the questions or their answers. Worked examples reduce many of the extraneous demands of problem solving and thereby preserve cognitive resources needed for learning.

II. How to Use Worked Examples to Enhance Learning

Deliberate practice (see Chapter D) is for advanced performance, while worked examples are for early learning. Worked examples are useful in domains where procedural fluency is important and a goal is efficient, errorless performance (see Chapter K).

There are three ways to bolster the effects of worked examples for learning. The first is to adhere to a few design principles. The second is to set up the instructional tasks that wrap around the worked example. The third is to choose the right level of task decomposition.

CREATING WORKED EXAMPLES

To create effective worked examples, <u>reduce distracting complexity</u>. The goal is to avoid any extraneous cognitive load that detracts from focusing on the steps of the solution. If students are following a diagram, remove labels that are irrelevant to the worked example. Furthermore, <u>avoid splitting attention</u>, such as making students jump and back forth from a block of text to a diagram

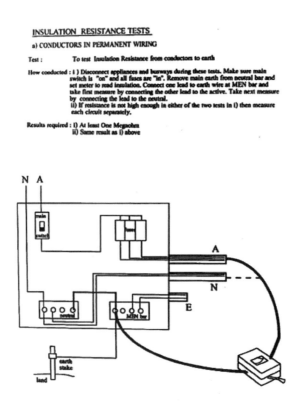

Figure W.1. Original instructions for a wiring diagram. (From Chandler and Sweller, 1991.)

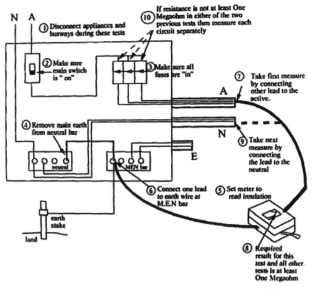

FIGURE 2   Example of the instructional format presented to the modified group of Experiment 1.

Figure W.2. Redesigned instructions to reduce cognitive load. See if you can notice the different design principles the authors used to improve the instructions. (From Chandler and Sweller, 1991.)

(Mayer, Heiser, & Lonn, 2001). <u>Eliminate the need to search for information</u>—if you have followed assembly instructions for furniture, you may have experienced the nuisance of shifting from the written instructions to the diagram of the next step and then to yet a third document that indexes the different screws and parts. Finally, <u>highlight the subgoals</u>, and consider whether it will be useful to explain their reasons. In cases where learners can (and will be able to) explain to themselves the reason for each subgoal, the answer may be no. In other cases, providing explanations can help learners understand why they are doing each step, so they can generalize to other situations.

A wonderful example is provided by Chandler and Sweller (1991). Figure W.1 shows an original set of instructions. Figure W.2 shows how they improved the instructions. The two examples make a great pair of contrasting cases. See if you can notice whether the authors followed all the underlined-design principles described in the preceding paragraph.

INSTRUCTIONAL TASKS

Additional activities can enhance the benefits of worked examples. One easy trick is to interleave worked examples with problems. For example, alternate a worked example with a similar problem that students have to solve on their own. This can help motivate students to engage and understand the worked example, because they will have to solve similar problems. Moreover, solving a follow-up problem on their own helps students remember the solution better.

A harder trick is to encourage self-explanation. Self-explanation refers to the mental monolog that people use to work out the meaning of a text or diagram. For instance, people can ask themselves what-if questions to see if they have thought through the implications of what they are reading. Because worked examples typically provide procedural instructions rather than conceptual explanations, it is up to learners to make sure they understand the purpose of the procedure in a larger context. Even if a worked example includes explanations for each step, learners still need to make sure they understand those explanations. People do not always naturally self-explain, because it is effortful. Chapter S provides some examples of prompts that encourage self-explanation.

TASK DECOMPOSITION

Making a worked example that leads to flexibility depends on many decisions about the level of detail to include. Consider the differences in the following algebra transformations:

(a) $3x = 6$
$\rightarrow x = 2$
(b) $3x = 6$
$\rightarrow 3x \div 3 = 6 \div 3$
$\rightarrow x = 2$

Example (a) is appropriate for advanced students. Example (b) is better for beginners, because it shows the hidden step of dividing by 3 on both sides. For some, the following worked example (c) would be even better, because it shows why the 3s disappear:

(c) $3x = 6$
$\rightarrow 3x \div 3 = 6 \div 3$
$\rightarrow (3 \div 3)x = 6 \div 3$
$\rightarrow (1)x = 2$
$\rightarrow x = 2$

A major task for the designer of worked examples is choosing the right level of decomposition for a student's incoming knowledge. Experts can be bad at this, because they have an expert blind spot (Nathan & Petrosino,

2003). They forget what it was like to be a novice, and they do not realize how much they have chunked their knowledge where lots of substeps are combined into one big step.

When designing instruction, it is often useful to work with a content expert and play the intelligent novice. Keep asking, "Why did you take that step?" For example, "Why did you divide both sides by three?" This way you can figure out how to decompose the steps for a novice. This is a form of cognitive task analysis, where you use problem-solving interviews to try to figure out each cognitive step needed to solve a problem. Learners need to understand these steps or subgoals, so they can transfer components of the overall solution procedure to a new situation (Catrambone & Holyoak, 1990). If they do not learn the subgoals and purposes of the relevant steps, they will only be able to use the whole cloth procedure for identical problems.

III. The Outcomes of Worked Examples

The most natural outcome of worked examples is early procedural skill. Beginners learn the steps to take with no-nonsense efficiency, so they can get started with effective problem solving sooner (Salden, Koedinger, Renkl, Aleven & McLaren, 2010). From there, learners can begin to apply, refine, and customize those steps in actual problem solving.

Worked examples are especially good for well-defined domains, such as algebra, where there are known moves and clear goals. (Ill-defined domains, such as solving poverty, do not have a clear set of moves or subgoals that will achieve a solution.) Worked examples, by themselves, are not a natural fit for conceptual knowledge, because understanding concepts often requires making very many connections among ideas. Expressing all those connections in a worked example can overwhelm the simple elegance and cognitive parsimony of a good worked example. However, combining worked examples and self-explanation can support conceptual understanding.

Worked examples have shown benefits for learning over unaided problem solving in domains including algebra, geometry, physics, and computer programing (Atkinson, Derry, Renkl, & Wortham, 2000). Returning to our algebra example from earlier, here is a prototypical example of a study that uses different instructional conditions to show that worked examples are superior to problem solving.

Problem-Solving-Only condition:

(1) Solve for a. (2) Solve for h.
$(a + b)/c = d$ $(h + k)/g = a$

Worked-Example condition:

(1) Solve for *a*.   (2) Solve for *h*.

$(a + b)/c = d$ $(h + k)/g = a$

$(a + b)/c \times c = dc$

$a + b = dc$

$a + b - b = dc - b$

$a = dc - b$

Students are typically first introduced to a topic through a lecture or reading. Then students in the Problem-Solving condition solve a set of problems as they might during homework or seatwork (or in a computerized environment). In contrast, students in the Worked-Example condition go through a set of problem pairs. In the pairs, one problem is set up as a worked example that students can follow, and the second is a similar problem the students have to answer themselves. Finally, a posttest measures their abilities to apply the solutions to relatively similar kinds of problems. Most of the time, the worked-example group comes out ahead.

IV. Can People Learn to Teach Themselves with Worked Examples?

To our knowledge, nobody has examined whether students can be taught to seek out worked examples. One reason is that people do this pretty naturally, if there are examples to be had. For example, homeowners might look up a video on YouTube about how to paint their kitchen. Someone learning to draw a cartoon might look for step-by-step instructions from a book.

People can help themselves learn better from worked examples by employing self-explanation. For example, they can try to predict the next step in problem solving and check if they are right, or they can ask themselves why a particular step in the solution is important. When worked examples are coupled with self-explanations, learners gain more (Renkl, Stark, Gruber, & Mandl, 1998).

V. Risks of Worked Examples

Most risks of worked examples can be captured by an analogy to automobile navigation systems. When a car navigation system leads drivers step by step, drivers take those steps and arrive at the desired location. However, the next time they drive to the same location, they cannot remember the steps very well on their own. Even if they do remember the steps, they cannot consider any possible variations, because they did not experience any variation during initial learning. They do not know how the navigation system made its decisions among alternative routes.

To mitigate the risk of students blindly following worked examples without remembering, it can be useful to (a) alternate worked examples and problems as described above and (b) fade worked example support. For instance, one might take a page from the generation playbook (see Chapter G) and slowly remove pieces of the worked example, which students need to fill in from memory. Alternatively, one might simply begin to withhold the worked examples or add an incentive to stop looking at the worked examples (e.g., it begins to cost players points in a game after the first two peeks at a worked example). It is a natural tendency to want to get the solution if it is available, so sometimes it takes extra steps to push students to figure it out on their own (Roll, Aleven, McLaren, & Koedinger, 2011).

To avoid the risk of students being unable to handle variation, provide students some variation during learning, for example, by showing negative instances where the solution procedure does not work. It can also be useful to provide students with two worked examples side by side, where each achieves the same outcome but through a slightly different route (Rittle-Johnson & Star, 2007).

A common risk of being told solutions is that people pay attention to the solution more than they pay attention to the context in which the solution should be applied (Schwartz, Chase, Oppezzo, & Chin, 2011). When relying on the car's navigation system, people often pay more attention to the instruction "turn left in 100 feet" than to the specific landmarks they can use to recognize when to take the turn in the future. The consequence is that they will not recognize when to use the turn-left procedure on their own. Similarly, with worked examples students may not notice the conditions that give rise to the problem, and they will fail to recognize those conditions later, and fail to apply their knowledge. One possible way to avert this risk is to use worked examples with just-in-time telling (see Chapter J): provide students with an opportunity to explore the problem space before delivering the efficient solution in a worked example.

Another risk of worked examples is that students might come to expect that they should quickly know the correct solution strategy to apply to problems. When given a difficult open-ended problem that they have not been taught how to solve, students may resist, or they may just apply what they do know instead of learning what is new (see Chapter K).

VI. Examples of Good and Bad Use

One good use is for the early introduction of procedures in homework assignments. Provide worked examples along with similar problems students have to solve themselves. For example, when trying to help students learn a new procedural skill, such as creating a histogram chart in an Excel spreadsheet, create a worked example they can follow, giving step-by-step instructions with pictures and labeling each step. Indicate how the solution could be generalized. Instead of writing, "Highlight cells C2:C4," write "Highlight cells C2:C4, or whichever cells hold the data you want to plot." Afterward, students should create their own chart with new data.

A bad use is to provide worked examples as part of an end-of-term problem set on material already covered. If students already have a good understanding of the material, the worked examples are unnecessary, and time spent problem solving would be more beneficial.

VII. References

Atkinson, R. K., Derry, S. J., Renkl, A., & Wortham, D. (2000). Learning from examples: Instructional principles from the worked examples research. *Review of Educational Research, 70*(2), 181–214.

Catrambone, R., & Holyoak, K. J. (1990). Learning subgoals and methods for solving probability problems. *Memory and Cognition, 18*(6), 593–603.

Chandler, P., & Sweller, J. (1991). Cognitive load theory and the format of instruction. *Cognition and Instruction, 8*(4), 293–332.

Mayer, R. E., Heiser, J., & Lonn, S. (2001). Cognitive constraints on multimedia learning: When presenting more material results in less understanding. *Journal of Educational Psychology, 93*(1), 187-198.

Nathan, M. J., & Petrosino, A. J. (2003). Expert blind spot among preservice teachers. *American Educational Research Journal, 40*(4), 905–928.

Renkl, A., Stark, R., Gruber, H., & Mandl, H. (1998). Learning from worked-out examples: The effects of example variability and elicited self-explanations. *Contemporary Educational Psychology, 23*(1), 90–108.

Rittle-Johnson, B., & Star, J. R. (2007). Does comparing solution methods facilitate conceptual and procedural knowledge? An experimental study on learning to solve equations. *Journal of Educational Psychology, 99*(3), 561-574.

Roll, I., Aleven, V., McLaren, B. M., & Koedinger, K. R. (2011). Improving students' help-seeking skills using metacognitive feedback in an intelligent tutoring system. *Learning and Instruction, 21*(2), 267–280.

Schwartz, D. L., Chase, C. C., Oppezzo, M. A., & Chin, D. B. (2011). Practicing versus inventing with contrasting cases: The effects of telling first on learning and transfer. *Journal of Educational Psychology, 103*(4), 759-775.

Salden, R. J., Koedinger, K. R., Renkl, A., Aleven, V., & McLaren, B. M. (2010). Accounting for beneficial effects of worked examples in tutored problem solving. *Educational Psychology Review, 22*(4), 379–392.

Sweller, J. (1994). Cognitive load theory, learning difficulty, and instructional design. *Learning and Instruction, 4*(4), 295–312.

W IS FOR WORKED EXAMPLES

What is the core learning mechanic?
Worked examples involve demonstrating step by step how to complete a procedural task.

What is an example, and what is it good for?
A self-help video shows how to install a faucet and explains each step of the repair. Watching the video can save novices a great deal of time learning how to install the faucet compared with the inevitable doing and undoing that happens when they try on their own.

A second application is showing the solution steps for an algebra problem.

Solve for a:
$(a + b)/c = d$
$a + b = dc$
$a = dc - b$

When people do not know how to solve problems, worked examples are useful for initial learning. They help novices attend to the key steps, which helps them solve highly similar problems later.

Why does it work?
Worked examples build on observational learning. They allow the learner to observe and imitate well-defined steps. Ideally, they also share expert thinking processes, particularly how and why to segment complex problems into subgoals. A worked example can be more efficient than problem solving for initial learning. The worked example reduces unnecessary floundering and distractions, so people can focus on the actual steps that give the right solution.

What problems does the core mechanic solve?
- Students have no idea where to start when trying to solve problems.
  - A young student has never seen a variable and confronts $3 + x = 5$.
- Students have limited time to learn a set of procedures.
  - People need to complete safety training before they can start working.
- Students observe a model behavior but cannot imitate it very well.
  - A child cannot learn how to tie a shoelace by watching adults tie their shoes.

Examples of how to use it

- If students are first learning a specific algebra operation, provide a worked example followed by a similar problem for students to solve on their own.
- When trying to help students learn a new procedural skill, such as creating a histogram chart in an Excel spreadsheet, create a worked example they can follow, giving step-by-step instructions with pictures and labeling each step.

Risks

- Students may imitate the procedures of the worked example without understanding why each step is needed.
- Students may not learn when to use the procedures shown in a worked example.

is for eXcitement

Turning up attention and arousal

EXCITEMENT IS A physiological state of heightened arousal. It comes with increased heart rate, increased blood pressure, moist palms, focused attention, higher emotion. Moderate levels of arousal improve performance and memory encoding. Too much arousal leads to performance impairments, especially during difficult activities.

Imagine you are sitting in a college lecture in a dimly lit auditorium. There are three hundred other students and a professor on a faraway stage. It is the forty-fifth of seventy slides in biochemistry. In a burst, a student pops up and shouts, "I found Waldo!" Across the room, another student leaps from his chair dressed in a striped turtleneck, and both dash out of the room. A titter rises from the startled class, the professor rolls her eyes, and the lecture resumes.

Was this just a momentary distraction? Not necessarily—it may have improved your learning of the class material, even though Waldo had absolutely nothing to do with the lecture content.

I. How Excitement Works

People perform better when they are aroused (we are talking general arousal here, not sexual arousal). This makes intuitive sense, because low levels of arousal amount to drowsiness, which makes it hard to accomplish anything.

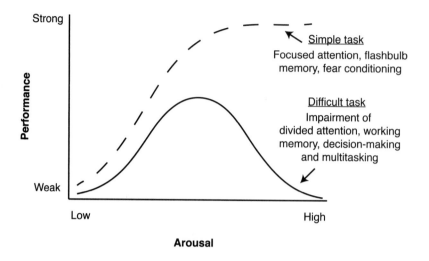

Figure X.1. Idealized graph of the relations among task difficulty, arousal, and performance. (From Diamond, Campbell, Park, Halonen, and Zoladz, 2007.)

Conversely, you can probably recall an occasion when you felt a little nervous before an event—a test, a meeting, a race—and you may have found that being amped up pushed you to better performance. Researchers describe the relation between arousal and performance as the *Yerkes-Dodson law* (Yerkes & Dodson, 1908).

Figure X.1 shows the changes in performance as arousal increases (Diamond, Campbell, Park, Halonen, & Zoladz, 2007). For simple tasks (dashed line), arousal pushes performance until it reaches a plateau where performance cannot increase any more. For difficult tasks, shown by the solid line, too much arousal hurts performance. Being too excited can cause a loss of focus and even a crash and burn for complex tasks.

The Yerkes-Dodson law describes performance using known skills, not learning new ones. Fortunately, moderate levels of arousal also facilitate learning, especially memory. Biologically, when an arousing event occurs, the body releases adrenaline and cortisol, which respectively initiate the "fight-or-flight" response and the stress response. The hormones travel to an emotion-processing center of the brain called the amygdala, which then modulates memory regions of the brain. The result is a change in memory processing, such that arousing events are remembered better than neutral events.

Emotions color arousal. Though both are arousing, anger feels different from unfettered joy. Hebb, an early scholar of arousal and performance, claimed that arousal "is an energizer, but not a guide; an engine but not a

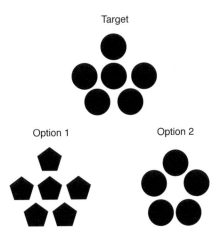

Figure X.2. Which is more similar to the target: option 1 or option 2? (Based on Fredrickson and Branigan, 2005).

steering gear" (1955, p. 249). Recent brain research indicates that positive and negative emotions serve as a steering gear that drives the engine of arousal towards different memory circuits. Arousal from pleasant emotions engages the brain's reward circuitry, while arousal from unpleasant emotions does not (Colibazzi et al., 2010).

Positive and negative feelings also steer attention. As an example, look at the target shapes in Figure X.2. Which option do you think is more similar to the target? If you had just watched a film that produced a positive emotional arousal, you would be more likely to choose option 1, which shares big-picture features with the target—the arrangement of shapes. (As described in Chapter A, they share the same deep structure.) If you watched a film that elicited a negative emotional arousal, you would be more likely to choose option 2, which shares a common surface feature: circles. Different emotions dictate attention to different information, which affects what people encode and remember (Fredrickson and Branigan, 2005).

Scientists have yet to agree on how emotion and arousal interact to influence learning. There are very many emotions to investigate including sadness, joy, and anger. For the remainder of the chapter, we consider arousal more generally, irrespective of emotional valence.

II. How to Use Excitement to Enhance Learning

There are many ways to increase arousal. Two methods commonly used by researchers are videos of violent or sexual acts (arousal is a primitive response!), but these would be bad choices for the classroom. We discuss a few ideas that might be more acceptable.

SOCIAL INTERACTION

People perform better when other people are around, called *social facilitation*. Cyclists go faster with a peer (Triplett, 1898). Billiards players shoot better with an audience (Michaels, Blommel, Brocato, Linkous, & Rowe, 1982). Even ants excavate more tunnels in the company of other ants (Chen, 1937). To explain social facilitation, Zajonc (1965) proposed that the mere presence of others induces general arousal. In turn, arousal enhances prepotent responses, or behaviors that are well known. He drew an unhappy implication for learning: arousal activates prepotent responses, which interfere with learning new responses. Zajonc concluded, "One practical suggestion . . . advise the student to study all alone, and to arrange to take his examinations in the company of many other students " (1965, p. 274). So much for collaborative learning! But wait . . .

Recent research has amended Zajonc's conclusion. Babies learn language better from a real person than from a video of a person (Kuhl, Tsao, & Liu, 2003). Adults learn science concepts better in the presence of real people. Okita, Bailenson, and Schwartz (2008) conducted a study that simply manipulated people's beliefs about whether they thought they were interacting with a person or a computer. Participants first read a science passage for about 5 minutes. They then put on virtual reality (VR) equipment to interact with a virtual female character, as shown in Figure X.3. The participant's job was to ask the character a set of scripted questions about the science reading, and the

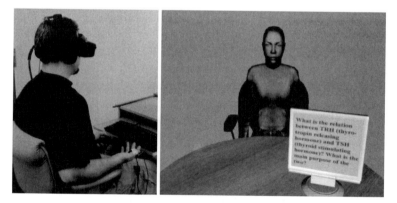

Figure X.3. Participants wore an immersive virtual reality headset and an arousal sensor on their finger (left). They read questions aloud to a visible character and heard the character's answers (right). (From Okita, Bailenson, and Schwartz, 2008.)

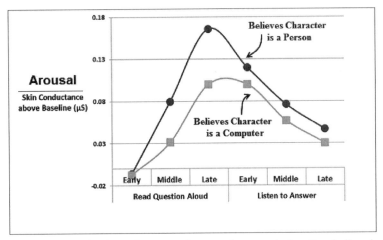

Figure X.4. People showed a greater increase in arousal when they believed they were reading a question to a person than when they believed they were reading to a computer (based on data from Okita et al., 2008).

character spoke her answer. Half of the participants were told that the female character was controlled by a computer program. The other half were told that the character was controlled by a woman whom they had just met. In reality, the female character delivered the same prerecorded answers to every participant. After the interactive session, participants removed the VR gear and answered questions to determine what they had learned.

People who thought the female character represented a real person learned about 25 percent more of the science content, even though the people in the two conditions had read the passage before entering VR and had identical VR exchanges. The mere belief of a social interaction improved learning. Why? Arousal was in play. The researchers tracked people's arousal by measuring their skin moisture. As people become more aroused, their skin moistens and a small current passes along the surface more easily. Figure X.4 shows the average time course of arousal for a single question-answer pair. When people read the question to the character, their arousal went up, and when they listened to the character's answer, it came down again. When an individual exhibited higher arousal when reading a question, the person was better at answering that same question on the posttest. Participants who thought they were talking to a person had a larger increase in arousal, so they did better on the posttest (Okita et al., 2008).

One interpretation is that social communication increases arousal, which prepares people to attend to and learn more from the responder. The authors corroborated this hypothesis. Another group of individuals also thought the VR character was a real person, but they did not read the questions aloud, so they were not communicating. They did not learn as much as participants who thought the character was a person and communicated the questions aloud (Okita et al., 2008). The study has an ironic implication for classroom lectures. In-person lectures may be social compared with reading a textbook, but they may not be social enough to take advantage of social facilitation for learning. To see real benefits, learners may need to take social actions, such as communicating to others or asking questions in class.

DON'T JUST SIT THERE

Simple things keep arousal from flatlining. One is caffeine, which helps learning (Borota et al., 2014) and shares some biological mechanisms with general arousal. Another technique is exercise. Cognition is often impaired during exercise, but a temporary boost in performance and learning occurs after exercise ends (Lambourne & Tomporowski, 2010). Active learning also helps. College lectures can intersperse multiple-choice questions. Students vote for their preferred answers (anonymously with "clickers") and then discuss the questions with their neighbor. A decade of research has shown that college physics students learn more through active learning compared with straight lectures (Crouch & Mazur, 2001). Arousal is likely one of the many mechanisms at play.

ENGAGE CURIOSITY AND INTEREST

When people say, "I'm excited about what I'm learning," they usually mean they are curious or interested, rather than feeling physiologically aroused. Interest and curiosity may act by different brain mechanisms than general emotional arousal. Emotional memory correlates with increased brain activity in the amygdala, whereas interest-related memory does not (Hamann, Ely, Grafton, & Kilts, 1999). Nevertheless, interest-based excitement does help learning, so it is worth considering.

Gruber, Gelman, and Ranganath (2014) asked participants to rate their curiosity for a set of trivia questions (e.g., "What is the actual meaning of the word *dinosaur*?"). They then completed an fMRI brain scan to measure how their brain responded to a series of questions. (FMRI uses the same machine that scans a torn up knee, but the machine is set to detect blood flow to areas of the brain rather than map tissue structure.) Participants saw each trivia question appear on a screen, followed by a random face, and then the answer to the triva question. Later, as one might suspect, they were able to remember more answers to questions about which they were initially curious. The surprising part involves the faces interspersed between the questions and answers. The faces were not famous and had nothing to do with the trivia topic. Nevertheless, participants remembered the faces that appeared just after the high-curiosity questions. Curiosity activated their reward circuits—the same circuits that activate when people receive external rewards such as money. The reward circuitry reinforced memory for any information in the time window of curiosity, relevant or not.

III. The Outcomes of Excitement

Excitement increases arousal, and arousal increases attention and improves memory (as long as arousal is not too great). Sometimes arousal even affects people's memory for information that came before the arousal, which has interesting implications for learning.

On the plus side, arousal can improve memory consolidation (see Chapter Z). Nielson and Arentsen (2012) lectured college students about the psychology of language. After the lecture, half of the students watched a short video of live-action oral surgery—very arousing, though not very happy. The other students watched a dull video about cardiovascular strength and depression. Both videos were unrelated to the lecture content. The group that watched the arousing video scored over ten percent higher on a test of the lecture material that had been presented before the video.

On the minus side, arousal can also interfere with memory formation. Lang, Newhagen, and Reeves (1996) showed this by asking people to watch a typical evening news story. In the video clip that accompanied the news report, some people saw a strongly negative and arousing video, and others saw something more bland. The negative video clip hindered people's memory of the news presented just before the video, compared with the milder video.

How can we make sense of these confusing results? Arousal improves memory for incidental information in one study, but interferes in another. One theory is that arousal leads to competition for memory (Mather & Sutherland, 2011). As an example of how it works, Wang (2015) asked people to watch an arousing video after memorizing a set of words. This helped people's memory of the words, but it hurt their memory of whether the words were read by a male or female speaker. Arousal helps people consolidate focal information, as in the case of the diligent college students learning about the psychology of language. Arousal pushes out nonfocal information, as in the case of the students watching a news report in a laboratory.

Returning to our original Where's Waldo? scenario, your memory for the biochemistry lecture material would be improved by the Waldo stunt, but only if you were actually focused on the lecture when the interruption occurred. This way the information would be salient in your mind and heightened by the arousal bias. If you were zoning out at the time of the interruption, the lecture would be peripheral in your mind, and it would get pushed toward forgetting by the arousing experience. Arousal plus proper attention is the best recipe.

IV. Can People Learn to Teach Themselves to Use Excitement?

People intuitively, and correctly, believe they learn more when they are excited. What people do not know is that *excitement does not need to come from the content of the learning material to improve memory.* Physical movement, loud noises, social interaction, and evidently the violent videos in all those studies can trigger excitement in the form of arousal. It should not be hard to teach people to self-administer these things, especially now that you can explain that it improves their memory. In fact, go drink a cup of coffee right now, so you can better remember what comes next.

V. Risks of Excitement

Before you leap to create the next killer homework arousal app, there are two things to keep in mind. The first is that the effects of excitement may be due to the change in arousal, not the actual level of arousal. A steady state of high alert may not yield benefits. (Your constantly excited friend may not be learning any better.) The second is that too much arousal causes performance declines. You may be tempted to have your app continuously increase arousal, but it cannot keep increasing arousal without ultimate catastrophe. The solution is to dish out excitement in timely doses.

Here is a huge risk: arousal and anxiety create a toxic brew. The catastrophe model of arousal (Fazey & Hardy, 1988) proposes that if a person feels high levels of anxiety in advance of a performance, then even moderate levels of arousal can cause a steep performance drop—this is also known as choking. Beilock (2010) proposes two concurrent processes behind the phenomenon. First, worrying or anxiety triggers the prefrontal cortex to exert conscious control over behaviors that would normally be automatic. For example, people overthink their golf swing when they are anxious. Second, anxiety disrupts prefrontal cortex function, stealing cognitive resources. With high anxiety and high arousal, people rely on a part of their brain that is less practiced for the task at hand, yet it is also temporarily impaired—a setup for failure.

Another risk is that people misinterpret their own arousal. Many scholars believe that the chain of emotion begins with arousal and ends with an interpretation of the arousal, called an emotion. Once people feel aroused, they try to develop an interpretation of the aroused feeling using surrounding evidence. For example, if it is good situation, they might interpret the arousal as joy. The risk is that people can make misattributions. Take the case of people who report themselves as lonely. They often have the skills needed for social interaction, but anxiety causes them to choke. In one study, Knowles, Lucas, Baumeister, and Gardner (2015) changed people's attribution toward their arousal. Participants received a drink and heard that it had a great deal of caffeine, when actually it had zero. The belief led to better social performance among lonely participants. Why? Because participants were able to (mis)attribute their nervous, jittery feeling to the caffeine, rather than to their own anxiety about being in a social situation. They were then able to apply their social skills unhampered by anxiety (and worrying about their anxiety).

A final curious risk is that emotionally arousing events give people a false sense of good memory. Talarico and Rubin (2003) asked people to recall how they learned about the World Trade Center attack of September 11, 2001. People were very confident in their memories, presenting vivid and detailed stories. However, their accuracy was actually no better than their memories of more mundane events that occurred around the same time. Similar results have been reported about the *Challenger* explosion in 1986 (Neisser & Harsch, 1992), for which people reported being very confident in their memories, but were mostly inaccurate.

VI. Examples of Good and Bad Use

Good: Add a little interactivity into a lecture. This should boost arousal just enough to improve attention memory for content. Students will also be grateful.

Good: Introduce a variable reward system in a video game, which increases arousal. Arousal is higher when people do not know whether or how much reward they will get, compared to when they get a standard reward every time (Howard-Jones, Demetriou, Bogacz, Yoo, & Leonards, 2011). Making a math videogame "jucier" by adding explosions will also help, but it is important to recognize that people will also learn to associate violent explosions with math, which we humbly suggest is not a great outcome (see Chapter R).

Bad: Induce anxiety before a test. This can put people on the downslope of the Yerkes-Dodson performance curve.

Bad: Dance around in a Waldo outfit. Not worth it.

VII. References

Beilock, S. (2010). *Choke: What the secrets of the brain reveal about getting it right when you have to.* New York: Free Press.

Borota, D., Murray, E., Keceli, G., Chang, A., Watabe, J. M., Ly, M., . . . Yassa, M. A. (2014). Post-study caffeine administration enhances memory consolidation in humans. *Nature Neuroscience, 17*(2), 201–203.

Chen, S. C. (1937). Social modification of the activity of ants in nest-building. *Physiological Zoology, 10*(4), 420–436.

Colibazzi, T., Posner, J., Wang, Z., Gorman, D., Gerber, A., Yu, S., . . . Peterson, B. S. (2010). Neural systems subserving valence and arousal during the experience of induced emotions. *Emotion, 10*(3), 377–389.

Crouch, C. H., & Mazur, E. (2001). Peer instruction: Ten years of experience and results. *American Journal of Physics, 69*(9), 970–977.

Diamond, D. M., Campbell, A. M., Park, C. R., Halonen, J., & Zoladz, P. R. (2007). The temporal dynamics model of emotional memory processing: A synthesis on the neurobiological basis of stress-induced amnesia, flashbulb and traumatic memories, and the Yerkes-Dodson law. *Neural Plasticity, Article ID 607703*,1-33.

Fazey, J. A., & Hardy, L. (1988). *The inverted-U hypothesis: A catastrophe for sport psychology.* Leeds, UK: National Coaching Foundation.

Fredrickson, B. L., & Branigan, C. (2005). Positive emotions broaden the scope of attention and thought-action repertoires. *Cognition and Emotion, 19*(3), 313–332.

Gruber, M. J., Gelman, B. D., & Ranganath, C. (2014). States of curiosity modulate hippocampus-dependent learning via the dopaminergic circuit. *Neuron, 84*(2), 486–496.

Hamann, S. B., Ely, T. D., Grafton, S. T., & Kilts, C. D. (1999). Amygdala activity related to enhanced memory for pleasant and aversive stimuli. *Nature Neuroscience, 2*(3), 289–293.

Hebb, D. O. (1955). Drives and the C.N.S. (conceptual nervous system). *Psychological Review, 62*(4), 243–254.

Howard-Jones, P., Demetriou, S., Bogacz, R., Yoo, J. H., & Leonards, U. (2011). Toward a science of learning games. *Mind, Brain, and Education*, 5(1), 33-41.)

Knowles, M. L., Lucas, G. M., Baumeister, R. F., & Gardner, W. L. (2015). Choking under social pressure: Social monitoring among the lonely. *Personality and Social Psychology Bulletin, 41*(6), 805–821.

Kuhl, P. K., Tsao, F. M., & Liu, H. M. (2003). Foreign-language experience in infancy: Effects of short-term exposure and social interaction on phonetic learning. *Proceedings of the National Academy of Sciences of the USA, 100*(15), 9096–9101.

Lambourne, K., & Tomporowski, P. (2010). The effect of exercise-induced arousal on cognitive task performance: A meta-regression analysis. *Brain Research, 1341*, 12–24.

Lang, A., Newhagen, J., & Reeves, B. (1996). Negative video as structure: Emotion, attention, capacity, and memory. *Journal of Broadcasting and Electronic Media, 40*(4), 460–477.

Mather, M., & Sutherland, M. R. (2011). Arousal-biased competition in perception and memory. *Perspectives on Psychological Science, 6*(2), 114–133.

Michaels, J. W., Blommel, J. M., Brocato, R. M., Linkous, R. A., & Rowe, J. S. (1982). Social facilitation and inhibition in a natural setting, *Replications in Social Psychology, 2,* 21-24.

Neisser, U., & Harsch, N. (1992). Phantom flashbulbs: False recollections of hearing the news about *Challenger.* In E. Winograd & U. Neisser (Eds.), *Affect and accuracy in recall: Studies of "flashbulb" memories* (pp. 9–31). New York: Cambridge University Press.

Nielson, K. A., & Arentsen, T. J. (2012). Memory modulation in the classroom: Selective enhancement of college examination performance by arousal induced after lecture. *Neurobiology of Learning and Memory, 98*(1), 12–16.

Okita, S. Y., Bailenson, J., & Schwartz, D. L. (2008). Mere belief in social action improves complex learning. In P. A. Kirschner, F. Prins, V. Jonker, & G. Kanselaar (Eds.), *Proceedings of the 8th International Conference for the Learning Sciences* (Vol. 2, pp. 132–139). Utrecht, Netherlands: International Society of the Learning Sciences.

Talarico, J. M., & Rubin, D. C. (2003). Confidence, not consistency, characterizes flashbulb memories. *Psychological Science, 14*(5), 455–461.

Triplett, N. (1898). The dynamogenic factors in pacemaking and competition. *American Journal of Psychology, 9*(4), 507–533.

Wang, B. (2015). Negative emotion elicited in high school students enhances consolidation of item memory, but not source memory. *Consciousness and Cognition, 33,* 185–195.

Yerkes, R. M., & Dodson, J. D. (1908). The relation of strength of stimulus to rapidity of habit-formation. *Journal of Comparative Neurology and Psychology, 18,* 459–482.

Zajonc, R. B. (1965). Social facilitation. *Science, 149*(3681), 269–274.

X IS FOR eXCITEMENT

What is the core learning mechanic?
Excitement increases physiological arousal, which focuses attention and improves memory acquisition.

What is an example, and what is it good for?
In the middle of a long lecture, a professor asks students to stand up and look around. Activity increases arousal, which in turn improves attention and memory for the material.

Why does it work?
Excitement is a physiological change associated with primitive flight-or-fight responses. Heart rates increase, palms become moist, attention focuses. Emotion colors arousal with positive or negative feelings. Positively arousing emotions activate the brain's reward system and the amygdala, both of which help lay down memory traces. The exciting event does not have to be relevant to the instructional content. Arousal after the fact can sometimes improve memory for what happened earlier.

What problems does the core mechanic solve?
- Students are not paying attention.
  ◦ A long lecture becomes so dull that students are close to sleeping.
- An instructor needs to emphasize a point.
  ◦ In the middle of a lecture, there is a key point that students have to remember.

Examples of how to use it
- Add arousing components to an educational video game.
  ◦ Introduce a variable reward system in a video game, such that players don't know exactly how much reward they will receive, rather than giving a constant reward each time.
- Include opportunities for social interaction.
  ◦ In a lecture class, give students a chance to talk to one another occasionally, which will increase their arousal.

Risks
- Too much excitement interferes with performance and learning.
- Arousal and anxiety combine to cause choking under pressure.
- If people are not paying attention to the target content, arousal can interfere with learning.

Y is for Yes I Can

Increasing self-efficacy

YES I CAN refers to self-efficacy—people's belief that they have what it takes to accomplish a goal. When people believe success is within reach, they approach activities more readily, persist longer, persevere in the face of failures, and accomplish more.

How do you convince yourself to try something? One argument is the payoff—a million-dollar lottery has an attractive payoff, so you try it. This part of the calculus is often called the utility or value. Sometimes, students do not perceive any utility in what they are supposed to learn, so they don't bother. (Chapters M, P, Q, and R address this issue.)

The second part of the calculus is whether you can succeed or not—your expectancy. This partially involves estimating the probability of success: maybe buying the lottery ticket wasn't such a good idea after all. People also have expectations about their abilities to cause success (self-efficacy): maybe you believe you can rig the lottery, so you play. If the utility of an endeavor is high and your expectancy for accomplishing that endeavor is high, you approach and persist.

Low self-efficacy is a tragedy for learning. Albert Bandura pinpoints the concern: "Self-belief does not necessarily ensure success, but self-disbelief assuredly spawns failure" (1997, p. 77). When students believe they cannot succeed, they give up easily and set low goals for themselves. They handicap their chances for learning, regardless of the odds. We address how to foster a sense of Yes I Can. An outstanding question is whether it is possible to foster a person's can-do attitude in general, or whether it always varies by activity, such as for baseball but not homework.

I. How Yes I Can Works

In Bandura's formulation, self-efficacy differs from self-esteem and self-confidence, which both involve people's overall sense of worth. People can have different feelings of self-efficacy for different tasks. Chase (2013) studied relatively accomplished scholars in mathematics and literature. She gave both groups of scholars an accessible but difficult problem in math (a tricky math problem) and in literature (a tricky poem). The mathematicians persisted on the math problem and noted the components of the problem that made it tricky. But when they received the poem, they said, "I've never been good at this stuff." Conversely, the literature scholars persisted on the poem and blamed the poet for being bloated, but blamed themselves for not being able to do the math problems, which they said they were never good at anyway. Perceived self-efficacy in one domain does not entail self-efficacy in another. This is a good thing, because few things are more dangerous than ignorant overconfidence. Bandura nails the point again: "The objective of education is not the production of self-confident fools" (1997, p. 65).

Bandura (1997) described four factors that influence people's self-efficacy: (1) mastery experiences: having had past success; (2) vicarious experiences: seeing others like you achieve the goal; (3) social persuasion: hearing you are efficacious; and (4) physiological signals: noticing the effort and time involved while doing an activity. Since Bandura's original work, most contemporary versions of self-efficacy include some form of self-attribution. People attribute a causal role to themselves for successes and failures. An example of attributional thinking comes from the fundamental attribution error (Ross, 1977): Americans tend to believe that other people's bad behavior is caused by bad personalities, whereas their own bad behavior is caused by the environment. For example, when driving to work, a car cuts you off, and you think the driver is a jerk and a bully, but when you cut someone off, it is because your boss would fire you for being late again. People regularly make motivation-relevant attributions that reveal the fundamental attribution error: "I cannot do this task well because my teacher is being mean."

Attributions can broaden the reach of a particular feeling of self-efficacy. This occurs through the existence of schemas. A schema is a general representation for a common class of situations. People have a schema for eating out that includes sitting down, ordering food, eating, and paying the bill (and maybe tipping). People can form an attribution toward a schema rather than just a specific instance ("I am good at eating out" versus "I am good at eating out at Moe's Greasy Spoon"). Of special relevance, learners can develop a self-attribution about their abilities toward the all-important generalized schema of school.

Carol Dweck (2006) has identified a pair of important self-attributions that often apply to the schema of school: fixed mindset and growth mindset. A fixed mindset holds that intelligence is innately fixed rather than learnable—some people are smart and some are not, and there is nothing you can do about it. The attribution that people do not have the causal power to improve their minds leads to poor learning behaviors. In contrast, with a growth mindset people believe that intelligence and abilities in school can grow with effort. Here are some key differences in the behaviors that come with a growth and fixed mindset:

Learners with growth mindset	Learners with fixed mindset
Focus on learning	Focus on performing
Persist in the face of challenge	Give up easily
Think of failure as an opportunity to learn	Avoid failure because it displays a lack of ability
Choose more challenging activities	Choose easier activities

The generalization of a mindset is likely a function of whether learners schematize two situations as similar or not. Students might have a growth mindset for a class that emphasizes making and inquiry but have a fixed mindset for a class that emphasizes single correct answers, or vice versa. Alternatively, they may subsume both types of instruction under the single schema of school and exhibit the same mindset for both.

The following are examples of mind-set survey questions. People answer by choosing from options that range from disagree a lot to agree a lot:

- You can learn new things, but you cannot really change your basic level of intelligence.
- I like work that I'll learn from even if I make a lot of mistakes.
- To tell the truth, when I work hard, it makes me feel as though I'm not very smart. (Mindset Works, n.d.)

You can match these questions more precisely to the motivational contexts you hope to address by asking students to indicate their level of endorsement of a more specific schema: "You can learn new things *in math* . . . "

At an even more general level of self-motivation, studies suggest people have self-attributions and emotional dispositions that operate on the scale of years. Damon has examined long-term purpose, which he defines as follows: "Purpose is a stable and generalized intention to accomplish something that is at once meaningful to the self and consequential for the world beyond the self" (2008, p. 33). Notice how this expands the notion of utility—it is not just about one's personal benefit but also about the world's benefit. Adopting large meaningful goals for life, such as wanting to become a doctor to help others, can lead learners to achieve positive outcomes (Yeager & Bundick, 2009).

Duckworth, Peterson, Matthews, and Kelly (2007) have adopted the term *grit* to refer to a collection of behaviors, strategies, and dispositions that drive long-term persistence. These largely fall under the rubric of noncognitive skills. Of course, they are not really noncognitive, because they often depend on memory, causal attributions, self-narratives, and strategies. A better term for noncognitive skills might be "things not tested by current achievement or IQ tests but that nevertheless predict important life and school outcomes." But then, that is just not a pretty name at all.

Grit especially emphasizes persistence and a passion for long-term goals. How strongly would you say the following statements apply to you?

(a) I finish whatever I begin.
(a) I become interested in new pursuits every few months.
(c) I have overcome setbacks to conquer an important challenge.
(d) I have been obsessed with a certain project or idea for a short time but later lost interest. (adapted from Duckworth, 2007)

If you strongly agree with statements A and C and do not think statements B and D sound like you, you would get a high grit score. Grit scores correlate with Ivy League GPAs, spelling bee success, and class retention at West Point (Duckworth et al., 2007). The grit score's degrees of association with these outcomes exceeds that for IQ.

Research on how to help people develop their capacity for grit and purpose is limited, and it is unknown whether training would help. It may depend on accreting many years of purposeful experiences, just like it takes athletes many years to build their abilities. As scientific constructs go, these are relatively new. For now, they provide insight enough, in a world of rampant tests of content mastery, to consider that character can influence people's success.

II. How to Use Yes I Can to Enhance Learning

There are two compatible approaches for improving students' can-do attitudes: Changing their self-attributions and improving their skills so they can experience a bolstering sense of success. We consider each in turn.

CHANGING ATTRIBUTIONS

One approach to improving self-efficacy is to change people's causal attributions about their abilities to control their own success. Just telling students they can succeed may be insufficient. But if we can teach students a simple causal mechanism for how their actions can control their success, it may improve their attributions dramatically. The premiere example comes from *Brainology*, a program that instills a growth mind-set (see http://www.mindsetworks.com). It teaches students that our brain grows and the neurons make connections when we try, emphasizing the malleability of the mind. The intent is to convince students to work hard to cause their brains to grow, rather than just worrying about how smart they are. Brainology has been successful with children grades 5–9, as well as older ages (Blackwell, Trzesniewski, & Dweck, 2007).

A second approach helps students appreciate the twisting path to success, so they do not mistake failure for incompetence. Except for sports-related advertisements, where we see examples of great effort, failure, sweat, and success, students do not normally see the nitty-gritty of achievement. This creates room for filling in all sorts of crazy ideas, such as successful people do not have to try hard, so if students try hard they must be stupid. Hong and Lin-Siegler (2012) helped students understand that success does not come easy, and they should not be deterred by their own challenges. They told stories about the struggles of famous scientists (Einstein, of course, but also Marie Curie.) Compared with hearing about the scientists' achievements (the usual presentation in books) or nothing at all, the students who heard stories of struggles exhibited better outcomes in attitudes and learning. Similarly, Schunk, Hanson, and Cox (1987) found that role models who display struggle and coping strategies work better than models who dismiss their struggles.

A third approach is to provide students with a successful peer who helps them believe that they, too, have the power to learn. Bartsch, Case, and Meerman (2012) used peer models in a statistics course. The students had started the course with high academic achievement generally but low self-efficacy in statistics. Half of the students listened to a live presentation from a prior student of similar age who spoke about her experiences, stress-management strategies, study methods, and eventual success in the course. She was portrayed as having incoming qualifications similar to those of the current students. The other half of the students imagined a successful statistics student and wrote about this person's time management, study methods, and stress-management skills. The group that witnessed the peer presentation increased in statistics self-efficacy. (See Chapter O for more on social models.) Those who wrote about an imagined successful student decreased in self-efficacy, perhaps because the students imagined a wide gulf between themselves and the imagined ideal. Using a "star pupil" as a role model can backfire if it leads learners to believe success is unattainable by mere mortals.

SKILL AND WILL

A major contributor to self-efficacy is the feeling of success. Pep talks can go only so far if people continually fail. In addition to improving people's will, we need to improve their skill. This book describes many ways to improve people's abilities at specific tasks, such as reading and hobbies. Researchers have also examined whether they can improve people's abilities at learning in general from school-based tasks under the rubric of self-regulated learning (Zimmerman & Schunk, 1989). Self-regulated learners know they have control over their learning. They set goals, organize, and self-evaluate their knowledge growth. People who do not use self-regulated learning can lack learning awareness, such as one of our sons, who regularly believed he had aced a test only to discover later that he got a D. (He turned out just fine, in case the gentle reader is worried.)

In an early study of self-regulated learning (before it was even called self-regulated learning), Schunk and Gunn (1985) taught nine- to eleven-year-olds who were struggling with division. Children worked on a packet of division problems for four days. Each day started with an adult modeling how to solve problems. The study had two manipulations that took place during the adult modeling. The first was whether students received training in developing good achievement beliefs. For instance, the adult said, "Students who do the best in division think that they can solve problems, work hard, and that they're getting pretty good in division. In this problem, you might think at first, 'I can do this one.' As you're working on it you might think, 'I can finish it if I work hard,' and when you finish it you might think, 'I'm getting pretty good at this.'" The second manipulation was whether students received training in the importance of good task strategies, such as, "Students who do the best in division also are careful when they multiply and subtract." The study was small (only ten students per condition), but the results are striking. Students completed a pretest and posttest of eighteen division problems. They also rated their self-efficacy for doing the problems.

	Self-efficacy gains		Skill gains	
	Achievement beliefs	No achievement beliefs	Achievement beliefs	No achievement beliefs
Task strategies	53%	36%	47%	43%
No task strategies	26%	15%	17%	20%

Table Y.1. Gains in self-efficacy and skill from lessons on division among nine- to eleven-year-old children (data from Schunk & Gunn, 1985)

Table Y.1 shows the gains from pretest to posttest for the four conditions. The combination of receiving achievement beliefs and task strategies was key for improving self-efficacy, and achievement beliefs without strategies did not help much. One interpretation is that the achievement beliefs may have helped children initially, but without the task strategies, the children encountered difficulties in solving the problems, which undermined the effect of being told, "Yes, you can."

Skilled performance can bring evidence of success, which in turn can increase students' willingness to try. Unfortunately, it is difficult to sense our own learning gains to feel success. If you are a college instructor and you want to improve end-of-semester course ratings, give students the same task at the start and end of the class, and let them see their two answers side by side just before rating your class. This will help them detect how much they have learned, and they will be more generous in their course ratings.

Less self-serving, we can also provide students appropriate feedback indicative of success. Schunk and Lily (1984) provided a simple demonstration. Middle school students learned a new arithmetic operation (finding a remainder without dividing). After instruction, students completed a series of problems designed to be challenging but ultimately to yield success. The students received simple feedback indicating the correct answer after each problem. The researchers found that early on, girls reported lower self-efficacy on the activity than boys, but after doing the worksheet and receiving simple feedback showing that they could, in fact, do the operation, girls reported self-efficacy equal to that of the boys. Of course, this study doesn't answer the question of where the gender difference in self-efficacy came from to begin with—it is likely the result of the pernicious and incorrect stereotype that girls cannot do math (see Chapter B). Instructors should attend to their responsibility of taking early steps to change attributions of low self-efficacy that arise from social stereotypes or other sources of negative information.

III. The Outcomes of Yes I Can

Self-efficacy influences both what we choose to do and how we interpret and respond to events. Self-efficacy has been shown to be an important factor in (a) approach behaviors, including career choice (Hackett, 1995); (b) persistence behaviors, including effort and perseverance in the face of obstacles or adversity; and (c) responses to effort, including stress and depression (Bandura, 1997). Over time, positive self-efficacy accumulates into an upward trajectory of learning and achievement.

An example comes from managers who interacted with a decision-making simulation in a business studies program (Bandura & Wood, 1989). The managers largely reported similar levels of self-efficacy at the start of the study. Half of the managers were prompted to believe that complex decision making is an acquirable skill developed through practice, and the simulation provided a vehicle for cultivating decision-making skills. The other half of the managers received prompts toward a fixed-capacity view: they were told that complex decision making depends on inherent cognitive capacities and that the simulation "provides a vehicle for gauging the underlying cognitive capacities" (p. 410). Ouch!

Over time, those prompted with the acquirable-skill mindset reported an increasing rise in self-efficacy when interacting with the simulation, whereas those in the fixed-capacity condition reported steady declines in self-efficacy. Moreover, those in the acquirable-skill condition increasingly used analytic strategies systematically and effectively, and they set more challenging goals. By the end, the acquirable skill condition had an average 20 percent higher simulated productivity than the fixed-capacity condition. Self-efficacy fuels its own success.

IV. Can People Learn to Teach Themselves Using Yes I Can?

Most approaches to helping people self-regulate their motivations involve some form of self-attributional talk: "My brain can grow, even though this is hard." These are demonstrably helpful strategies. Outside of school, people also need to set their own goals, and simple acronyms can help them create goals that can yield feelings of self-efficacy. For example, SMART goals are specific, measurable, achievable, relevant, and timely.

Unfortunately, it is exactly at those times when temptation is greatest that rationality is weakest. The motivational tank may be so empty that people have no reasoned will remaining (Baumeister & Vohs, 2007). Oppezzo and Schwartz (2013) examined a self-regulation strategy that does not require convincing oneself in the final hour. They gave high school students the goal of increasing the amount of fruits and vegetables in their diets. Then the students underwent training on how to distribute their motivational supports to the environment, for example, by putting reminders and rewards into their environment. A familiar example of a distributed strategy for losing weight is to keep fattening foods out of the house and to arrange a friend to give praise for a good day. They found that teaching students to distribute their motivational supports caused the students to consume more fruits and vegetables compared with students who were taught self-talk strategies.

V. Risks of Yes I Can

Risks of self-efficacy come from both sides of the fence. On one side, underestimating the importance of self-efficacy can rob students of agency. On the other side, encouraging it blindly or in the wrong way can result in misguided foolishness. We elaborate below.

BLAMING THE VICTIM

The belief that effort and persistence result in success resonates with the familiar puritan work ethic. A major risk is assuming that if students do not succeed, it is their fault for not working hard enough. It would be a mistake for an educator to abnegate responsibility for creating an effective learning environment, believing students should just try harder. If the environment is poorly designed for learning, we cannot blame the student for not being able to work hard enough to succeed.

A striking example involves learned helplessness. Animals that cannot avoid a harsh environment give up. In one study (Seligman & Maier, 1967), dogs received shocks they could not stop. Later, the dogs were put in a new box where the floor administered shocks. They could avoid the shocks by jumping over a barrier to a nonelectrified floor. They sat still, accepting the painful shocks. In contrast, other dogs who did not receive the uncontrollable shocks earlier leapt over the barrier to escape the electrified floor. People also exhibit learned helplessness, where they give up escaping shocks, loud noises, and other aversive stimuli (e.g., Thornton & Jacobs, 1971). Negative classrooms that are out of children's control may eventually lead to a collapse of self-efficacy, even when children switch to a new classroom where they could have some control if they just tried.

ASSUMING SELF-EFFICACY IS ALWAYS GOOD

Self-efficacy, mindset, and grit can be applied to any arena of life, including less than admirable ones. For instance, Hitler was likely one of the grittiest people in history, single-mindedly sticking to his goals through failed battles, logistical hang-ups, and global opposition. But most people would not call his grittiness good. Motivational tools need direction as well as strength.

PRAISING THE LEARNER, NOT THE EFFORT

"You're so smart," "you're so pretty"—praising learner traits can backfire, because it implicitly creates a belief in native ability rather than effort. Researchers praised fifth-graders after completing a set of easy puzzle problems (Mueller & Dweck, 1998). For half the students, the praise was directed at their intelligence, "You must be smart at these problems." For the other half it was directed at their effort, "You must have worked hard at these problems." Next, students picked whether they wanted to try easy or hard problems; 92 percent of the effort-praised students chose harder problems, compared with 33 percent of intelligence-praised students.

On a longer time scale, researchers found that one- to three-year-old children who received more parental praise for their behaviors (e.g., "I like how you covered your mouth") also exhibited more attributes of growth mindsets when they were seven to eight years old (Gunderson et al., 2013). These researchers did not demonstrate a causal connection, but it is an intriguing association.

VI. Examples of Good and Bad Use

Corno and Xu (2004) have called homework the job of childhood. Homework shares many characteristics with the work world, such as the challenge of self-discipline, motivation, and—dare we say it— soulless chores. So, as a parent, how could you help your child develop homework self-efficacy?

Bad (fixed mind-set): "Ugh. I was never good at science either. Let's just try to finish."

Bad (praising intelligence): "Wow. That was a really hard problem and you got it. You're so smart!"

Good (praising effort): "Wow. You worked super hard on that problem. It really paid off!"

So-so (only addressing will): "This is something that takes time and practice to learn. I am sure you can get this if you really work at it."

Good (addressing will and skill): "This is something that takes time and practice to learn. I am sure you can get this if you really work at it. Why don't you look at the strategies your teacher suggested in the handout."

VII. References

Bandura, A. (1997). *Self-efficacy: The exercise of control*. New York: W.H. Freeman.

Bandura, A., & Wood, R. E. (1989). Effect of perceived controllability and performance standards on self-regulation of complex decision-making. *Journal of Personality and Social Psychology, 56*, 805–814.

Bartsch, R. A., Case, K. A., & Meerman, H. (2012). Increasing academic self-efficacy in statistics with a live vicarious experience presentation. *Teaching of Psychology, 39*(2), 133–136.

Baumeister, R. F., & Vohs, K. D. (2007). Self⊠regulation, ego depletion, and motivation. *Social and Personality Psychology Compass, 1*(1), 115–128.

Blackwell, L. S., Trzesniewski, K. H., & Dweck, C. S. (2007). Implicit theories of intelligence predict achievement across an adolescent transition: A longitudinal study and an intervention. *Child Development, 78*(1), 246-263.

Chase, C. C. (2013). Motivating persistence in the face of failure: Equipping novice learners with the motivational tools of experts. In J.J. Staszewski (Ed.), *Expertise and Skill Acquisition: The Impact of William G. Chase* (pp. 59-84). New York: Psychology Press..

Corno, L., & Xu, J. (2004). Homework as the job of childhood. *Theory into Practice, 43*(3), 227–233.

Damon, W. (2008). *Moral child: Nurturing children's natural moral growth*. New York: Free Press.

Duckworth, A. (2007). Twelve-item grit scale. Retrieved August 1, 2015, from http://upenn.app.box.com/12itemgrit

Duckworth, A. L., Peterson, C., Matthews, M. D., & Kelly, D. R. (2007). Grit: Perseverance and passion for long-term goals. *Journal of Personality and Social Psychology, 92*(6), 1087-1101.

Dweck, C. (2006). *Mindset: The new psychology of success*. New York: Random House.

Gunderson, E. A., Gripshover, S. J., Romero, C., Dweck, C. S., Goldin⊠Meadow, S., & Levine, S. C. (2013). Parent praise to 1⊠to 3⊠year⊠olds predicts children's motivational frameworks 5 years later. *Child Development, 84*(5), 1526–1541.

Hackett, G. (1995) Self-efficacy in career choice and development. In A. Bandura (Ed.), *Self-efficacy in Changing Societies* (pp. 232-258). New York: Cambridge University Press.

Hong, H. Y., & Lin-Siegler, X. (2012). How learning about scientists' struggles influences students' interest and learning in physics. *Journal of Educational Psychology, 104*(2), 469-484.

Mindset Works (n.d.). What's My Mindset? (for age 12 to adult) [Measurement instrument]. Retrieved July 1, 2015, from http://community.mindsetworks.com/my-mindset?force=1.

Mueller, C. M., & Dweck, C. S. (1998). Praise for intelligence can undermine children's motivation and performance. *Journal of Personality and Social Psychology, 75*(1), 33-52.

Oppezzo, M., & Schwartz, D. L. (2013). A behavior change perspective on self-regulated learning with teachable agents. In R. Azevedo and V. Aleven (Eds.), *International handbook of metacognition and learning technologies* (pp. 485–500). New York: Springer.

Ross, L. (1977). The intuitive psychologist and his shortcomings: Distortions in the attribution process. In L. Berkowitz (Ed.), *Advances in experimental social psychology* (Vol. 10, pp. 173–220). New York: Academic Press.

Schunk, D. H., & Gunn, T. P. (1985). Modeled importance of task strategies and achievement beliefs: Effect on self-efficacy and skill development. *Journal of Early Adolescence, 5*(2), 247–258.

Schunk, D. H., Hanson, A. R., & Cox, P. D. (1987). Peer-model attributes and children's achievement behaviors. *Journal of Educational Psychology, 79*(1), 54-61.

Schunk, D. H., & Lilly, M. W. (1984). Sex differences in self-efficacy and attributions: Influence of performance feedback. *Journal of Early Adolescence, 4*(3), 203–213.

Seligman, M. E., & Maier, S. F. (1967). Failure to escape traumatic shock. *Journal of Experimental Psychology, 74*(1), 1-9.

Thornton, J. W., & Jacobs, P. D. (1971). Learned helplessness in human subjects. *Journal of Experimental Psychology, 87*(3), 367-372.

Wood, R., & Bandura, A. (1989). Impact of conceptions of ability on self-regulatory mechanisms and complex decision making. *Journal of Personality and Social Psychology, 56*(3), 407-415.

Yeager, D. S., & Bundick, M. J. (2009). The role of purposeful work goals in promoting meaning in life and in schoolwork. *Journal of Adolescent Research, 24*(4), 423-452.

Zimmerman, B., & Schunk, D. (1989). Self-regulated learning and academic: Theory, research, and practice. New York: Springer-Verlag.

Y IS FOR YES I CAN

What is the core learning mechanic?
Enabling learners to believe that they can succeed helps them take on a challenging activity, persist longer, persevere in the face of failures, take on more challenges, and ultimately accomplish more.

What is an example, and what is it good for?
As Albert Bandura, the father of self-efficacy, wisely notes, "Self-belief does not necessarily ensure success, but self-disbelief assuredly spawns failure" (1997, p. 77). A novice rock climber with high self-efficacy will choose to tackle paths that look difficult and will get right back on the climbing wall when she falls. A novice with low self-efficacy will attempt new paths only when necessary and respond to a fall by giving up and trying an easier route.

Why does it work?
One part of the motivation equation is the perceived utility of success. The second part is whether people believe they can succeed. People make attributions about whether they can cause their own success. Improving these attributions increases the likelihood they will engage and persist in a challenging task.

What problems does the core mechanic solve?
- People do not think they can cause themselves to improve, so they do not try.
  - "I'm bad at math. I'm just not a math person."
- People blame their environment for their failures.
  - "Nothing I do in the organization matters. My employers don't listen, and it wouldn't make a difference even if they did."
- People avoid challenges that they could probably meet if they tried.
  - A child wants to try only puzzles she knows she can solve.

Examples of how to use it
- Students believe they cannot learn math no matter how hard they try.
  - Explain that trying hard grows important connections in the brain, even if they do not succeed this time.
- Toddlers are learning to solve problems.
  - Praise their effort and behavior ("You worked so hard—it really paid off!"), and avoid praising a presumed trait ("You're so smart").
- Let peer models be living examples for current students.
  - In a life-skills class for people newly released from prison, bring in a

speaker of similar age and background who was formerly in prison and has since successfully transitioned to free life. Ask her to speak about her challenges, coping mechanisms, and ultimate success.

Risks

- Instructors may focus so much on student attitudes that they forget they need to create a good learning environment.
- Building self-efficacy without an attention to useful goals can create overconfidence.
- Praising intelligence or talent may inadvertently steer learners to easier challenges.

Z is for Zzzzzz...

Consolidating the memories of the day

GETTING YOUR ZZZ'S means getting your sleep. Over half a century ago, John Steinbeck wrote, "A problem difficult at night is resolved in the morning after the committee of sleep has worked on it" (1954, p. 54). The past fifteen years of sleep research has supported his insight. Sleep improves memory, physical skills, and insight. We close this book with a basic piece of advice: for learning to be deep, be kind to your sleep.

We all do it, we all need it, and we all try to cheat it. Yet sleep always wins in the end, which is a good thing for learning. Sleep's relevance to learning is twofold. First, it helps us stay alert during waking hours so we can learn new things. Second, it consolidates the day's memories into long-term storage. This consolidation improves memory for the day's events, and it increases the probability of finding patterns in our memories.

Lau, Alger, and Fishbein (2011) conducted a study that demonstrated the effects of sleep on pattern finding. People memorized many Chinese characters without knowing that they had a structure: conceptually similar characters shared radicals. Figure Z.1 shows that three water-based characters share the water radical (circled in the diagram). Many characters were intermixed during the memorization phase, so participants would not notice this structure right away. After memorizing the characters and their definitions, people

Alcoholic drink   River   To swim

Figure Z.1. The radical for "water" in three Chinese characters.

either took a nap or stayed awake. Those who took a nap were more likely to abstract the common structure in the characters they had previously memorized. They were better able to guess the meaning of a new character that shared one of the radicals they had seen before and to guess the meaning of the radicals when presented in isolation.

I. How Does Sleep Work?

Sleep occurs in repeated ninety-minute cycles. Periods of dream-filled, rapid-eye-movement (REM) sleep take turns with a deeper, slow-wave sleep (SWS). Figure Z.2 provides a schematic of a typical bout of sleep. At the onset of sleep, people fall quickly into deep SWS and then transition to REM sleep. They switch back and forth throughout the night, with SWS dominating the first hours of sleep and REM sleep dominating the last hours.

Dreamless SWS is the major player in memory consolidation. Falling into SWS after a day of living and learning gives way to a complicated dance of neural signals in your brain. While awake, the brain's circuits busily buzz to their own purposes. But while sleeping, large networks of neurons synchronize operations, turning on and off together at about one cycle per second. While on, the neurons send out a heavy wave of signals, and while off, they go silent. *Slow-wave sleep* is named after these slow (for the brain, at least) on-off oscillations. Researchers know SWS is related to learning because the waves are stronger after a day of heavy learning (after studying for finals) and weaker if not much learning has occurred (a lazy summer day). They also show up in predictable brain locations. If a person learns a motor routine during the day, like a finger-tapping pattern, then areas of the brain responsible for movement processing will show increased amplitude of sleep oscillations compared with a day of little motor learning (Huber, Ghilardi, Massimini, & Tononi, 2004).

The synchronized oscillations of SWS drive memory reactivation. Say a person learns a new driving route and plans to use it again in the

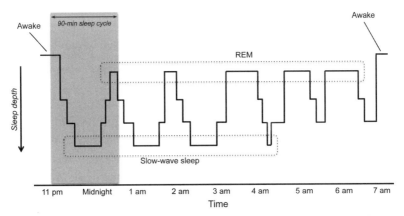

Figure Z.2. Sleep cycles of a typical night of sleep. Slow-wave sleep is the deepest phase of sleep, and it dominates early in the night. Rapid-eye-movement sleep is a lighter phase of sleep during which dreaming occurs. It prevails in later sleep cycles. (Based on Rasch and Born, 2013.)

future. While the person learns, a set of neurons fires up to encode the route. Later, during the "on" phases of SWS, the same neurons reactivate repeatedly in a subconscious fast-forward replay of the learned route. The reactivations start in the hippocampus, a part of the brain associated with episodic memory (memory of events) and, after a short delay, echo in other areas of the brain associated with long-term memory. The evidence suggests that memories are literally moving from the hippocampus to other brain areas, transferring the day's memories into long-term memory storage.

Finally, these patterns of neural activity lead to neural plasticity, or physical changes to neurons. The phenomenon has been witnessed only recently, though it has been assumed for years. During sleep after learning, neurons grow new spine-like protrusions that receive incoming information from nearby neurons. These new dendritic spines strengthen the communication between neurons, which is one way the brain creates new learning. Interestingly, when researchers used a drug to block memory reactivation during SWS, spine growth was hindered (Yang et al. 2014). However, if they instead blocked REM sleep (but allowed SWS reactivation), spine growth proceeded as usual. Thus, the researchers showed measurable brain plasticity during sleep linked to memory reactivations during SWS.

In the complex dance of sleep, all the players fall in step to drive learning with no conscious effort. As the saying goes, while the cobbler sleeps, the elves are hard at work.

II. How to Use Sleep to Enhance Learning

Sleep occurs in all mammals. Despite vulnerability while sleeping, the risk-reward balance has kept sleep from evolving out of existence for millions of years. There are several strategies you can use to take advantage of the need for sleep.

GET ENOUGH SLEEP

People who have gone twenty-four hours without sleep are cognitively impaired to the equivalent of a 0.1 percent blood alcohol level (over the legal driving limit). If one undersleeps repeatedly, the debt accumulates. A ten-hour recovery sleep will help recover function, but the recovery will not last throughout the day (Cohen et al., 2010). You cannot cheat your way out of sleep. Make efforts to get sufficient sleep on a regular twenty-four-hour cycle.

How much sleep is sufficient? It depends on the person, but you can test yourself with the Multiple Sleep Latency Test (Carskadon et al., 1986). In the middle of the day, lie down in a darkened room. Hold a spoon over the side of the bed with a large plate on the floor underneath. Check the time and try to go to sleep. When you fall asleep, the spoon will fall from your hand and clatter on the plate, waking you up. If less than five minutes has passed, this indicates severe sleep deprivation. If fifteen to twenty minutes has passed, it (usually) means you are doing fine in the sleep department.

TAKING SMART NAPS

The key to napping involves the sleep cycles. A sleep cycle starts with light sleep, transitioning into deep SWS, and ending with a stretch of lighter REM sleep. Waking up from the SWS can cause extreme grogginess for up to half an hour. With that in mind, here is what the research says about optimal nap duration:

Nap duration	Result
10–15 minutes	Temporary memory boost: a 10-min nap improves memory for a previously learned list of words; benefits fade within a week. Increased alertness. No grogginess.

30 minutes	More memory benefits than the short nap.
	~30 min of grogginess upon waking.
60 minutes	Long-lasting memory improvement. Less grogginess (SWS phase has ended).
90 minutes	Full benefits of a sleep cycle, including improved emotional, procedural, and declarative memory and increased creativity, with minimal grogginess. (summarized from Lahl, 2008; Alger, Lau, & Fishbein, 2012; Brooks & Lack, 2006)

Unless you have time for more than an hour of rest, a fifteen-minute power nap will provide the biggest bang for your buck. Need even more energy? One trick is to drink coffee just before the fifteen-minute nap (Horne & Reyner, 1996). The caffeine will start to kick in just as you are waking up.

PROMPTED SLEEP REACTIVATION

Studying is hard. Time is short. If only there were a way to learn while asleep. While not quite ready for the home market, the science is getting close by using *prompted reactivation*. For example, in one study (Ngo, Martinetz, Born, & Mölle, 2013), people memorized word pairs. When they slept, the researchers tracked the SWS waves and set an audible metronome to the rhythm of the brain waves. This amplified the brain waves. The treatment nearly doubled the benefits of sleep for remembering the word pairs.

Reactivation can also work by reminding the brain during SWS. Antony, Gobel, O'Hare, Reber, and Paller (2012) showed how this works for learning to play a simple piano melody. They asked participants to learn two melodies by following video game-like instructions on a screen (à la *Guitar Hero*). Later, during SWS, they played a recording of one of the melodies on repeat, causing memories of that specific melody to reactivate in participants' brains. When they awoke, the participants performed both melodies again and, astoundingly, did better on the one that was played while they slept, even though their practice times and performances on both melodies were equal before sleep. Participants reported no awareness of the sleep playback, so the "extra practice" was essentially effortless.

Using another interesting technique, people learned information about card locations (Rasch, Büchel, Gais, & Born, 2007). While they were learning, the researchers released a rose scent into the room. Later, during sleep, the rose scent was readministered, prompting memory reactivation and improving memory for the card locations.

Before you run off to set up a sleep reactivation station of your own, keep in mind some of the limitations of the idea. First, despite the enthusiasm for playing classical music for a sleeping infant, there is zero evidence that people learn new memories during sleep. *Sleep only strengthens previous learning.* Listening to foreign language audiotapes only during sleep will not help people learn a foreign language. But, if people taking a foreign language class remind themselves of the day's vocabulary during sleep, they will likely get a memory boost (Schreiner & Rasch, 2014). Second, there may be unidentified downsides of external sleep reactivation. For example, boosting specific memories through reactivation could hamper consolidation of other memories (Antony et al., 2012). Still, the limitations should not dampen reader enthusiasm. The possibilities abound, and a recent surge in sleep learning research makes this an exciting time to think about practical applications.

III. The Outcomes of Sleep

Health-wise, sleep prevents fatigue, disease, and death. For instance, during early sleep, the brain flushes out toxic elements that build up during the day as a by-product of metabolism (Xie et al., 2013). Sleep also has numerous positive outcomes for learning. Here are a few, with learning outcomes that may be surprising.

Decreased forgetting: A classic study showed that after learning nonsense syllables, taking a nap helps people to forget less than staying awake does. Even when tested as little as one hour after learning, participants forgot more syllables if they stayed awake than if they napped during that hour (Jenkins & Dallenbach, 1924). Interestingly, different types of memory seem to be boosted preferentially during different sleep stages: emotional, implicit, and procedural memory may be boosted during REM sleep, while declarative memory and insight learning may benefit more from SWS.

Greater athletic performance: Mah, Mah, Kezirian, and Dement (2011) asked Stanford University basketball players to extend their nighttime sleep by two hours, to a minimum of ten hours in bed (alone) per night for about six weeks. Mah and colleagues found improvement in sprint times, free-throw percentage, and three-point shot success, even though the athletes reported already feeling at the peak of their athletic skill before the start of the study. Was the additional two hours of sleep per day (and the concurrent loss of two waking hours) worth a 10 percent gain in shooting accuracy? As they say, beauty is in the eye of the beholder.

Improved insight: Sleep is the original incubator of ideas. Unrecognized patterns in one's experience come together and eventually bubble to the surface. Here are two of our favorite studies. Diekelmann, Born, and Wagner (2010) asked people to memorize word triplets (e.g., *night, dark, coal*). Each triplet shares a secret untold theme word (*black*). Researchers then asked people to recall the words later. If people accidentally introduced the theme word, it indicated they tightly integrated the triplet theme around the hidden theme. People who napped after learning the triplets were more likely to introduce the theme words into their recall than were people who stayed awake. This is likely due to sleep memory consolidation, during which people's recent learning integrates with their prior knowledge. This integration with prior knowledge helps make connections among the words.

Beijamini, Pereira, Cini, and Louzada (2014) showed that sleep boosts problem-solving insight in a video game context. They challenged people to play a commercial video game in which the goal is to move a character toward a balloon using a mouse and logical reasoning. Each level increased in difficulty, and when people hit a level they could not complete in ten minutes, the playtime ended. Soon after, half of the players took a ninety-minute nap. People who napped subsequently passed their challenge level more easily than those who did not nap, revealing a sleep-driven insight into how to solve the level.

IV. Can People Learn to Teach Themselves with Sleep?

Smart napping and remaining vigilant to one's sleep needs are straightforward, if hard to implement given the demands of life. Self-cued memory reactivation should work in theory, but the evidence so far is only anecdotal. If people have trouble falling and staying asleep, we recommend the National Sleep Foundation (see http://www.sleepfoundation.org) as a starting point for tips for a better night's sleep.

V. Risks of Sleep

The major risk involves getting too little sleep. The risk is especially keen for teenagers, who normally get seven hours of sleep per night but actually need more than nine, according to the National Sleep Foundation. People feel sleepy when their bodies start to secrete the hormone melatonin. For an average American teen, this secretion runs from 11 p.m. through 8 a.m. Unfortunately, this biological factor clashes with the schedule of school. Teens often need to wake up between 6:00 and 6:30 a.m. to get to school on time. Of course, sleep times are malleable (just ask any parent of a toddler), so why can't teens just shift their sleep time earlier? The general wisdom is that cultural factors, including homework and social opportunities, make this impractical, especially coupled with teens' observations that they "just don't feel tired!" The result? Zombies in first-period biology. Some schools have delayed school start times by an hour. Students at these schools report longer nighttime sleep and less daytime sleepiness; teachers report that students are more alert; and, schools report higher rates of attendance (Wahlstrom, 2002).

A second risk of sleep deprivation is susceptibility to memory confabulations. Suppose a person witnesses a crime in the morning but is told a contradictory account of the event soon after. People who are awake all night before the crime are more likely to falsely remember witnessing what they were told rather than what they saw (Frenda, Patihis, Loftus, Lewis, & Fenn, 2014). It is one reason that eyewitnesses should not be subjected to strong suggestion during interviews with police and lawyers.

Can too much sleep be a risk? The postnap grogginess that many people attribute to too much sleep is likely due to simply waking up during SWS. It is unclear whether it is possible for a healthy person to sleep too much. One study showed that people who habitually sleep more than nine hours are more likely to have a host of health issues, including diabetes, weight gain, and stroke (Liu, Wheaton, Chapman, & Croft, 2013). However, the study was correlational, so it is possible that health issues caused sleep extension, not the other way around.

VI. Examples of Good and Bad Use

- *Good:* Nap either fifteen or ninety minutes to brighten your mood and your memory.
- *Good:* Maintain a consistent sleep schedule to ensure your circadian rhythm aligns with your sleep.
- *Good:* Use light therapy to fix jet lag. Exposure to bright light in the evening pushes one's waking hours later. Bright light in the morning moves waking hours earlier.
- *Bad:* Drinking coffee or alcohol before bed disrupts sleep—forget the nightcap.
- *Bad:* Napping at your most alert time of day or within a few hours of bedtime is counterproductive. You won't be able to fall asleep at your most alert times of day due to forces of your circadian rhythm. And a nap after 3 p.m. can hinder nighttime sleep.
- *Bad:* Choosing to stay up all night accelerates forgetting. Instead, "sleep on it" to help declarative memory and to find underlying patterns in what you've learned.

VII. References

Alger, S. E., Lau, H., & Fishbein, W. (2012). Slow wave sleep during a daytime nap is necessary for protection from subsequent interference and long-term retention. *Neurobiology of Learning and Memory, 98*(2), 188–196.

Antony, J. W., Gobel, E. W., O'Hare, J. K., Reber, P. J., & Paller, K. A. (2012). Cued memory reactivation during sleep influences skill learning. *Nature Neuroscience, 15*(8), 1114–1116.

Beijamini, F., Pereira, S. I. R., Cini, F. A., & Louzada, F. M. (2014). After being challenged by a video game problem, sleep increases the chance to solve it. *PLoS One, 9*(1), e84342.

Brooks, A., & Lack, L. (2006). A brief afternoon nap following nocturnal sleep restriction: Which nap duration is most recuperative? *Sleep, 29*(6), 831-840.

Carskadon, M. A., Dement, W. C., Mitler, M. M., Roth, T., Westbrook, P. R., & Keenan, S. (1986). Guidelines for the Multiple Sleep Latency Test (MSLT): A standard measure of sleepiness. *Sleep, 9*(4), 519–524.

Cohen, D. A., Wang, W., Wyatt, J. K., Kronauer, R. E., Dijk, D. J., Czeisler, C. A., & Klerman, E. B. (2010). Uncovering residual effects of chronic sleep loss on human performance. *Science Translational Medicine, 2*(14), 14ra3.

Diekelmann, S., Born, J., & Wagner, U. (2010). Sleep enhances false memories depending on general memory performance. *Behavioural Brain Research, 208*(2), 425–429.

Frenda, S. J., Patihis, L., Loftus, E. F., Lewis, H. C., & Fenn, K. M. (2014). Sleep deprivation and false memories. *Psychological Science, 25*(9), 1674–1681.

Horne, J. A., & Reyner, L. A. (1996). Counteracting driver sleepiness: effects of napping, caffeine, and placebo. *Psychophysiology, 33*(3), 306-309.

Huber, R., Ghilardi, M. F., Massimini, M., & Tononi, G. (2004). Local sleep and learning. *Nature, 430*(6995), 78–81.

Jenkins, J. G., & Dallenbach, K. M. (1924). Obliviscence during sleep and waking. *American Journal of Psychology, 35*(4) 605–612.

Lau, H., Alger, S. E., & Fishbein, W. (2011). Relational memory: A daytime nap facilitates the abstraction of general concepts. *PLoS One, 6*(11), e27139.

Liu, Y., Wheaton, A. G., Chapman, D. P., & Croft, J. B. (2013). Sleep duration and chronic diseases among US adults age 45 years and older: Evidence from the 2010 Behavioral Risk Factor Surveillance System. *Sleep, 36*(10), 1421-1427.

Mah, C. D., Mah, K. E., Kezirian, E. J., & Dement, W. C. (2011). The effects of sleep extension on the athletic performance of collegiate basketball players. *Sleep, 34*(7), 943-950.

Ngo, H. V. V., Martinetz, T., Born, J., & Mölle, M. (2013). Auditory closed-loop stimulation of the sleep slow oscillation enhances memory. *Neuron, 78*(3), 545–553.

Rasch, B., & Born, J. (2013). About sleep's role in memory. *Physiological Reviews, 93*(2), 681–766.

Rasch, B., Büchel, C., Gais, S., & Born, J. (2007). Odor cues during slow-wave sleep prompt declarative memory consolidation. *Science, 315*(5817), 1426–1429.

Schreiner, T., & Rasch, B. (2014). Boosting vocabulary learning by verbal cueing during sleep. *Cerebral Cortex, 25*(11), 4169–4179.

Steinbeck, J. (1954). *Sweet Thursday.* New York: Viking.

Wahlstrom, K. (2002). Changing times: Findings from the first longitudinal study of later high school start times. *NASSP Bulletin, 86*(633), 3–21.

Xie, L., Kang, H., Xu, Q., Chen, M. J., Liao, Y., Thiyagarajan, M., . . . Nedergaard, M. (2013). Sleep drives metabolite clearance from the adult brain. *Science, 342*(6156), 373–377.

Yang, G., Lai, C. S. W., Cichon, J., Ma, L., Li, W., & Gan, W. B. (2014). Sleep promotes branch-specific formation of dendritic spines after learning. *Science, 344*(6188), 1173–1178.

Z IS FOR ZZZS

What is the core learning mechanic?
Sleeping allows recent memories to consolidate into long-term storage and integrate with prior knowledge.

What is an example, and what is it good for?
An afternoon nap or a regular night's sleep improves memory for facts and skills learned earlier in the day, and it helps people find patterns in their experiences.

Why does it work?
Sleep is a like a personal postgame roundup for your day. During sleep the brain settles down into introspection mode, with no more new challenges or new information coming in. Memories of the day reactivate in fast-forward, over and over again, and start to connect with knowledge already stored in long-term memory. This reduces forgetting and exposes relations among ideas that were previously hidden.

What problems does the core mechanic solve?
- Students are sleepy in class.
- A person is stumped by a tough problem and needs a little insight.

Examples of how to use it
- Nap for fifteen minutes for a burst of alertness and a small memory boost. Nap sixty to ninety minutes for greater memory benefits.

Risks
- Not sleeping enough: a twenty-four-hour bout of sleep deprivation leads people to act about the same as if they have a 0.1 percent blood-alcohol level. Chronic sleep deprivation over days or weeks negatively affects alertness, vigilance, memory, and mood.
- Waking up during slow-wave sleep causes grogginess. To avoid grogginess after a nap, avoid twenty- to thirty-minute naps.

Figure Credits

Figure B.2: Reproduced with permission from "Psychological insights for improved physics teaching," by L. Aguilar, G. Walton, and C. Wieman, 2014, *Physics Today, 67*(5), p. 43. Copyright 2014, American Institute of Physics.

Figure C.1: Reproduced with permission of Lawrence Erlbaum Associates Software & Alternative Media, Inc., from "A Sketch of a Cognitive Approach to Comprehension," by J. D. Bransford and N. S. McCarrel, 1974, in W. Weimer and D. S. Palermo (Eds.), *Cognition and the symbolic processes.* Hillsdale, NJ: Lawrence Erlbaum; permission conveyed through Copyright Clearance Center, Inc.

Figure C.2: Reproduced with permission of Lawrence Erlbaum Associates Software & Alternative Media, Inc., from "A Sketch of a Cognitive Approach to Comprehension," by J. D. Bransford and N. S. McCarrel, 1974, in W. Weimer and D. S. Palermo (Eds.), *Cognition and the symbolic processes.* Hillsdale, NJ: Lawrence Erlbaum; permission conveyed through Copyright Clearance Center, Inc.

Figure C.3: Adapted with permission of John Wiley & Sons, from "Perceptual learning modules in mathematics: Enhancing students' pattern recognition, structure extraction, and fluency," by P. J. Kellman, C. M. Massey, and J. Y. Son, 2010, *Topics in Cognitive Science, 2*(2). Copyright 2009, Cognitive Science Society, Inc.

Figure C.8: Reprinted from *Cognitive Psychology, 11*(3), by R. S. Nickerson and J. J. Adams, "Long-term memory for a common object," pp. 287-307, copyright 1979, with permission from Elsevier.

Figure D.3: From K. A. Ericsson, R. T. Krampe, and C. Tesch-Römer, "The role of deliberate practice in the acquisition of expert performance," *Psychological Review, 100*(3), p. 369, 1993, publisher American Psychological Association. Reprinted with permission.

Figure E.3: Reprinted from "The productive agency that drives collaborative learning," by D. L. Schwartz, in P. Dillenbourg (Ed.) *Collaborative learning: Cognitive and computational approaches*, pp. 197-218, copyright 1999, with permission from Elsevier.

Figure F.3: Reprinted from "Posterlet: A game based assessment of children's choices to seek feedback and revise," by M. Cutumisu, K. P. Blair, D. B. Chin and D. L. Schwartz, *Journal of Learning Analytics, 2,* 2015, p. 56.

Figure H.2: Adapted from *Cognitive Psychology, 38*(3), by D. L. Schwartz, "Physical imagery: Kinematic versus dynamic models," p. 440, copyright 1999, with permission from Elsevier.

Figure H.3: Adapted from "Learning to see less than nothing: Putting perceptual skills to work for learning numerical structure," by J. M. Tsang, K. P. Blair, L. Bofferding and D. L. Schwartz, *Cognition and Instruction, 33*(2), 2015. Reprinted by permission of the publisher (Taylor & Francis Ltd, http://www.tandfonline.com).

Figure H.4: Adapted from "Learning to see less than nothing: Putting perceptual skills to work for learning numerical structure," by J. M. Tsang, K. P. Blair, L. Bofferding and D. L. Schwartz, *Cognition and Instruction, 33*(2), 2015. Reprinted by permission of the publisher (Taylor & Francis Ltd, http://www.tandfonline.com).

Figure J.3: From D. L. Schwartz, C. C. Chase, M. A. Oppezzo, and D. B. Chin, "Practicing versus inventing with contrasting cases: The effects of telling first on learning and transfer," *Journal of Educational Psychology, 103*(4), p. 761, 2011, publisher American Psychological Association. Reprinted with permission.

Figure M.4: Available: https://scratch.mit.edu/projects/10859244/#editor

Figure O.1: From "Imitation of facial and manual gestures by human neonates," by A. N. Meltzoff and M. K. Moore, 1977, *Science, 198,* p. 75. Reprinted with permission from AAAS.

Figure O.2: From "Theory of mind: mechanisms, methods, and new directions" by L. J. Byom and B. Mutlu, 2013, *Frontiers in Human Neuroscience, 7.*

Figure O.3: From "The role of imitation in personality development," by A. Bandura, 1963, *The Journal of Nursery Education, 18*(3). Reprinted with permission of the author.

Figure O.4: From "The role of imitation in personality development," by A. Bandura, 1963, *The Journal of Nursery Education, 18*(3). Reprinted with permission of the author.

Figure Q.1: From "Personal inquiry: Orchestrating science investigations within and beyond the classroom," by M. Sharples et al., 2014, *Journal of the Learning Sciences, 24*(2), pp. 1-34.

Figure S.2: Reprinted with permission of John Wiley & Sons from "The role of a mental model in learning to operate a device," by D. E. Kieras & S. Bovair, 1984, *Cognitive Science, 8*(3), p. 259. Copyright 1984, Cognitive Science Society, Inc.

Figure V.6: Reprinted with permission of John Wiley & Sons from "The construction and analogical transfer of symbolic visualizations," by D. L. Schwartz, 1993, *Journal of Research in Science Teaching, 30*(10), p. 1309-1325. Copyright 1993, Wiley Periodical, Inc., A Wiley Company.

Figure V.8: Reprinted with permission of Cambridge University Press from "Spatial representations and imagery in learning," by D. L. Schwartz & J. Heiser, 2006, in K. Sawyer (Ed.), *Handbook of the learning sciences*, p. 283-298.

Figure V.9: From "A pragmatic perspective on visual representation and creative thinking," by L. Martin & D. L. Schwartz, 2014, *Visual Studies, 29*, Taylor & Francis. Reprinted by permission of the publisher (Taylor & Francis Ltd, http://www.tandfonline.com).

Figure W.1: From "Cognitive load theory and the format of instruction," by P. Chandler & J. Sweller, *Cognition and Instruction, 1991*, Taylor & Francis. Reprinted by permission of the publisher (Taylor & Francis Ltd, http://www.tandfonline.com).

Figure W.2: From "Cognitive load theory and the format of instruction," by P. Chandler & J. Sweller, *Cognition and Instruction, 1991*, Taylor & Francis. Reprinted by permission of the publisher (Taylor & Francis Ltd, http://www.tandfonline.com).

Figure X.1: Reprinted from "The temporal dynamics model of emotional memory processing: a synthesis on the neurobiological basis of stress-induced amnesia, flashbulb and traumatic memories, and the Yerkes-Dodson law," by D. M. Diamond, A. M. Campbell, C. R. Park, J. Halonen, & P. R. Zoladz, *Neural Plasticity, 2007.*

Figure X.3: Reprinted from "Mere belief in social action improves complex learning," by S. Y. Okita, J. Bailenson, & D. L. Schwartz, in P. A. Kirschner, F. Prins, V. Jonker, & G. Kanselaar (Eds.), *Proceedings of the 8th International Conference for the Learning Sciences, 2*, pp. 132-139. Copyright 2008, International Society of the Learning Sciences.

Figure Z.2: Based on "About sleep's role in memory," by B. Rasch & J. Born, 2013, *Physiological Reviews, 93*(2), p. 682. Permission from the American Physiological Society.

The ABC Animals

Alligator
Bear
Cow
Deer
Elephant
Frog
Giraffe & Gorilla
Hippopotamus
Iguana
Jaguar
Kangaroo & Koala
Lion
Mouse
Numbat
Ostrich
Panda & Penguin
Quail
Rhinoceros & Raccoon
Saint Bernard
Toucan
Uakari
Vulture
Warthog
Xenarthra
Yak
Zebra

Problem-Focused Index

Index

About the Authors

Daniel L. Schwartz, PhD, is the Dean of the Stanford University Graduate School of Education and holds the Nomellini-Olivier Chair in Educational Technology. He is an award-winning learning scientist, who also spent eight years teaching secondary school in Los Angeles and Kaltag, Alaska. His special niche is the ability to produce novel and effective learning activities that also test basic hypotheses about how people learn.

Jessica M. Tsang, PhD, is a researcher and instructor at Stanford University's Graduate School of Education who studies how to design instruction that naturally recruits students' native capacities for learning and understanding. Her interdisciplinary research bridges between cognitive neuroscience and the design of effective classroom practices. She has previously worked in the field of education philanthropy, urban school reform, and educational media technology.

Kristen P. Blair, PhD, is a Senior Research Scholar and Instructor at Stanford University's Graduate School of Education. She develops technologies to support students' learning in math and science, and she studies child development and learning in classroom and in family contexts. She holds a PhD in Learning Sciences and Technology Design and a BS in Mathematical and Computational Science, both from Stanford University.